MAX DÉCHARNÉ is an author, songwriter and musician. He has recorded numerous albums and singles, and eight John Peel Sessions as the singer with The Flaming Stars. A regular contributor to *Mojo* magazine since 1998, his books include *Hardboiled Hollywood*, *King's Road*, the jive-talk dictionary *Straight From The Fridge, Dad* and *A Rocket in my Pocket* (Serpent's Tail, 2010), a history of rockabilly music, as well as the 2016 work *Vulgar Tongues: An Alternative History of English Slang*.

'Max Décharné's engaging book *Vulgar Tongues* is a spectacular feat, collating information from a mind-boggling range of sources – from jazz lyrics to dime novels, from eighteenth-century brothel directories to 1960s criminal autobiographies.' Lynne Truss, *New Statesman*

'A detailed delight … The entertainment to be found within this etymology is legion … Luckily for us, Décharné is a master of the manifold, who wields a light touch over a heavy amount of esearch … Décharné's work ably demonstrates that the creation of slang is something hardwired in us, the need to mock suppression being the mother of its invention – one brilliant argument for never keeping a civil tongue.' Cathi Unsworth

'Décharné, a musician and songwriter, has written extensively on music, crime and noir, and his great gift is to connect his ency-:lopaedic knowledge of more recent slang to that of the past. His mind is a trivia-trap of the first order, and the book is a bracing historical tour of the lexicons of sex, prostitution, crime, alcohol, drugs, popular music and military slang.' *New York Times Book Review*

MAX DÉCHARNÉ

★

VULGAR
TONGUES

An Alternative History of
English Slang

This paperback edition published in 2017

First published in Great Britain in 2016 by Serpent's Tail,
an imprint of Profile Books Ltd
3 Holford Yard
Bevin Way
London
WCIX 9HD
www.serpentstail.com

1 3 5 7 9 10 8 6 4 2

Designed by Sue Lamble
Typeset in Jenson by MacGuru Ltd
Printed and bound by CPI Group (UK) Ltd, Croydon CRO 4YY

A CIP record for this book can
be obtained from the British Library

ISBN 978 1 84668 828 7
eISBN 978 1 84765 941 5

MAX DÉCHARNÉ

VULGAR TONGUES

An Alternative History of English Slang

FRANCIS GROSE ESQ.ʳ F.A.S.

Published by J. Sewell, Cornhill, June 1, 1797.

To Captain Francis Grose (1731–1791), whose books sent me down this path thirty-five years ago, and to my father John (1932–2011), who knew an appropriate slang word for most situations, good and bad.

Contents

ACKNOWLEDGEMENTS

I am deeply grateful to Rebecca Gray, my editor at Serpent's Tail – who first suggested that I write a history of English slang after hearing me on the radio in 2010 talking about the works of Captain Francis Grose – for all her sound advice, good humour and support along the way.

Heartfelt thanks as always to my good friend and literary agent Caroline Montgomery at Rupert Crew Ltd, for reading and providing insightful comments on each chapter as the book progressed, and for much else besides, and also to Fen Oswin and Doreen Montgomery from Rupert Crew for all their help through the years.

Many thanks also to Pete Ayrton, Anna-Marie Fitzgerald, Cecily Gayford, Ruth Petrie, Hannah Westland, Penny Daniel and all the other lovely people at Serpent's Tail – it's a real pleasure to work with you.

I am indebted to the staff at the Westminster Reference Library, the Guildhall Library and the British Library, and commend those who work in public libraries up and down the country at a time when many local councils seem bent on destroying these institutions. I would also like to thank all those behind that vast and invaluable work of scholarship, the Oxford English Dictionary.

A raised glass and a tip of the hat for help and inspiration to Mark & Karen Rubenstein, Gary Valentine, Sarah Martin, Ann Scanlon, Cathi Unsworth, Michael Meekin, Paul Willetts, Travis Elborough, Clive Phillips, Martin Stiles, Janet Dickinson, Frank Key, Mike Jay, David Yates, Tom Nancollas, John Williams, Richard Dacre, Randall Eiger and Andrea Jutson. A very special thank you to Margaret and Geoffrey, Derek and Fiona, and Jamie and Eleanor.

Finally, the most thanks and all my love to Katja, without whom there would simply have been no book at all.

THE MARK OF A
DECADENT MIND

Slang, n.

a. The special vocabulary used by any set of persons of a low or disreputable character; language of a low and vulgar type.

b. The special vocabulary or phraseology of a particular calling or profession; the cant or jargon of a certain class or period.

c. Language of a highly colloquial type, considered as below the level of standard educated speech, and consisting either of new words or of current words employed in some special sense.

Oxford English Dictionary

'If I say , "Come, lass", I am using familiar English; if I address her as "Dear girl", I am using ordinary Standard English; and if I say, "Come, sweet maid", I am using Literary English. If, however, I allude to the girl as a dame or a Jane, I am employing slang; if as a moll, I am employing cant; if as – but perhaps I had better not particularize the vulgarisms for "girl" or "woman".'

Eric Partridge, *Here, There and Everywhere* (1950)

FOR CENTURIES AFTER THE NORMAN CONQUEST, the majority of the rich, the powerful and the learned in England were curiously reluctant to speak English. Latin and French held sway, both in conversation and in written documents or the printed word. It was considered courtly, polite and cultured.

For the great mass of common people, however, English was the sole option – a forthright, earthy language which did not shrink from calling a spade a spade, or anything else for that matter. There was a street in Oxford in the 13th century named Gropecuntlane, and another in London called Gropecontelane; a variant spelling but the same meaning. In fact, this street name appeared in towns across the country in medieval times, often denoting the presence of a brothel. Not for nothing was the everyday speech of the common people known as the vulgar tongue.

Times changed, literacy rates improved, newspapers blossomed and by the 18th century, many words and phrases which had previously been standard English began to be considered improper or, in some cases, obscene. This may have cut some ice in polite and well-heeled circles, but the common people had their own modes of speech, and just as the former group attempted to raise written and spoken English to new heights of elegance and correctness, the latter took an inventive and instinctive delight in the development of slang.

The word *slang* acquired its current meaning only during the reign of George III. Back in the 1500s, it was the name for a type of cannon, and from 1610 it could also refer to a narrow strip of land. When Dr Johnson was compiling his *Dictionary of the English Language* in the mid-18th century, a long-established and rich underworld language could be found all around him in areas like Covent Garden and St Giles. However, if you look up the word 'Slang' in the *Dictionary*, the only entry Johnson provides is this quotation from the Bible:

> SLANG. The preterite of *sling*.
> David *slang* a stone, and smote the Philistine.
>
> I. Sam. xvii

Yet if you search in the same dictionary for the word *cant*, his fourth entry under this heading is as follows:

CANT
4. Barbarous jargon.
The affectation of some late authors, to introduce and multiply *cant* words, is the most ruinous corruption in any language.
Swift

Such talk was associated in the main with thieves, beggars and those on the margins of society. It was known as flash language, cant or pedlars' French, and often looked down on – the common fate of slang through the ages. Yet within twenty years of the publication of Johnson's dictionary, a character in Hugh Kelly's play *School for Wives* (1773) was given the line: 'There is a language which we sometimes talk in, call'd Slang', and this eventually became the main term for all variants of insider speech.

Tracing the threads over several centuries and across international borders, *Vulgar Tongues* is the story of how the English language of Shakespeare's day fragmented and twisted into all kinds of shapes, as people like pickpockets, beggars, sailors, musicians, gangsters, whores, politicians, gypsies, soldiers, gays and lesbians, policemen, rappers, cockneys, biker gangs and circus folk seized the King's or Queen's English by the throat and took it to places it would probably regret in the morning.

Perfectly ordinary banter, Squiffy

THE SLANG DEVELOPED BY VARIOUS GROUPS or closed communities sets them apart from the everyday population. To belong, you need to understand the lingo. The World War II fighter pilots in Monty Python's RAF Banter sketch (1974) experience a momentary communication failure when their squadron leader comes back from his mission and makes his report:

> Eric Idle: 'Bally Jerry pranged his kite right in the how's-your-father. Hairy blighter, dicky birdied, feathered back on his sammy, took a waspie, flipped over on his Betty Harpers, caught his can in the Bertie.'
>
> Terry Jones: 'Er... 'fraid I don't quite follow you, Squadron Leader.'
>
> Eric Idle: 'Perfectly ordinary banter, Squiffy...'

Other members of the squadron look equally bemused, then Michael Palin enters, uttering various phrases that no one else can understand, including the magnificent 'sausage squad up the blue end'. This idea was adapted in recent years by the comedy team of Armstrong and Miller, who had wartime RAF pilots speaking in contemporary youth slang ('I bought some really nice trousers in Camden. They is well hardcore with all pockets an' shit'). All of which highlights two essential points; it's no use coming out with the hippest phrases in town if no one else has a clue what you are on about, and up-to-date slang can sound absolutely ridiculous when used by anyone not part of the group.

The continuing popularity over the years of various slang dictionaries – which attempt to explain for the benefit of the general public the mysterious phrases employed by one group or another – shows the hold that such language exerts upon the imagination, yet it has a habit of slipping away even as it is pinned down. Much slang starts out as a kind of low-level guerrilla warfare directed at straight society, designed to keep out the squares, or annoy them, or both, and is then abandoned by the group which originated it once the words have become common currency.

Groovy was the hip new jazz word of the early 1940s, batted around carelessly by bebop musicians and pulp novelists. Twenty years later it was as mainstream as they come, co-opted by every branch of the media – so that today it is routinely taken for a sixties phrase. Fortysomething former members of the bongo-banging set were probably choking on their beards listening to Simon & Garfunkel in the '59th Street Bridge Song' (1966) singing about 'feeling groovy', as a once-exclusive in-word suddenly flooded the airwaves. Having become indelibly linked with images of flower power, love-ins and psychedelia, its original context is lost. Also in 1966, when Bob Dylan was singing 'Everybody must get stoned' in 'Rainy Day Women #13 & 35', old-school drinkers and members of the Rat Pack could have been forgiven for thinking that he was talking about the booze, rather than drugs, because formerly the word had meant a state of drunkenness.

Having the barclays

SLANG CAN BE THE GATEWAY to another world. When I interviewed Cynthia Plastercaster of Chicago – a delightful woman who has pursued a singular career since the 1960s making plaster impressions of rock stars' genitals, Jimi Hendrix among them (an artefact dubbed the *Penis de Milo*) – she told me that as a teenage American girl around 1965, she developed an interest in cockney slang purely in an effort to better understand her favourite British Invasion groups. As luck would have it, there was a band living locally who hailed from the UK and explained a few suggestive phrases for her:

> They were called the Robin Hood Clan. Nobody I know has ever heard of them, from anywhere, but anyway, they came

from Britain. They were slightly older guys, and there were six of them, that resided somewhere in Chicago. They taught us *charver, barclays bank* – rhymed with *wank* – and *hampton wick*. Those were the three, and that's all I needed...

Armed with these nuggets of wisdom, Cynthia felt confident enough to approach touring musicians, such as the Rolling Stones as they passed through Chicago. *Hampton wick* is the well-known rhyming slang for *dick* or *prick*, while readers of the superb diaries of Kenneth Williams will have encountered his familiar end-of-day phrase recording a successful bout of masturbation – 'had the Barclays' (or, on another occasion, 'a great session of Arthur's Erotica', also rhyming slang: *J. Arthur Rank, wank*). *Charver*, however, had survived in common parlance for over a century before the Robin Hood Clan taught it to Cynthia. A slang term for the act of sex, and also for a prostitute, it can be found in that indispensable 1846 collection of London low-life knowledge, *The Swell's Night Guide*, whose full title left little doubt as to its contents:

> *The swell's night guide, or, A peep through the great metropolis, under the dominion of nox: displaying the various attractive places of amusement by night. The saloons; the Paphian beauties; the chaffing cribs; the introducing houses; the singing and lushing cribs; the comical clubs; fancy ladies and the penchants, &c., &c.*

Largely the work of Renton Nicholson (1809–61) – self-styled Lord Chief Baron of the Garrick's Head and Town Hotel, Bow Street, and author of the posthumously published *Autobiography of a Fast Man* (1863) – it contains the following recommendation of a young lady: 'An out and outer she is and no mistake, a rattling piece and a stunning charver.'

Although one of the popular explanations for the development of slang is quite rightly that certain groups, such as criminals and beggars, have used it as a way of disguising their speech in front of straight society, other slang is adopted in certain circles purely as a way of defining a group identity. English public schools and certain universities have a long history of this. When the future Poet Laureate John Betjeman arrived at Marlborough College at the start of the 1920s, he needed to swiftly adapt his speech in order to fit in, as his biographer Bevis Hillier records:

> The 'new bug' at Marlborough had to learn the school slang in his first few weeks, on pain of beatings. Grey trousers were 'barnes'. The cushion-cum-bag in which he carried his books was a 'kish'… A characteristic word in the Marlborough argot was 'coxy'. Suggestive of 'cocksure' and 'coxcomb', it had roughly the same meaning as the slang word 'uppity'.

This was a way of enforcing a sense of identity, as well as distinguishing the pupils of one establishment from those at other schools nearby, or, heaven forbid, boys from the local town. In Anthony Buckeridge's post-war English school stories featuring a pupil named Jennings, a similar state of affairs applies:

> 'You great, prehistoric clodpoll, Darbi,' he complained, as he led the way up the cliff path. 'What did you want to go and make a frantic bish like that for?'

A *bish*, or mistake, is genuine primary-school slang, and was listed by Eric Partridge in his 1937 *Dictionary of Slang* as having first been used at Seaford College in Sussex from around 1925. It probably comes as no surprise to learn that Buckeridge himself attended Seaford as a child, and by using such terms in his vastly popular stories, he helped spread them among further generations of schoolchildren from 1950 onwards.

Scurft at the gaff and kept in lumber

NEWSPAPERS HAVE GENERALLY BEEN KEEN to give their readership an insight into the ways of slang. The *Observer*, a mere year after its first publication in 1791, was informing the public that 'the *Slang technical* term for persons in the pillory is *babes in the wood*', and later, when reviewing Disraeli's novel *Sybil, or the Two Nations*, in 1845, noted that the hero, Charles Egremont, becomes 'acquainted with some phrases in the slang of high society – for high society has its slang as well as low society – and there is little to choose between them on the score of fitness or elegance'.

As for an even older newspaper, *The Times*, it entered enthusiastically into a detailed description of current pickpocket slang when reporting the following speech from a sixteen-year-old thief who'd been operating at the Croydon Fair in 1805:

> 'Why, I have had good luck, me and the kid (pointing to a boy about fourteen years of age) have *shook a dummy* (slang for picking a pocket) at the *gaff* (the fair), with about 20*l*. of *screens* (Bank Notes)'; and observed the boy, his companion, was as good a *kid* (boy) as little Jack Parker, who was lately *lagged* (been transported), and that they had *shook* (picked pockets), and had got twenty-two *fogills* (pocket handkerchiefs) that morning. He had been *scurft* (taken into custody) at the *gaff*, for *drawing* (slang for taking any thing out of a pocket) a *reader* (a pocket-book), but he had *dinged it* (thrown it away); he was kept in *lumber* (confinement), and then they kicked him and let him go.

A century and a half later, the newspapers' urge to explain was just as strong, whether the subject was the latest teenage craze, or politics. Here is the *Daily Express* in 1963, giving UK parents the lowdown on surfer-speak in their regular column, *This Is America*:

After phone-box packing and glue-sniffing, this year the hip fad is healthy surf-riding... This week the record companies jumped on the surf-board by issuing new rock'n'roll numbers with a beating surf background. Sample titles: 'Hot Doggen' (a doggen is an accomplished surfer), 'Walking The Board,' 'Happy Gremmie' (in teenage slang a gremmie is a surf crowd follower, too young to risk it).

Moving forward a decade, there was more advice on transatlantic slang for UK readers, this time courtesy of a 1976 *Daily Mirror* article about President Ford's new running mate, Bob Dole:

In American political slang Dole is known as a 'gun slinger' and in the teenage slang of a senator's daughter sizing up his sex appeal he was labelled 'a fox'.

While it is tempting to imagine readers of the paper forming a mental image of a politician living in an underground burrow, occasionally hunted by packs of dogs, this is just one of the pitfalls of unexplained slang. At least it was a marginally more interesting usage than the example chosen by Oxford Dictionaries, at the time of writing, as their 'international word of the year, 2013'. *Selfie* is a blindingly obvious slang term for an action which is pretty much as old as the camera itself, but it apparently beat off fierce competition from the likes of *twerk* to win the accolade. As a news report issued by Australian Associated Press proudly stated, 'it seems almost certain the selfie originated in Australia with a young drunk first using the word to describe a self-portrait photograph more than a decade ago'.

Young and mentally immature

As widespread as it is, there have always been those who have deplored the use of slang. In addition to reporting new words, newspapers have long enjoyed making fun of slang phrases or denouncing the various groups who use them. For instance, in 1920, a writer named H. Addington Bruce published an article in the *Milwaukee Journal* claiming that 'only the young and the mentally immature can possibly regard slang as witty'. Mr Bruce, author of timeless family favourites such as *Scientific Mental Healing* (1911) and *Nerve Control and How to Gain It* (1918), was the 'psychological advisor' to the Associated Newspapers group. He asserted that 'All slang is essentially vulgar and in bad taste', and concluded with a terrible warning that 'devotees of slang are further liable to suffer by being excluded from intimate association with truly cultivated people'.

This view was hardly confined to America alone. In England in 1925, the Leader of the Opposition (and future Labour prime minister) Ramsay MacDonald declared that using slang in conversation was the mark of 'decadent minds', and that such language 'murders truth itself'.

Someone who would very likely have taken issue with this kind of opinion at the time was the poet Carl Sandburg, who defined slang simply as 'language that takes off its coat, spits on its hands and goes to work'. However, whether it goes to work or not, people have often determined that it should be kept away from school. In October 2013, UK newspapers reported that a London academy was attempting to outlaw the use of certain slang words and phrases among its pupils, to help them perform well at interviews for universities and jobs. To that end, the school put up signs which read:

BANNED WORDS

COZ		AINT
LIKE		BARE
EXTRA		INNIT
YOU WOZ	*and*	WE WOZ

Beginning sentences with BASICALLY

Ending sentences with YEAH

Leaving aside the mild irony of an educational establishment which leaves out the apostrophe in *ain't* while trying to give a lesson in language, the objectives sound essentially well intentioned. Mind you, a school district authority in North Carolina went considerably further in 2006, banning all 1,508 pages of the *Cassell Dictionary of Slang*, reportedly under pressure from 'conservative Christian groups'. Since slang has often been used as a way of saying the unsayable – from the scurrilous and the obscene all the way through to the shocking and the tragic – it is not hard to see why authorities of all kinds, whether educational, religious or political, have long tried to suppress it.

The most obvious cultural reference point for this impulse is, of course, *Nineteen Eighty-Four* (1949), George Orwell's masterful summary of the mindset of totalitarian regimes, in which state control of language is central to the control of the population. On the face of it, the ruling party's three key slogans are a denial of the meaning of words: *War is Peace, Freedom is Slavery, Ignorance is Strength*. In constructing its own language, *Newspeak*, the authorities are gradually outlawing thousands of words and the concepts behind them. The central character, Winston Smith, is given a lesson in the purpose of all this by his colleague, Syme, one of the people working on an updated edition of the Newspeak dictionary, which is getting smaller month by month:

Every concept that can ever be needed, will be expressed by exactly *one* word, with its meaning rigidly defined and all its subsidiary meanings rubbed out and forgotten.

While such aims might bring joy to the heart of any would-be dictator – and the occasional school authority – they attack the very impulse which gives rise to slang; a type of speech which revels in multiple layers of meaning and alternative readings of familiar words.

Orwell's novel gave a name to the concept of *thoughtcrime*. Since the rise of the political-correctness movement in the 1980s, there are a fair number of slang phrases which, if uttered or written today by a public figure, would be enough to swiftly terminate their career, causing them to be hounded out by the massed ranks of media pundits, bloggers and Twitter users. The business of shutting down opinions or words which are considered offensive was more often associated in the past with despots and totalitarian regimes. Various high-profile court cases from the sixties onwards – in particular the *Lady Chatterley* trial in 1960, which led to several respectable UK newspapers printing the word *fuck* in full for the first time – might, at the time, have led some to envisage a world where society became gradually more free from censorship of the written and spoken word, barring libel and slander. However, in recent decades, things have changed significantly.

It is still common to quote Voltaire's much-praised sentiment 'I disapprove of what you say, but I will defend to the death your right to say it' (a phrase actually coined by Evelyn Beatrice Hall, writing as S. G. Tallentyre, in her 1906 biography *The Friends of Voltaire*). However, unpopular views and words are now routinely banished to the outer darkness, although the internet comment pages have lifted the lid on all manner of discredited sayings and opinions which continue to bubble to the surface as fast as online moderators can delete them.

On British television, the critic Kenneth Tynan deliberately uttered the word *fuck* one night on the BBC's *BBC3* show in 1965, breaking another cultural taboo. These days, it is a commonplace to expound the view that American television shows are vastly superior to those produced in the UK, and yet the only reason excellent, slang-heavy shows like *The Sopranos* can be made is that they are funded by and broadcast on the subscription channel HBO, and therefore free from the normally very censorious mainstream US TV arbitrators, who blush with horror at the slightest 'wardrobe malfunction' or swear word. Not so *The Sopranos*, whose elderly character Corrado 'Junior' Soprano responds to the sharp pain of falling over in the bath and hurting his spine with the choice expression 'Your sister's cunt!' Similarly, in literature, the language of the streets can surface in a mixture of slang, swearing and multi-faceted abuse, such as in the following tirade directed at a black street-preacher in late 1950s Chicago by a group of passing black youths:

> You shit-coloured, square-ass poor mother-fucking junkman. Stop bullshitting the people. Ain't no God for Niggers. Fuck you and your peckerwood God in the ass, and fuck the Virgin Mary, too.
>
> Iceberg Slim, *Trick Baby* (1967)

Just thirty words, but there's something there to offend everybody – and that was, of course, the point. Iceberg Slim (Robert Black) had been a long-time pimp and serial jailbird before he turned to crime writing, so he knew his material inside out, and the language he employed was authentic. *Trick Baby* even came with a glossary of street terms, such as *pull coat* ('to inform or alert') and *peckerwood* ('contemptuous term referring to white men').

If the phrases employed by criminals tend to be abrasive, so, too, do those employed by soldiers. Most front-line troops in wartime are generally not long out of school, heavily armed and scared to death, and the slang they use to describe their day-to-day struggle for survival is generally brutal, often bitterly funny and right to the point. RAF pilots in the Battle of Britain wouldn't say that a friend had crashed; they would employ the bleakly deadpan expression 'Newton got him'. Or, as one Vietnam veteran told the journalist Mark Baker: 'If someone you're close to dies, you feel the pain in your heart, naturally. But the attitude you pick up quick is, "Oh. Shit. Dime a dozen. Travel light and carry a heavy bag." A heavy bag was a bag of dope.'

Pretending, in speech and drama, that all sections of society live life as if it were one continual vicarage tea party is a cultural dead end. (Mind you, it is easy to imagine a clergyman nowadays mildly berating someone who has done something stupid with the quaint old term *nincompoop* – a seemingly innocuous word – unaware that in the 18th century this was an obscene insult, as a contemporary slang compendium had it, for 'one who never saw his wife's ****').

Slang generally exists at the sharp end of the vulgar tongue, which is why so many of its dictionaries in earlier times were clandestine publications, and frequently anonymous. In the 1990s, Graham Linehan and Arthur Matthews, scriptwriters of the *Father Ted* series, famously satirised the censorship impulse by having Ted and Dougal protesting outside a cinema holding placards which read 'Careful Now' and 'Down With This Sort Of Thing'. Today, however, newspaper items about people taking offence at a huge variety of word usage seem to appear almost daily. Attempting to ban or suppress certain phrases – in effect, to declare 'I disapprove of what you say, and I will pillory, fine or imprison you because you say it' – is at best an urge to return to the days when Dr Bowdler and his family took a puritan axe to the collected works of Shakespeare, and at worst a way of lining yourself up with the kind of regimes which Orwell had in his sights when writing *Nineteen Eighty-Four*.

All right, Dad, shed the heater...

IF THERE IS ONE WRITER whose continuing worldwide success proves beyond doubt that the liberal use of slang is no barrier to understanding, then it is probably the great Raymond Chandler. His seven novels and various short story collections have been continually in print ever since they first began appearing in the 1930s. After an apprenticeship writing short, hard-boiled tales for pulp magazines like *Black Mask*, he secured his reputation with his 1939 debut novel, *The Big Sleep*, which gloried in the tough-talking, slangy narration of its detective Philip Marlowe, and whose title is itself a slang term for death.

Naming a book after the sordid business of *climbing the six-foot ladder* went down so well that Chandler did it again in 1953 with *The Long Goodbye*. In his work, characters are either busily engaged brandishing *roscoes* (guns), being fitted for a *Chicago overcoat* (coffin), jumping in their *heap* (automobile), *dipping the bill* (drinking) or trying to make some *cabbage* (money). You don't need a dictionary in order to enjoy reading these stories, because the context usually gives the sense of the term even if it is unfamiliar, but it is these phrases which give the language such a distinctive flavour, and which lesser writers have been attempting to copy ever since.

In more recent times, Irvine Welsh came to international

prominence with his 1993 novel *Trainspotting*, shot through with Edinburgh street expressions and slang, which reached an audience way outside those who might themselves employ such language. For instance, someone at a middle-class suburban dinner party, rising to go to the lavatory because of over-indulgence in alcohol, and also wished to stress that they were not carrying any drugs at that moment, would be unlikely to phrase it in quite the following way:

> Ah've been oan the peeve fir a couple ay days, mate. Ah'm gaun fuckin radge wi the runs here. Ah need tae shite. It looks fuckin awfay in thair, but it's either that or ma fuckin keks. Ah've nae shit oan us. Ah'm fuckin bad enough wi the bevvy, nivir mind anything else.

Here, as in Chandler's novels, the context usually provides the meaning, whether readers have encountered specific phrases before or not. Many terms have a life of a decade or two, then pass out of common use. A fair few of the bewildering variety of expressions employed by 18th- or 19th-century Londoners would not be recognised by its citizens today, but some words and phrases seem almost indestructible. For instance, *keks* (trousers) and *bevvy* (beer or drink), which appear in the above passage, both date back to Victorian times but are still part of today's everyday speech. Similarly, the word *radge*, meaning *mad* in this context, has come a long way since it was first recorded in J. Sullivan's *Cumberland and Westmorland, the People, the Dialect, Superstitions and Customs* (1857), pausing briefly to make an appearance in 'I Can't Stand My Baby', the 1977 debut single by Edinburgh punk band The Rezillos. *Shite*, in the above quote, is to excrete, but *shit* is heroin.

Memorable balls

THE TROUBLE WITH SLANG, and language generally, is that it doesn't stay still; meanings shift and mutate with the passing of time or the coming of new associations, and yesterday's plain speech can become today's double entendre. The children's author Shirley Hughes wrote a popular tale in 1977 about a boy and his battered soft toy of the canine variety. It was called *Dogger*, and the colloquial meaning of that particular word has changed beyond all recognition over the past few decades, conjuring up images of semi-clad figures scrabbling around in car parks looking for sex. A similar problem afflicts the title of one of the great pre-war jazz novels, Dorothy Baker's thinly disguised fictionalisation of Bix Beiderbecke's life story, *Young Man with a Horn* (1938) – a title to send *Viz* magazine's double-entendre-obsessed Finbarr Saunders into paroxysms of spluttering. (Indeed, when the book was filmed under that title in 1950 starring Kirk Douglas and Lauren Bacall, the picture was prudently renamed for its UK release *Young Man of Music*.) Yet here was a case of new slang meeting old slang; 20th-century jazz musicians habitually referred to the instrument they played as their *horn*, but as an English slang term for an erection, *getting the horn* dates at least as far back as Shakespeare's day.

A fine selection of volumes whose titles were left high and dry by the changing meanings of words over the years was rounded up by Russell Ash and Brian Lake in their entertaining 1985 collection *Bizarre Books*. These included *Perverse Pussy*, a children's story about a cat published in 1869 by the American Sunday School Union; J. Osborne Keen's *Suggestive Thoughts for Busy Workers* (1883), issued by the Bible Christian Book Room; *Memorable Balls* (1954), James Laver's recollection of dances attended; and John Denison Vose's immortal university story

The Gay Boys of Old Yale (1869). Taken together, all of these have titles which would give any self-respecting customs official pause, yet seekers after filth would surely retire disappointed – although doubtless better informed – after having perused them.

It might be thought that the originators of a popular jazz dance back in the 1930s called The Shag had seen the title of their creation given an unfortunate double entendre with the passing of time. However, the word was current in the 1780s, and listed in Captain Francis Grose's indispensable slang compilation the *Classical Dictionary of the Vulgar Tongue* ('*Shag*. To copulate'). As for the bebop fraternity, always keen to distinguish themselves from the squares, they shared that sentiment with the London underworld of the 1780s, who termed any man who would not steal, anyone honest, a *square cove* – from the Masonic fraternity's description of a trusted person as *on the square*, one of us.

Plenty of these words are old, some of them ancient even in Captain Grose's day. There are also many phrases which sound deceptively new, yet date back much further than people imagine. For instance, anyone familiar with the 1979 Neil Young song 'Hey, Hey, My, My (Into the Black)' would be pulled up short when chancing upon the words of the philosopher Bishop Richard Cumberland (1631–1718), a school friend of Pepys, who asserted that 'It is better to wear out than to rust out'. A shock of a greater kind awaits any Robert Browning enthusiast of a delicate disposition encountering his lengthy poem *Pippa Passes* (1841), not because it contains the much-quoted lines 'God's in His heaven / All's right with the world', but rather because of these:

> Then, owls and bats,
> Cowls and twats,
> Monks and nuns, in a cloister's moods,
> Adjourn to the oak-stump pantry!

The reason why a distinguished and respectable Victorian poet publicly employed a slang term for the female pudenda is very simple – he had no idea what it meant. Or, to be precise, he thought it was an article of clothing worn by nuns, yet for two hundred years the word *twat* had meant exactly what it means today. Browning's confusion seems to have arisen from his misinterpretation of an anonymous satirical poem from 1660, 'Vanity of Vanities, or Sir Harry Vane's Picture', which read in part:

> They talk't of his having a Cardinall's Hat,
> They'd send him as soon an Old Nun's Twat

All things considered, Browning would have been better off reading the playwright Thomas D'Urfey's *Wit and Mirth* (1719), where the meaning is marginally more clear:

> I took her by the lilly white Hand, And by the Twat I caught her.

Hip to be hep

ONE OTHER OBVIOUS DRAWBACK for the slang user is that sometimes the hip word of today will turn unexpectedly into the embarrassingly square word of tomorrow. Indeed, the word 'hip' itself became hip only after its predecessor 'hep' fell out of favour, as noted by Blossom Dearie in the song 'I'm Hip' (1966), written by Dave Frishberg and Bob Dorough – 'When it was hip to be hep I was hep'. One example of this kind of change has a personal resonance for me. In the year 2000 I published a book of words and phrases drawn from a lifetime's obsession with the language of vintage pulp crime fiction, film noir and jazz, blues, hillbilly, rockabilly and rock'n'roll music. I called the book *Straight from the Fridge, Dad*, which was an adaptation of a slang phrase meaning 'cool' that I'd heard in that jewel among teenage exploitation films, *Beat Girl* (1960). The implication being that the book was a compendium of phrases associated with the hipper or more outré fringes of society – musicians, mobsters, beatniks, con artists, etc. – as they existed during the first half of the 20th century – the language of outsiders, not the straights and the conformists. In the book's subtitle, I used a sobriquet which most jazz musicians of the late 1940s bop era would have been proud to bear – *hipster* – which meant someone who was one of the best, the sharpest, the most in the know, a *solid sender*, a *cool operator*. The rockers and delinquents of the 1950s adopted the term, and there it remained, a proud flag of suavedom for decades to come, so that I had no problem subtitling my book 'A Dictionary of Hipster Slang'.

Two years after it was published in the UK and US, an American book appeared called *The Hipster Handbook* by Robert Lanham, full of nerdy lifestyle material seemingly aimed at Ivy League squares, and somehow this has become almost the default modern meaning of the term, firstly in America and then in the UK. Geek chic. People who, according to Lanham, enjoy 'strutting in platform shoes with a biography of Che Guevara sticking out of their bags'. Leaving aside the question of why anyone would think it was cool to carry a book about a man who enthusiastically lined up significant numbers of his fellow citizens in front of firing squads, it also shows the extreme distance the word *hipster* has travelled since the days of 1940s originals such as alto sax giant Charlie Parker or boogie pianist Harry 'The Hipster' Gibson. For whatever reason, in England these days, to call someone a *hipster* is to insult them, in much the same way that, in the punk days of the late 1970s, one of the most damning labels you could hang on anyone was to call them a *poser*.

Times change, meanings change.

Yo, Jimbo…

BY THE SAME TOKEN, the slang greeting 'Yo!' has taken a long strange path over the years. When hard-line rappers Public Enemy named their 1987 debut LP *Yo! Bum Rush the Show*, this was very much the language of the street. Yet fast-forward two decades to an off-air private conversation between two politicians at the G8 summit in Switzerland, as jive-talking George W. Bush greets the then British prime minister Tony Blair:

> GWB: Yo! Blair, how are you doing?
> TB: I'm just…
> GWB: You're leaving?
> TB: No, no, no, not yet. On this trade thingy…

This kind of language is a long way from the formal, statesman-like way in which Hollywood or the BBC have traditionally portrayed conversations between world leaders. A little later in the conversation, Bush talks about the need 'to get Hizbullah to stop doing this shit' – another slangy phrase. Mind you, this is a man who warned a Washington audience in 2004 about 'these hateful few who have no conscience, who kill at the whim of a hat', and assured a New Hampshire Chamber of Commerce in 2000 that 'I know how hard it is for you to put food on your family', so he clearly had a special relationship not so much with England but with the English language.

At first glance, this might look like a straightforward case of a politician making a lamentable attempt to be 'down with the kids'. Yet the conversation between Bush and Blair was recorded without their knowledge, and there was no thought of trying to impress the younger members of the electorate with this language. Which is not to say that politicians are immune to such behaviour. Such toe-curling verbal anachronisms were roundly satirised by a sketch on the British TV show *Do Not Adjust Your Set* (1968), in which Eric Idle appears as a newly groovy Tory minister giving a party political broadcast:

> Good evening, and hello young electors, or may I call you cats. I'm Daddy-O Smythe, formerly known as Lance Captain Sir Archibald Barrington-Smythe – but you can call me Duggie – and I'm here to tell you about the new, switched-on, trendy, swinging, extremely psychedelic Conservative Party happening group thing... So do make like hippy hippy go-go people. Be like granny, take a trip along to your polling boutique, and put your tip for the top on us at the next vote-in. Swinging...

In 2016, having apparently learned nothing from this, the Britain Stronger in Europe campaign group – headed by Conservative peer Lord Rose and partly bankrolled by a number of prominent hedge-fund managers – attempted to persuade young people to vote in favour of remaining in the European Union by means of a much-mocked, supposedly *streetwise* advert, complete with obligatory hashtag:

> WORKIN, LEARNIN, EARNIN, SHOPPIN, RAVIN, CHATTIN, ROAMIN, MAKIN, MEETIN, SHARIN, GOIN, LIVIN... Make sure you're #VOTIN

If the word *yo* was considered hip in certain circles in 1986 when Public Enemy used it, that status probably took something of a beating two years later when MTV launched the show *Yo! MTV Raps*, seemingly in response to complaints earlier in the decade that showing any kind of black music on screen was pretty much the last thing they had in mind. Yet George W. Bush grew up in Texas from the late 1940s onwards, and the word *yo* was certainly in use as a slang form of greeting in the American South in that era. For example, here is a quote from John D. MacDonald's 1953 Florida-based crime novel *Dead Low*

Tide, in which the narrator, a white real-estate contractor, goes to a local bar with a woman from his office:

> We went in. Some fans were humming. I gave a self-conscious, 'Yo' to a couple of commercial fishermen I knew.

MacDonald had moved to Florida in 1949, so his dialogue would have sounded right for the time and location. Similarly, when I interviewed legendary 1950s Italian–American doo-wop star Dion DiMucci a few years ago, he began with his habitual greeting, the word 'Yo', and he is a man who started out in the Bronx, not South Central LA. Turning back much further, to 19th-century London, James Redding Ware's *Passing English of the Victorian Era* (1909) cites the expression *Yo, Tommy* – 'Amongst the lower classes it is a declaration of admiration addressed to the softer sex by the sterner'.

So is *yo* a black expression which has turned white, or white slang which has turned black and then back again? It certainly does not appear in Clarence Major's *Black Slang – A Dictionary of Afro-American Talk* (1970), whose words were drawn from 'every-day conversations in the black community, biographies, films, periodicals and the compiler's own black experience'. Major does lay claim to the word *pad*, however, meaning 'one's home, room, apartment'. Fair enough, you might think – given the fondness of 1940s jazz musicians for the term – except that if you go back more than two centuries to the anonymous London publication *The Life & Character of Moll King* (1747), you will find a character exclaiming 'He doss in a pad of mine! No, Boy, if I was to grapple him, he must shiver his Trotters at Bilby's Hall.' Among the capital's poor in those days, the word *pad* signified anywhere you could lay your head for the night, which was often just a rough mattress in the corner of a crowded room – literally a pad of material. As years went by, it came to signify the dwelling itself. Those

Londoners who fell foul of the law would be, if not 'turned off' by the hangman at Tyburn, transported to the colonies, which, before 1776, often meant America. Naturally, they took their slang with them, where it spread among hoboes, itinerant musicians, travelling players, carnival folk and criminals, both white and black, and *pad* finally went mainstream and global by the 1960s.

Passing through the mouths of illiterate clowns

THE ENGLISH LANGUAGE HAS ALWAYS ABSORBED overseas influences; *Yacht*, for instance, is an Anglicisation of the Dutch word *jaght* (now spelt *jacht*), denoting a fast, light vessel, which first began appearing in English towards the end of the 16th century; *arse*, that classic staple of the language which has been in use for the best part of a millennium, derives from the Germanic, in which today's equivalent is the word *arsch*.

Eighteenth-century slang lexicographer Francis Grose, writing in his pioneering work *A Provincial Glossary, with a Collection of Local Proverbs, and Popular Superstitions* (1787), complained of 'words derived from some foreign language, as Latin, French or German, but so corrupted by passing through the mouths of illiterate clowns as to render their origin scarcely discoverable'.

Half a century later, William Holloway made an attempt to record local English sayings, county by county, in *A General Dictionary of Provincialisms* (1839). He notes, for instance, that it would be said in Norfolk, Hampshire and Sussex of someone distinctly lacking in intelligence 'that his Upper-Storey is badly furnished' – a slang phrase which later surfaces in mid-20th-century American crime novels.

Whereas two hundred years ago, it might take a slang word many years to reach from the county of its origin to London (or vice versa), cultural developments in the intervening years have greatly speeded up this process. The growth of the cinema as an international art form has certainly played its part in this, and long before television appeared in most homes, the cinema encouraged young people in places such as Penzance or Dundee to imitate the speech patterns of Bogart or Cagney. A far-sighted 1929 *Daily Mirror* article, 'Will the Talkies Change Our Language?', written by Tom Patch, addressed this question just as silent films were giving way to sound:

> I remember many years ago being very much amused by a notice that stood on the counter of a shop in a well-known resort in the South of France. It said: 'English spoken – American understood.' Now the talkies have arrived over here in force, and there seems to be some danger that our mother tongue will be almost wiped out of existence. ... I gather from some of the more responsible Americans whom I know that what the talkies are pouring into the receptive ears of the youth of this nation is not so much the American language as its slanguage. ... It has never sounded right to me when I have heard a full-throated singer from Lancashire giving voice to vocal Americanisms about 'Sweeties' and 'Cuties' and 'Doggone wows.' Similarly, I am horrified at the thought of a good old Londoner – a hearty fellow born within the sound of Bow Bells, allowing his extremely attractive vernacular to become clogged up with expressions from across the Herring Pond, however snappy and up-to-date they may be.

It is hard to fault the accuracy of this prediction, as cockney and other regional UK slang has gradually given way on its home territory to that derived from American and other sources, mostly spread by means of film, television or music. With modern technology, these changes are now happening ever faster.

Each year, newspapers run their annual 'new words of the year' articles, in which we are told, for example, that *twerking* has been brought in from the wilderness. This word for a type of dancing has been around in rap circles for roughly two decades – and in terms of song lyrics, it first surfaced in a 1993 New Orleans bounce track by DJ Jubilee called 'Do The Jubilee All' – yet its meaning would not have meant much to the residents of Basingstoke or Brussels until very recently. *Twerking* came to worldwide prominence as a result of a performance by Miley Cyrus and Robin Thicke on 25 August 2013 at MTV's annual Video Music Awards – held, as aficionados of cockney rhyming slang will perhaps have noted – at the Barclays Centre in New York.

Within weeks, riding the media storm generated by the performance, Miley had appeared alongside Justin Bieber singing vocals on a single by rapper Lil Twist. The song was called, with the deathless logic of a corporation at full cry in search of a dollar, 'Twerk'. As blogger Perez Hilton put it, 'On the heels of Miley Cyrus' twerktastic evening at the VMAs comes the single that is going to BLOW YOUR TWEEN MIND!' Or not, as the case may be. Among the comments left by fans below this news item were 'puke', 'gross', 'this song sucks', and the considerably more eloquent 'I think this song signals there is no hope for us, it's over, we had a good run, society, however, has failed'.

Owing to the internet and the globalisation of 24-hour rolling media, the word *twerk* went from cool to embarrassing in record time. Its recognition factor spreading so far outside its original core group that *Private Eye* magazine was able to print a cartoon just weeks after the MTV controversy which showed a group of elderly gents in cloth caps gyrating arthritically in a building labelled 'Twerking Men's Club', confident that their readers of all ages would understand the meaning of the word.

But enough of the present; where did it all begin?

Vagabond Speech and Rogue's Latin

EVERYDAY SPEECH USED TO BE largely a transient thing. Today, though, the spread of mobile devices has enabled millions to capture random moments of passing life in sound and vision. The current social-media-obsessed age seems to have an urge to record for posterity virtually every aspect of life, however trivial. Given that agencies of government are apparently also logging and eavesdropping on every phone call, email or mouse click made by their electors with a thoroughness that would make the Stasi green with envy, the historians of the future will be positively drowning in evidence of how 21st-century people dressed, thought, acted and spoke.

Of course, this was not always the case. Consider the musician Robert Johnson. Arguably the most famous bluesman of all time, he cut a series of recordings in the 1930s which by the sixties were being hailed as all-time classics, yet it was not until 1986 that a single authenticated photograph of him was discovered. Even today, the count has risen only to three. Now imagine how many individual photographs have been taken, both officially and at concerts, of any member of whichever transient boy band happens to be bothering the charts this year. Turning to the written word, William Shakespeare has been world famous for centuries, yet there are just six surviving examples of his signature known to exist. As for what he actually looked like, the arguments continue, with only two images considered authentic, neither of which was made in his lifetime.

If it is this difficult to establish such basic facts about certain well-known people from the distant and even the recent past, how did the slang of the everyday people survive – for example, the casual speech of the masses, such as those who lived in 17th-century England, when it was technically possible to be born and work, marry and be buried without leaving any trace in the written records whatsoever? Not all marriages took place in church, not all graves had a marker, and many who ploughed fields or thatched roofs for a living could neither read nor write. Speech, of course, was plentiful among the common people – sometimes referred to by their educated social superiors as the *mobile vulgus*; literally the fickle crowd, or, in its shorter version, the *mob* – but it generally left few traces.

'Peddelars Frenche or Canting'

IN 14TH- AND 15TH-CENTURY ENGLAND, everyday conversation was conducted in what is now termed Middle English, but legal and literary documents were often in French or Latin. Even the unauthorized publication of an English translation of the Bible at that time was fraught with danger, and open to charges of heresy. Later, however, under the reign of Henry VIII, the first officially sanctioned translation appeared, known as the *Great Bible* (1539), and its use in church services throughout the nation helped standardise the pronunciation and spelling of English. Religion still dominated the land, but for any 16th-century reader wanting to encounter a slightly different turn of phrase to 'These are the generacions of Pharez: Pharez begat Hezron:

Hezron begat Ram, Ram begat Aminadab, Aminadab begat Nahson,' there were shortly to be other options.

During the explosion of semi-legal and clandestine publishing activity which occurred in the later 16th century, mixed in among all the political and religious broadsides, some pamphlets appeared dealing with the activities of beggars, *cony-catchers* (cheats or swindlers) and notorious criminals, which inevitably recorded something of the language employed by such people. In much the same way that 1960s and 1970s television crews reported back from mud huts on the banks of the Amazon, so that comfortable families in Dorking or Harrogate would know something of the lives and customs of various tribes deemed to be still living a 'Stone Age' existence, the first slang compendiums were assembled by writers significantly more privileged than those they described. The prime source for the vagabond slang of Elizabethan times is a book entitled *A Caveat or Warening for Common Cursetors Vulgarely Called Vagabones* (1567) by Thomas Harman, a man of some substance in Kent, who claimed to have spent twenty years questioning any of the itinerant poor who called at his door asking for money. In addition to detailing the varieties of beggar at large in the kingdom, and naming some of the most well-known individuals, his book included a glossary of cant terms. This was the first written use of the word *cant*, defined by Harman as meaning both 'to aske or begge', and also to speak in the language or dialect of beggars and thieves.

Thomas Harman's stated purpose, however, was not to entertain his readers, but rather to alert them to the identities and likely tactics of such people, and advise them what to do if any of them appeared at their door. In the preface, addressed to his neighbour, the Countess of Shrewsbury – one of the wealthiest women in the country – he said that he had written a book about vagabonds:

...to the confusion of their drowsey demener and unlaw-
full language, pylfring pycking, wily wanderinge, and lykinge
lechery, of all these rablement of rascales that raunges about al
the costes of the same, So that their undecent, dolefull dealing
and execrable exercyses may apere to all as it were in a glasse,
that therby the Iusticers and Shréeves may in their circutes be
more vygelant to punishe these malefactores.

Small reward, then, for all the beggars who had shared the
secrets of their 'unlawful' language with him. Yet, whatever his
declared intentions, this seems to have been the first organised
attempt to set down such speech in a book or pamphlet, and was
such a success that it was pillaged as source material by writers
and dictionary compilers for at least the next two hundred years.

Harman fixed in the mind of the reader several stereotypes
concerning these 'wretched, wily, wandering vagabonds calling
and naming them selves Egiptians' (gypsies). According to him,
they lived completely immoral lives, bedding down indiscriminately on one occasion in a barn for drunken couplings, 'seven
score persons of men, every of them having his woman, except
it were two wemen that lay alone to gether for some especyall
cause'. As for their speech, 'which they terme peddelars Frenche
or Canting', Harman asserts that 'the first inventer therof was
hanged, all save the head; for that is the fynall end of them all,
or els to dye of some filthy and horyble diseases'.

In Harman's valuable glossary of the 'pelting speche' of
'these bold, beastly, bawdy Beggers', several slang words occur
which have remained part of everyday language since Shakespeare was young – such as *fylche*, meaning to rob – while others
are self-explanatory: *stampers* are shoes; a *prauncer* is a horse.
Nevertheless, anyone today attempting to use some of the other
expressions over a few jars at their local hostelry would probably
meet with blank incomprehension. *Maunde* (ask) your friend if

they can provide you with a *Lypken* (house to sleep in) during the *darkemans* (night), because you've just *mylled a ken* (robbed a house) – netting a *grunting chete* (pig), some *Rome bouse* (wine), a pair of *slates* (sheets), a *caster* (cloak), three *wyns* (pennies) and *halfe a borde* (a sixpence) – and they will very likely ask the landlord for a few pints of whatever you've been drinking.

Cony-catching and the upstart crow

A CAVEAT OR WARENING *for Common Cursetors Vulgarely Called Vagabones* sold in good quantities, and was used a decade later as source material by pioneering Elizabethan historian William Harrison over several pages of his landmark *Description of England* (1577). It also provided inspiration for the various cony-catching pamphlets by one of the most successful writers of the Elizabethan age, the playwright Robert Greene. In fact, any reader encountering the latter's *A Notable Discovery of Coosnage, Now daily practised by Sundry lewd persons, called Connie-catchers, and Crosse-biters* (1591) would have needed a fair understanding of vagabond slang merely to decode the title. *Coosnage* or *cozenage* was cheating or fraud; *connie-catching*, more usually called *cony-catching*, was the early word for a confidence trick (the victim – whom 20th-century con men would call the *mark* – being the *cony*, the original common name for a rabbit); while *cross-biting* is the business of cheating the cheater. Greene, who wrote at least three other works on a similar theme around this time, listed in *A Notable Discovery* the slang names given to the various thieves involved in such swindles; for example:

> The partie that taketh up the Connie, the Setter
> He that plaieth the game, the Verser
> He that is coosned, the Connie

He that comes in to them, the Barnackle
The monie that is wonne, Purchase

Another writer who lifted large sections from Harman's work was the anonymous author of *The Groundworke of Conny-Catching* (1592), while the poet and dramatist Thomas Dekker went on to reprint Harman's glossary of thieves' terms in his 1608 pamphlet *Lanthorne and Candle-light*.

During the last decade of the reign of Elizabeth I, Shakespeare had begun his rise to prominence on the London stage – indeed, the earliest mention of his theatrical career comes in a barbed attack from the very same cony-catching authority Robert Greene, in a work published shortly after the latter's death in 1592. Greene's fame as a playwright at this time far outstripped that of Shakespeare, yet he felt the need to make reference to the younger man in his splendidly titled valedictory effort, *Greene's Groats-worth of Wit, bought with a million of Repentance, Describing the follie of youth, the falshoode of make-shift flatterers, the miserie of the negligent, and mischiefes of deceiving Courtezans*:

> ...there is an upstart Crow, beautified with our feathers, that with his *Tygers hart wrapt in a Players hyde*, supposes he is as well able to bombast out a blanke verse as the best of you: and being an absolute *Iohannes fac totum*, is in his own conceit the onely Shake-scene in a countrey.

This sounds harsh, yet the *Dictionary of National Biography* states that Greene's work was in fact an influence on the Bard, and that Shakespeare later 'drew affectionately on *Pandosto* [Greene's prose romance from 1588] and the coney-catching pamphlets in *The Winter's Tale* (1610–11)'.

Groping for trouts in a peculiar river

By THE TIME OF SHAKESPEARE, the English language had developed an astonishing range of expressions. His plays are the second most frequently quoted source for words in the *Oxford English Dictionary* (second only to *The Times*, which has had upwards of two hundred years of publication, whereas the Bard's writing career lasted just twenty-four). It is impossible at this stage to determine how many of the thousands of words or phrases which make their first written appearance in Shakespeare's plays were ones which he himself coined, as opposed to those which were already part of common speech. In *Othello* (1603), for instance, Iago tells Desdemona's father, Brabantio, that his daughter has been sleeping with Othello:

> Sir, y'are rob'd, for shame put on your Gowne,
> Your heart is burst, you have lost half your soule
> Even now, now, very now, an old blacke Ram
> Is tupping your white ewe.

Here, the playwright is using the word *tup* – an existing agricultural expression for the mating of sheep – in its slang sense as a term for human sexual intercourse, but he was not the first writer to do this (it also appears in Sir Thomas Chaloner's 1549 English translation of *The Praise of Folie* by Erasmus). Later in the same scene, Iago uses another sex metaphor: 'your daughter and the Moore, are making the Beast with two backs'. Shakespeare's use seems to be the first recorded in English, yet it appears to derive from an older French slang phrase, *faire la bête à deux dos*, which occurs in the prologue to *Gargantua* (1534) by Rabelais – although the first English translation of that work did not appear until fifty years after *Othello* was written. (Of course, other playwrights of the time were also using slang terms: for example, in *Volpone* (1606), Shakespeare's contemporary Ben Jonson has *noddle* for head, and *four eyes* for spectacles).

Shakespeare's cosmopolitan audience, hearing this kind of speech in the very first era of England's licensed theatre, would have been well able to negotiate and decode such language. Whether his own coinages or not, they provide a rich record of vocabulary and phrases in Elizabethan and Jacobean English. Characters talk of the *Neapolitan bone-ache* (syphilis) in *Troilus and Cressida* (1602), and of someone *having his pond fished by his next neighbour* (being cuckolded) in *The Winter's Tale* (c. 1610/11), which is similar to a slang expression for sex in *Measure for Measure* (1603/04), *groping for trouts in a peculiar river.*

Small wonder that puritanical 19th-century editors such as Harriet Bowdler and her brother Thomas hacked their way through Shakespeare's works like novice chainsaw owners let loose in the Amazon rainforest, rooting out anything they considered even potentially smutty – often erroneously, as the *Monthly Review* commented at the time of the 1818 edition of the Bowdler *Family Shakespeare*:

> We cannot, however, avoid remarking that the editor has some-
> times shewn the truth of the old saw, that the *nicest* person has
> the *nastiest* ideas, and has omitted many phrases as containing
> indelicacies which we cannot see, and of the guilt of which our
> bard, we think, is entirely innocent.

The English Rogue

THE 17TH CENTURY IN ENGLAND saw civil war, a growth in literacy, and an increasing stream of pamphlets and broadsides – many of which dealt with the lives of notorious characters. Perhaps inspired by the enthusiasm of the reading public for such material, a sometime bookseller called Richard Head decided to begin writing his own sensationalist fare, which he then sold from his London premises. His biggest success, by far, was a rambling, episodic adventure novel called *The English Rogue* (1665), narrated by its dissipated hero, Meriton Latroon, using a wide variety of cant expressions. On one occasion, meeting a prostitute of his acquaintance, Latroon describes their sexual encounter entirely in nautical terms:

> I knew not whether this Frigate was English or Flemish built, but at last, hailing whence she was, I boarded her, and made her a lawful prize: mistake me not, I rummag'd not in her Hold, fearing she was a Fire-ship.

The last phrase, *fire-ship*, was a current term for one afflicted with venereal disease, and this is arguably its first appearance in print, although Head drew many of his other expressions from Thomas Harman's *Caveat*.

Slang phrases for sexual activity, or for drink and its effects, were of course nothing new. Libertines in earlier times spoke of *doing the flesh's service* (1315), of *chamber-work* (1450), and *the shaking of the sheets* (1577), while anyone interested in strong ale might have requested *merry-go-down* (1500), *mad dog* (1577) or *lift-leg* (1587). After a hard night of indulgence, the result would probably be a *hangover*, but since that word dates only from the start of the 20th century, the sufferer would have complained rather of *ale-passion* (1593) or a sensation known as the *pot verdugo* (1616).

Richard Head's English Rogue would have been no stranger to any of these as he stalked Restoration London in search of new sensations and old pleasures. In common with many writers looking to bring a selection of supposedly authentic criminal argot to the discerning public, the author – and his narrator – are at pains to establish that although he has had dealings with thieves, he is at least a man with an education, and something not too far from a gentleman. As with the Elizabethan pamphleteers, the task of preserving and recording the slang which has come down to us from the 17th century largely fell to those who had an interest in this world, but were not themselves truly a part of it. Like a modern tabloid newspaper reporting a drunken orgy – in shocked tones, but over several full-colour pages – they present their evidence for the benefit of a readership which might never have experienced that world directly, but enjoyed hearing of it second-hand:

> Having even wearied ourselves with drinking and singing, we tumbled promiscuously together, Male and Female in Straw, not confining ourselves to one constant Consort, we made use of the first that came to hand; by which means incests and adulteries became our pastimes.

This scene appears directly inspired by a passage in Thomas Harman's work of the previous century, and many of the words contained in Head's short list of cant terms are drawn from the same source, such as *fencing cully* ('one that receives stollen goods'), *heave a booth* ('to rob an House') and *shop-lift* ('one that steals out of shops').

In the light of the great success of the *English Rogue*, which ran to five editions in his lifetime, Head further explored the language in a book of 1673, reusing much of his previous material under the following title, which deserves quoting in full:

> The canting academy, or, The devils cabinet opened wherein is shewn the mysterious and villanous practices of that wicked crew, commonly known by the names of hectors, trapanners, gilts, &c.: to which is added a compleat canting-dictionary, both of old words, and such as are now most in use: with several new catches and songs, compos'd by the choisest wits of the age

Clearly it was felt that the reading public was by now conversant with a selection of such language, well used to talk of *hectors* (bullies or thugs), *trapanners* (con men) and *gilts* (burglars), and if they were tiring of the subject, there was little sign of it. Although Richard Head died in 1686, drowning on the short sea journey from the mainland to the Isle of Wight, his successors were already waiting in the wings.

When not reading books or pamphlets – or, indeed, attempting to avoid the plague (1665) and the Great Fire (1666) – many Londoners of the time of Charles II were avid playgoers. This was entirely understandable, since the theatres had only recently reopened after Cromwell's joyless puritans outlawed such entertainments during their time in power. Samuel Pepys records in his diary of the 1660s many visits to the playhouses, sometimes to see long-suppressed works of Shakespeare ('June 4, 1661: ...thence to the Theatre and saw "Harry the 4th," a good play'), but also to view early examples of what have become known as Restoration Comedies. In the latter plays, the language was explicit, knowing and slang-heavy. The leading male character in William Wycherley's *The Country Wife* (1675) has the surname Horner, because he makes a sport of cuckolding husbands, putting the *horns* on them under the guise of being impotent, and thus above suspicion. At one point, Horner goes offstage into another room to meet Lady Fidget, after conducting the following conversation in front of the closed door of the room with her husband Sir Jasper:

> Horner. Now, is she throwing my things about, and rifling all I have, but I'll get into her the back way, and so rifle her for it –
> Sir Jasper. Hah, ha, ha, poor angry Horner.
> Horner. Stay here a little, I'll ferret her out to you presently, I warrant.

[Exit Horner at t'other door]

Sir Jasper. Wife, my Lady Fidget, Wife, he is coming into you the back way.

Lady Fidget. Let him come, and welcome, which way he will.

Sir Jasper. He'll catch you, and use you roughly, and be too strong for you.

Lady Fidget. Don't you trouble yourself, let him if he can.

The canting crew and other frolicks

THE GAUNTLET THROWN DOWN by the *English Rogue* was picked up in fine style at the close of the century by an anonymous writer known only as B.E., whose landmark work, *A new dictionary of the terms ancient and modern of the canting crew, in its several tribes of gypsies, beggers, thieves, cheats &c.*, was published in London in 1699. Its preface gives much of the credit for this type of speech to gypsies, but the author – a gentleman, naturally, according to the title page – claims that it will be 'useful for all sorts of People (especially Foreigners) to secure their *Money*, and preserve their *Lives*'. B.E. himself, while clearly part of the literate class, was more likely also one of the growing breed of Grub Street journalists who turned out the lurid pamphlets advertised alongside the quack remedies and religious tracts in the back pages of emerging news-sheets such as the *Weekly Advertiser*, the *Daily Courant* or the *Post Boy*. There was a ready market for anything which told of the exploits of notorious thieves, and a canting dictionary offered a window into that murky but fascinating world. While much of the language in this particular work was said to have come directly from the lower classes, the author admitted that he could not resist the inclusion of a scattering of high-society slang:

> If some Terms and Phrases of better Quality and Fashion, keep
> so ill Company, as Tag-Rag and Longtail; you are to remember,
> that it is no less then Customary, for *Great Persons* a broad
> to hide themselves often in Disguises among the *Gypsies*; and
> even the late L. of *Rochester* among us, when time was, among
> other Frolicks, was not ashamed to keep the *Gypsies* company.

Viewed today, many of the expressions in this compilation
of outsider language have passed so thoroughly into everyday
usage that they are unrecognisable as slang. Few people would be
surprised that a *biggot* is defined as 'an obstinate blind Zealot', or
that to be *jilted* is to be 'deceived or defeated in ones Expectation,
especially in Amours'. Some of these words appeared here for the
first time in any printed source, such as *land-lubber* as a derog-
atory sailor's name for those on shore, *skin-flint* for a 'griping,
sharping, close-fisted fellow', or *harridan* as a term of abuse for a
woman, 'one that is half Whore, half Bawd'.

This is the language of the streets, the drinking dens and
the brothels, set out for the entertainment of an ever-more
literate society in which newspapers and gossip-sheets were
proliferating, freed from excessive government censorship by
an act of 1695. Whether sitting in an alehouse, tavern or one
of the numerous coffee houses which had sprung up since the
1650s, the gentleman-about-town could brush up his knowledge of all kinds of terms for criminal activities, drunkenness,
fighting and whoring. They might, perhaps, count themselves
among the *libertines*, defined by B.E. as 'Pleasant and profuse
Livers, that Live-apace, but wildly, without Order, Rule, or Discipline, lighting the Candle (of Life) at both Ends'. These would
be people who were familiar with London's *vaulting academies*
(brothels), occasionally pick up a *flapdragon* or the *Spanish gout*
(a dose of the clap) and sometimes *put a Churl upon a Gentleman* (drink ale or malt liquor immediately after wine). However,

persons of their social standing would probably be unlikely to *cloy the clout* (steal a handkerchief), *wear the wooden ruff* (be put in the pillory) or have a final appointment with the *nubbing cove* (public hangman).

The *Canting Crew* dictionary, however much it may have been aimed at the affluent reading public, was written from the point of view of the criminal or itinerant classes. The word *booze* still had an outsider's cachet when it was used by the 1940s Los Angeles biker gang the Booze Fighters, but in fact it was quoted in as respectable a source as the *Daily Telegraph* as early as 1895, and had been an all-purpose term for alcohol under its variant spellings *bouse* and *bowse* for at least three hundred years. Here, the members of the canting crew, safe in their favourite *bowsing-ken* (alehouse), recall a piece of good fortune:

> *The Cul tipt us a Hog, which we melted in Rumbowse* – the Gentleman gave us a Shilling, which we spent in Strong Drink

After which, they very likely raised a toast to the gentleman in question, a word which made its first recorded appearance here ('*Tost* – to name or begin a new Health'). When it was all over, the table would be littered with *dead-men* ('empty Pots or bottles on a Tavern-table'), another first usage which survives to this day.

The parson's mouse-trap

THE 18TH CENTURY PROVED EVERY BIT as fond of slang and its uses and practitioners as its predecessor. That great hit of the London stage, John Gay's *The Beggar's Opera* (1728), featured characters based on notorious highwaymen and criminals, who were given fictional names drawn from thieves' cant. One of the gang is called by the self-explanatory name Filch, while another is Nimming Ned (to *nim* was to steal, deriving from the German *nehmen*, to take). The female associates of the gang, unsurprisingly, are given surnames such as Doxy and Trull, both of which were slang terms meaning whore. The dialogue, too, is larded with choice expressions and ripe terms of abuse: 'You baggage! You hussey! You inconsiderate jade! Had you been hanged it would not have vexed me...'

Few of these low-life words would have been unknown to the packed houses at the Lincoln's Inn Theatre watching Gay's work. Many such expressions had been set out for the early Georgian public during the previous decade by a gentleman who wrote sensationalist memoirs of famous criminals under the name Captain Alexander Smith. One such, *A Complete History of the Lives and Robberies of the Most Notorious Highwaymen, Foot-pads, Shop-Lifts, and Cheats of both Sexes in and about London*, appeared in an expanded version in 1719 with a slang dictionary appended:

> The 5th Edition, with the addition of near 200 Robberies lately committed. To which is added the Thieves New Canting Dictionary, explaining the most mysterious Words, Terms, Phrases and Idioms used at this Time by our modern Thieves.

While the *Complete History* was essentially a series of short life-stories, similar to the pamphlets of malefactors' confessions issued by the Ordinary of Newgate for the previous half-century, Smith's *Canting Dictionary* at the end of the book contained a selection of old and newer underworld phrases, which ranged from the expressive to the bleak, such as:

> *Dup the boozing-ken, and booze a gage*, i.e. go into the ale-house and drink a pot
>
> *Will ye raise a cloud*, i.e. will ye smoke a pipe

The gentry mort has rum ogles, i.e. that lady has charming black eyes

Backt, dead: as, *he wishes the old man backt*, that is, he longs to have his father on six men's shoulders

Wap, to lie with a man. *If she won't wap for a winn, let her trine for a make*, i.e. if she won't lie with a man for a penny, let her hang for a halfpenny

Cant words also came to the attention of people whose interest in language was of a less sensational nature. The London-born lexicographer and schoolmaster Nathan Bailey, who published his *Universal Etymological English Dictionary* in 1721, updated that volume in 1727 to include, among other things, an appendix entitled *A Collection of the Canting Words and Terms, both ancient and modern, used by Beggars, Gypsies, Cheats, House-breakers, Shop-lifters, Foot-pads, Highwaymen, &c.* This naturally drew in part upon earlier works, including that of Captain Smith, and was certainly not prudish or censorious in the manner of some later dictionaries. Bailey's books reached a wide audience, remaining in print for well over a century, and those who later made use of them included statesmen such as William Pitt the Younger and Abraham Lincoln. Perhaps most important of all, it was the 1727 edition of Nathan Bailey's *Universal Etymological English Dictionary* which Doctor Johnson used as the model for his own *Dictionary of the English Language* (1755).

Readers of this particular edition of Bailey's work were informed that *To Blow off the loose corns* meant 'To lie now and then with a woman', *Oliver's Skull* – as in Cromwell – was a chamber pot, and *The Parson's Mouse-Trap* was marriage. While these expressions have long passed out of everyday use, some still have a contemporary ring, such as *Jayl-Birds* meaning 'prisoners', *Tipsy* for 'almost drunk' or *Peepers* for 'eyes'.

Dissertations on the art of wheedling

IN TANDEM WITH THE PROLIFERATION of dictionaries and criminal history broadsides, the 18th century saw the rise of the English novel as an art form. These naturally also shine a light on the language of the day, but there are pitfalls here. For instance, in Henry Fielding's *The History of Tom Jones, a Foundling* (1749) can be found the phrase *smart-money*, which strikes a deceptively modern note. These days, this would refer to a likely bet, the sensible course of action, but in Fielding's time this was simply a form of payment made to members of the armed forces who had been wounded, the word *smart* used in the sense of pain, not intelligence. There are, however, genuine cant expressions in the novel: in a discussion of 'certain philosophers', the narrator slyly refers to them as *finders of gold*, which sounds like a compliment, but was also a slang name for those who cleaned out cesspits.

In 1754, an anonymous successor to Captain Smith and Nathan Bailey compiled *The Scoundrel's Dictionary: or, An Explanation of the Cant-words used by Thieves, House-breakers, Street-robbers, and Pick-pockets about Town, To which is prefixed, Some curious Dissertations on the Art of Wheedling: And a Collection of their Flash Songs, with a proper Glossary*. The title page of this entertaining document further attempts to claim authenticity for its contents with a subtitle stating that every word was direct from the horse's mouth: *The Whole printed from a Copy taken on one of their Gang, in the late Scuffle between the Watchmen and a Party of them on Clerkenwell-Green; which Copy is now in the Custody of one of the Constables of that Parish.*

Regardless of the legitimacy or otherwise of that assertion, this publication is especially valuable for its language, and in particular its explanation of the hierarchy of thieves and the names they gave to their various illegal occupations:

Besides the strolling Beggars and pretended Egyptians, there are others that use the Cant, who are most of the Town Thieves; or such as harbour about London, and are distinguished by several canting Names and Titles, *viz.*

The High-Pad, or Highway-Man. The Low-Pad, or Foot-robber. The Budge, who makes it his business to run into Houses, and take what comes first to hand. The Diver, or Pick-Pocket. The Bulk, or one that is his Assistant, in creating Quarrels by jostling, &c to gather a Crowd that the Diver may have a better Opportunity to effect his Purpose. The Jilt is one that pretending Business in a Tavern or Alehouse, takes a private Room, and with Pick-locks opens the Trunks or Chests, and taking what he can conveniently, locks 'em again, pays his Reckoning and departs. The Prigger of Prancers is one that makes it his Business to steal Horses. The Ken-miller is one that robs Houses in the Night-time, by breaking them open, or getting in at the Window, and seldom goes alone.

She may be a punk

ON 14 APRIL 1755 – one year after the publication of *The Scoundrel's Dictionary* – a lexicographical work of a different kind appeared: Dr Johnson's *Dictionary of the English Language*, a towering achievement by any standards, and one of the most influential dictionaries of all time. It had been commissioned almost a decade earlier by a group of London booksellers for the extremely substantial advance of 1,500 guineas. The scope of the work was wide, but not unprecedented. In fact, as Johnson's biographer David Nokes observes, 'Nathan Bailey's *Dictionarium Britannicum* included fifty per cent more words', and he further notes that the good doctor avoided many of the more salty expressions of the English tongue. When the omission of rude words was noted with approval by some of his female friends, Johnson apparently replied, 'What, my dears! Then you have been looking for them?'

This, of course, is the problem with prudery: no one would be able to search for such words if they did not know them already, and also have a fair idea how to spell them. Where, then, is the shock in seeing them written down? By contrast, for the modern reader, the chief surprises afforded by Johnson's *Dictionary* come from words which have acquired secondary meanings in the intervening years (although the first example is perhaps nearer the mark than some):

> *To* RAP *out.* To utter with hasty violence.
> He was provoked in the spirit of magistracy, upon discovering a judge, who *rapped out* a great oath at his footman. *Addison.*
> HIP-HOP. A cant word formed by the reduplication of *hop.*
> Your different tastes divide our poet's cares;
> One foot the sock, t'other the buskin wears:
> Like Volcius, *hip-hop*, in a single boot. *Congreve.*
> PUNK. n. f. A whore; a common prostitute; a strumpet.
> She may be a *punk*, for many of them are neither maid, widow, nor wife. *Shakespeare.*

Then of course, any streetwise person these days speaking of their *posse* might – if they think about the origin of the word at all – logically assume it is of American origin, from the days of the Old West, where the town lawmen rounded up a group of locals and set off in pursuit of criminals. Which is fine, as far as that goes, but like many other phrases, this one also came over from England in the 18th century, as Johnson's *Dictionary* confirms:

> POSSE. n. f. [Lat.] An armed power; from *posse comitatus*, the power of the shires. A low word.
> As if the passion that rules, were the sheriff of the place, and came off with all the *posse*, the understanding is seized. *Locke.*

The amiable Captain Grose

IF DR JOHNSON'S *DICTIONARY* (1755) for the most part avoided cant and slang – hardly surprising, given that he defined *to cant* as to speak in 'jargon', while his entry for *jargon* simply reads, 'Unintelligible talk; gabble; gibberish' – this is not a charge that can be laid at the door of Captain Francis Grose. This gentleman unleashed a book some thirty years later containing a heroic number of slang terms and expressions which, through no fault of their own, had fallen completely outside the scope of Johnson's work. Eric Partridge, arguably the greatest slang lexicographer of the 20th century, called Grose's *Classical Dictionary of the Vulgar Tongue* (1785) 'by far the most important work which has ever appeared on street or popular language'. Partridge further stated that 'every entry bears the unmistakable imprint of the vivid accuracy and the jolly, jovial earthiness of the greatest antiquary, joker and porter-drinker of his day, and one of the happiest wits of the 18th century', a judgement with which it is hard to disagree.

The pages of Grose's work bring to life the teeming, bawdy street-life of 1780s London – in particular the drinking establishments and brothels around Covent Garden – at a time when its population was somewhere around three quarters of a million (compared to Paris at 550,000; Moscow, 175,000; Rome, 160,000; and New York, the largest city in North America, 30,000). Dr Johnson, of course, also knew these streets well – the bookshop where he first met James Boswell was in Russell Street, just off Covent Garden piazza – but what Grose had in mind was a dictionary of another type altogether. His purpose, outlined in the preface to the first edition, was to utilise 'the freedom of thought and speech, arising from, and privileged by our constitution, [which] gives a force and poignancy to the expressions of our common people, not to be found under arbitrary governments, where the ebullitions of vulgar wit are checked by the fear of bastinado, or of a lodging during pleasure in some gaol or castle'. As a declaration in favour of free speech, and a gauntlet thrown down against official censorship, moralists and the easily offended, this is hard to beat.

The *Classical Dictionary* provided a window into a world of *barking-irons* (pistols), *member mugs* (chamber pots) and *horse-godmothers* (large masculine women), where people *blow the gab* (confess) or decorate the *sheriff's picture frame* (the gallows), where a *Covent Garden Abbess* is a madam, and her workforce of whores *Covent Garden Nuns*. This is a place where people speak *St Giles Greek* ('the slang lingo, cant, or gibberish'). Some phrases have survived into the present day – to *screw* is to copulate, to *kick the bucket* is to die – while others, of course, have not. Even at the time, a fair few of them would have been used only in particular circles and not usually in print, which makes their appearance in this dictionary even more remarkable, and must also have seemed that way to its original readers. Johnson's *Dictionary* ranged far and wide, but it is impossible to imagine it containing entries such as the following ripe example from Grose, printed in its original somewhat censored form:

> A BITER, a wench whose **** is ready to bite her a—se, a lascivious, rampant wench

Captain Grose, as his title suggests, had been a military man for a fair number of years, first in the Howard's and then in the Surrey regiment. He was also an artist and antiquary, exhibiting regularly at the Royal Academy. However, like many before him, he turned to writing books of various kinds in order to try to reduce his considerable debts. A native Londoner, he seems by all accounts to have been an amiable gentleman, equally well able to converse with anyone from the members of the armed forces, pickpockets and card-sharps to the habitués of the euphemistically named *riding academies* in Covent Garden. He died suddenly on a visit to Dublin in 1791, but his dictionary stands alongside that of Dr Johnson as one of the most valuable records of 18th-century English.

Grose national products

THE 1785 FIRST EDITION of the *Classical Dictionary of the Vulgar Tongue* was successful enough that Grose issued a second, marked 'Corrected and Enlarged', three years later. However, readers who had enjoyed the first may have felt alarm when reading the preface to the new one, which claimed that 'some words and explanations in the former edition having been pointed out as rather indecent or indelicate' had now been 'omitted, softened, or their explanations taken from books long sanctioned with general approbation'. That may be, but, for example, the definition of the word *biter* quoted above survived word for word into the new edition. Indeed, it seems as if the good captain was jesting somewhat in his preface about 'softening' or 'omitting' indecencies, given that his original entry *s—t sack* ('a dastardly fellow') was not only also included in the second edition, but with a new and lengthy explanation as to exactly how the unfortunate man confined in a sack had come to soil himself in the first place. This entry was then followed by another one, not present in the first, for the equally decorous phrase *sh-t-ing through the teeth* ('Vomiting. Hark ye, friend, have you got a padlock on your a-se, that you sh-te through your teeth?')

Grose did, however, amend some entries, and left out many more potential candidates which he had collected in the interim, that are preserved handwritten in his own working copy, which came into the hands of a London bookseller in 2013. These lost phrases included *turd hampers* ('breeches') and *goose neck and giblets* ('a man's tackle').

These two editions were the only ones which appeared in the author's lifetime. However, the popularity of his dictionary continued to the extent that a third edition was issued in 1796, five years after his death. Confusingly, this was also marked 'Corrected and Enlarged', although the vast majority of entries remained unchanged from Grose's second edition. The coming of the new century saw it issued again in 1811, but with a different title and a parade of other persons, named and anonymous, attempting to take credit for the work, to the extent that it is surprising they managed to find space for the original author at all:

> *Lexicon Balatronicum* – *A Dictionary of Buckish Slang, University Wit, and Pickpocket Eloquence, Compiled Originally by Captain Grose, and now Considerably Altered and Enlarged, with the Modern Changes and Improvements, by a Member of the Whip Club, Assisted by Hell-Fire Dick, and James Gordon, Esqrs of Cambridge; and William Soames, Esq of the Hon Society of Newman's Hotel*

The most obvious change here to Grose's original title is the prominent use of the word *slang* itself. While it had only a walk-on part in the editions published in the captain's lifetime, taking a very secondary role to the standard 18th-century term *cant*, here it is placed centre stage. The new title was clearly intended to appeal to Regency dandies and students, while playing down somewhat the low-life angle. This was the era of Brummell and Byron, and wealthy young men ruining themselves gambling on games of Macao at exclusive gentlemen's clubs such as Watier's in Piccadilly. Inside, however, it soon becomes clear that the vast majority of the book was

Grose's third edition, almost verbatim. Considerably altered and enlarged? Not really. Yet it did record some of the newer names for slang, such as:

> *FLASH LINGO* – The canting or slang language
> *PATTER*. To talk. To patter flash; to speak flash, or the language used by thieves. How the blowen lushes jackey and patters flash; how the wench drinks gin and talks flash.

Also among the new entries was at least one which former student radicals who manned the barricades in 1968, or read *Oz* magazine and the *International Times* back in hippie days, would certainly recognise:

> *PIG*. A police officer. Floor the pig and bolt; knock down the officer and run away.

A little over a decade later, the writer Pierce Egan largely restored the original title, issuing the book as *Grose's Classical Dictionary of the Vulgar Tongue, Revised and Corrected, With the Addition of Numerous Slang Phrases, Collected from Tried Authorities*. Egan, whose own bestselling nightlife stories of two London characters, Tom and Jerry, were themselves larded with the slang and flash talk of the day, provided his own thoughtful preface to the edition. He also included a lengthy and sympathetic biographical essay about Grose, with insights into the nightly London explorations made by the late captain and his manservant, Batch, in search of material in the rookeries on the north-western edge of Covent Garden:

> The *Back Slums* of St Giles's were explored again and again; and the Captain and *Batch* made themselves as affable and jolly as the rest of the motley crew among the beggars, cadgers, thieves &c who at that time infested the *Holy Land*!

Also, as a measure of how the cultural landscape had shifted since the previous edition of the *Classical Dictionary*, one of the new entries coined by Egan read as follows:

> DANDY. In 1820, a fashionable non-descript. Men who wore stays to give them a fine shape, and were more than ridiculous in their apparel.

By the time this was published, Brummell was in exile and Watier's Club – the dandy haunt par excellence – had closed with many of its high-rolling members ruined. Instead of buckish slang, this edition gave more emphasis to sporting matters such as boxing, a particular interest of Egan.

During the intervening two centuries, it is the edition misleadingly renamed *Lexicon Balatronicum* that has most often been reprinted, usually under the equally inappropriate title *1811 Dictionary of the Vulgar Tongue*. This makes Grose's book sound like a product of Regency London, yet his world was the capital city's seedy underbelly of thirty years before, and he died long before the heyday of the dandies. The *Classical Dictionary* is a true 18th-century artefact, and should be recognised as such.

There iz no alternativ

PROBABLY THE EARLIEST ATTEMPT by a nation to put some distance between the English they used and the place where it originated was of course that of America. Noah Webster, the pioneering lexicographer of American letters – who, with his spelling books and dictionaries, did more than anyone else to influence and record the way that nation spoke and wrote – was, in the words of Eric Partridge, a man of 'intensely anti-British bias'. The War of Independence was probably far too recent for this situation to have been otherwise. Webster is the person who made a host of changes such as removing the 'u' from the word *colour*, but in his early works he wanted to go much further. Consider this radical approach to spelling from the introduction to Webster's work, *A Collection of Essays and Fugitiv Writings on Moral, Historical, Political and Literary Subjects* (1790):

> In the essays ritten within the last yeer, a considerable change of spelling iz introduced by way of experiment. This liberty waz taken by the writers before the age of Queen Elizabeth, and to this we are indeted for the preference of modern spelling over that of Gower and Chaucer. The man who admits that the change of *housebonde, mynde, ygone, moneth* into *husband, mind, gone, month*, iz an improovment, must acknowlege also the riting of *helth, breth, rong, tung, munth*, to be an improovment. There iz no alternativ.

Some would argue that there was indeed an alternative – throw away the language altogether if it bothers you that much, and come up with your own – but Webster never quite went that far. He did, however, much later in his career, attempt to do for the Bible what the Bowdlers had done to Shakespeare, making thousands of changes to the text of the King James Bible in an effort to root out anything of a supposedly 'lewd' nature. The study of slang meant little to Webster, and his pioneering *American Dictionary of the English Language* (1828) dismissed it in one short sentence: 'low vulgar unmeaning language', which suggests a prudish bias, since such words can mean a great deal, regardless of how they might offend certain listeners.

The first real attempt in the US to round up the many singular coinages of the nation came in 1848 with the publication of John R. Bartlett's *Dictionary of Americanisms*, which contained a great deal of valuable material, but like Webster, showed little fondness for slang as it was slung. As Bartlett said in his introduction:

A careful perusal of nearly all the English glossaries has enabled me to select what appeared to be the most desirable to embrace, and what to avoid, in an American book of a similar kind. Cant words, except such as are in general use, the terms used at gaming-houses, purely technical words, and those only known to certain trades, obscene and blasphemous words, have been discarded.

Of course, genuine American slang was coming into play at this time – it just was not usually considered respectable enough to merit inclusion in the dictionaries of a nation which often insisted upon *rooster* instead of the plain English word *cock*, and where mention of the word *leg* in some circles was considered indecent. The 19th-century American writer Richard Meade Bache objected to this tendency in his book *Vulgarisms and Other Errors of Speech* (1868), noting that he had 'heard a *lady* direct a waiter to bring her the *trotter* of a chicken'. As he put it:

> It is a shame that excellent words, which are a part of our language, and which have served our ancestors for hundreds of years, should be driven out of familiar use by prurient imaginations. Cock and Hen are generic names, distinguishing the male and the female of all kinds of birds; but The Cock and The Hen are the distinctive appellations of the barn-door fowls. Why then should we substitute *rooster* for *cock?*

Admirable sentiments, yet in the same book he issued a stern warning against slang, which, he claimed, 'pervades too much of the conversation even of the refined'. Considering the many complaints from British commentators in the 20th century that Hollywood and the record companies were teaching the youth of this country ever-increasing amounts of US slang, it is a mark of how much attitudes changed since the days when Bache offered the following tortuously worded cautionary tale:

> In the writer's hearing, not long since, a very respectable man,

who has some pretension to education, inasmuch as he is a
publisher, found no better expression to describe the position
of an influential person in a certain business, than to say, that
he was 'at the top of the heap.'

Perhaps not surprisingly, the golden age of American slang
lexicons would come later.

Say it again, Sam

AFTER THE TRAILBLAZING WORK of slang dictionary compilers from Tudor times up until the end of the 18th century, the
pattern was set, since which time it may have occasionally seemed
that there were few remaining low-life hangouts, gin-joints and
thieves' dens across the widening English-speaking world where
the underclass felt safe from lexicographical observation.

As such collections proliferated at an increasing rate
throughout the 19th and 20th centuries, much valuable work
was done – not least by John S. Farmer and W. E. Henley in
their vast, seven-volume work of the 1890s, *Slang and Its Analogues*. However, an unfortunate trend also developed, in which
some dictionary compilers with a regional or nationalist bias
attempted to claim wholesale chunks of the English language
for their own particular ends. In some cases, this was purely
because the lexicographer in question comprehensively noted
down everything remotely slang-oriented in the speech of a particular place, regardless of the phrase's history. This occurred in
the 1988 Australian slang work *The Dinkum Dictionary* – later
reissued and enlarged as *The Penguin Book of Australian Slang* –
whose author wrote, 'I had no difficulty in deciding whether or
not to include sayings that are not strictly Australian in origin
– I simply included them all.' The result of this policy is that,

although Australian slang has given the world an extremely large number of inventive and original coinages, those words are lined up here alongside numerous others such as *chatterbox* (talkative, English, 1770s) or *broken-hearted*, which occurs in Tyndale's 1526 translation of the Bible (*To heal the broken harted*, Luke iv, 18). The inclusion of words which although used in that country are no more a product of it than any other random English word such as *wardrobe* or *shoe* would seem to be counterproductive.

Of course, to an extent most slang dictionaries lay claim to words which are common to other groups or locations, but occasionally assertions are made, seemingly based upon nothing more than the desire of the author to rewrite history. One example of this was the publication in 2007 of a widely mocked book entitled *How The Irish Invented Slang* by Daniel Cassidy, the late American writer, in which he attributed the origins of such musical and counterculture words as *jazz* and *dig* to Gaelic words which might, after a long night on the sauce, sound a tiny bit similar if spoken by someone gargling with a mouthful of marbles. Here again, the very legitimate story of the many Irish slang coinages is submerged and obscured by the unsustainable assertions lined up alongside them.

Nation shall speak slang unto nation

INCREASINGLY, AS THE 18TH CENTURY gave way to the 19th, there was no longer just the slang of the British Isles and all its variants, but also colonial and post-colonial adaptations, and the myriad specialist argots of the armed forces, criminals, actors, students, musicians, schoolchildren, tradespeople and others. The language fragmented and fed back into itself as time passed, so that a cant word known in Sydney or San Francisco might also be used in Liverpool, and vice versa (often with each community taking the word to be a local coinage).

It was ever more a question of who you were, as well as where you were, that determined your slang usage – as it remains to this day. Rappers imitate other rappers, and computer geek speaks to computer geek, regardless of location.

ONE

The Beast With Two Backs

Long dismissed as a myth, it now appears that there really *are* at least fifty Eskimo words for snow. Whatever the case, the English language unquestionably has hundreds, probably thousands, for sex. Each generation naturally likes to think that they have come up with their own, yet for every genuinely new coinage there are others which have been doing service for years, or are simply new variations on old themes.

People have always sat around with their friends telling obscene jokes or risqué stories; whether on a girls' night out, among a group of lads on the way to the football, or a selection of club-going gentlemen breaking out the port and cigars after dinner. In the high days of *Playboy* magazine back in the 1960s – when its literary contributors included the likes of Graham Greene, Vladimir Nabokov and Ian Fleming, and most of the adverts were for top-grade whisky, jet-set holidays and expensive tailoring – they also found space in each issue for a page of bawdy after-dinner jokes.

If time machines existed, and it was possible to drop in on an 18th-century Covent Garden hostelry and listen to the late-night conversations, without doubt you would hear the widest variety of slang and plain English terms for sexual activities. Everyday speech in those days was seldom preserved, so what has survived of how our ancestors spoke when they talked about sex is of necessity gathered from private letters, and scandalous, suppressed or clandestine writings of the time – a fragmentary record, but valuable nevertheless. As with many subjects, the most surprising thing is how many of these words are still in regular use today, employed by many people who may have no sense how venerable some of these terms might be.

Only my roll of honour, darling

AS CENSORSHIP OF THE WRITTEN WORD has diminished considerably on both sides of the Atlantic, the boundary between high art and low life has become ever more blurred, and an incredibly varied range of written representations of the sex act have been set before the public. Consider the following examples:

> 'Are there any shots left in that gun?' she asked, 'or did you shoot them all with Mary?' I told her I had an unlimited supply of ammunition, and she said that was good because she wanted a good screwing.

> I was coming for about 5 minutes with my legs round him I had to hug him after O Lord I wanted to shout out all sorts of things fuck or shit or anything at all...

> We fucked – That glorious word expresses it all. Slowly, till urged by spermatic wants, that inner sovereignty or force, within my balls, hurrying to ejaculate itself; quicker and quicker went my thrusts, her buttocks responded, her cunt gripped...

> 'Oh Jock, what was that you made me touch?' To avoid being coarse at such a time I replied, 'Only my roll of honour, darling.' 'Good grief,' she retorted, 'It felt like a roll of wallpaper.'

> And then my body, like a cathedral, broke out into ringing. The hunchback in the belfry had jumped and was swinging madly on the rope.

A few of these words and phrases would still cause the average newspaper editor to start reaching for the asterisks, despite the fact that they would be hard pressed to encounter a reader who did not understand them – indeed, the whole business of printing f*** becomes somewhat futile if your audience cannot mentally fill in the gaps. As to the respective origins and literary merits of these particular excerpts: quote number one is from a pulp paperback called *The New Sexual Underground – The Real Book about Hippie Love-Ins, Group Sex Parties, Nude Happenings, Wife Swaps!* (1967); quote two is from *Ulysses* by James Joyce (1922); quote three is from the vast and anonymous Victorian sex diary of a wealthy gentleman, *My Secret Life* (1882); quote four is from a letter written by a Scottish soldier to *Mayfair* magazine (December 1974); and quote five is from the novel *Middlesex* by Jeffrey Eugenides, which won the *Literary Review* Bad Sex in Fiction Award, 2002.

I untrussed and got ready for the plunge

DESPITE THE FACT THAT SLANG WORDS with sexual connotations occur in the everyday speech of much of the population, those governing society have repeatedly attempted to shield their citizens from exposure to them. This attitude was exemplified by the *Lady Chatterley* obscenity trial at the Old Bailey in October and November of 1960, at which learned barristers, cultural critics and distinguished novelists were called upon to debate the literary merits of a book which used basic English slang terms such as *fuck* and *cunt*. Defence witness Richard Hoggart argued that 'these are common words. If you work on a building site, as I have done, you will hear them frequently.' In fact, said Hoggart, 'they seem to be used very freely indeed, far more freely than many of us know. Fifty yards from this Court this morning, I heard a man say fuck three times as I passed him. He was talking to himself, and he said, "fuck her, fuck her, fuck her". He must have been angry.'

Another trial witness, Sarah Jones, classics mistress at Keighley Grammar School, was asked by Gerald Gardiner, QC, for the defence, about the reading habits of the girls she taught:

> Q: 'Is there a great deal of literature available to them now on sexual matters?'
> A: 'Yes, and there are technical works, and what you might call "dirty" literature.'
> Q: 'How far do girls understand the four-lettered words?'
> A: 'I have inquired of a number of girls after they have left school, and most of them have been acquainted with them since about 10 years of age.'

The idea that most people would be shocked by such things is a flimsy construction usually put forward by moralists with an axe to grind, but the general public seem to be made of sterner stuff. Indeed, as Anthony Burgess once pointed out: 'it only needed Kenneth Tynan to say "fuck" on television in the Sixties for decent girls to glory in the language of bargees'. Burgess, of course, added a fair few slang expressions to the language during that decade with the publication of his breakthrough novel, *A Clockwork Orange* (1962). It was written in a hybrid language of his own called *nadsat* – a blend of cockney rhyming slang, Slavic borrowings and made-up phrases – in which breasts were *groodies*, something good was *horrorshow*, and intercourse was *plunging* ('real good horrorshow groodies they were that then exhibited their pink glazzies, O my brothers, while I untrussed and got ready for the plunge'). It is a measure of how much freer from censorship the written word in the UK was than on the cinema screen that *A Clockwork Orange* had to wait until the

following decade before it was filmed – although there were pro-
posals in the mid-1960s to make a version in conjunction with
Mick Jagger, The Beatles, Andy Warhol and others. Whether
this would have proved to be *horrorshow* in its newer or more
traditional meaning is hard to say.

To jape, to sard, to fucke, to swive, to occupy

THE MOST COMMON OF THOSE EXPRESSIONS that the press
call four-letter words have a venerable history. Such terms were
originally standard English, but from the late 18th century to
the mid-20th were usually excluded from mainstream dictionaries, reclassified as vulgar slang and best avoided in polite society.
However, during their years of censorship, they could nevertheless be found in expensive works printed privately for the
well-heeled collector, and eventually in under-the-counter pulp
novels aimed at the one-handed trade, high-minded literature
of the trailblazing sort and any number of magazines offering
pornography of varying strengths and persuasions.

In England a thousand years ago the word *play* did service
as a general term for sexual intercourse, and was regularly
employed in this context up until the 17th century. Other terms
which came into use during that span of time were to *couple*,
felter, *mell*, *gender* and *converse*, but at some time during the 1500s
our old friend *fuck* made its first documented appearances – for
example, in the works of the appropriately named Scottish cour-
tier Sir David Lyndsay of the Mount, who, in 1568, composed
the line 'Ay fukkand lyke ane furious Fornicatour'. Yet initially,
fuck was just one word among many for this activity.

Back in the 14th century, Chaucer referred to the basic act
itself as *swiving*, which was still in regular use 300 years later,

such as in Robert Fletcher's 1656 translation of Martial's *Epigrams* ('I can swive four times in a night'). Indeed, half a century before Fletcher's book appeared, Shakespeare's contemporary, John Florio, in his pioneering volume *A Worlde of Wordes, or Most Copious and Exact Dictionarie In Italian and English* (1598), translated *fottere*, the Italian word for having sexual intercourse, as 'to jape, to sard, to fucke, to swive, to occupy'. Florio, born in London to an English mother and a Tuscan father, taught Italian at Oxford University for a while. His dictionary was aimed largely at the titled and the wealthy – hardly a clandestine publication – yet this frank attitude to terms for sexual activity is reflected throughout Florio's English definitions. Presumably, he felt that such expressions might prove useful to his readers when visiting Italy. Hence, in addition to such normal phrases as *giorno di festa*, 'a holyday', or *prodotti*, 'the fruites or gaines of any mans labour', he included *bardascia*, 'a buggering boy', *catanace*, 'an herb used of witches to provoke love and lust', and *valle de acheronte*, 'a womans privie parts or gheare. Also hell.'

The urge to equip the adventurous traveller with a variety of expressions to cope with any potentially erotic situation continues to this day. In the 1990s, I bought a basic phrase book before visiting Japan. In addition to the usual chapters devoted to shopping, dining and hotel life, it also contained a short section entitled 'Chatting Someone Up', which moved on the same page from innocuous gambits such as the Japanese for *you have such beautiful eyes* swiftly on to *we have to be careful about AIDS*. This admirable urge to provide for all eventualities pales, however, beside that heroic work of Messieurs Richard and Quétin, *English and French Dialogues* (1876), whose concept of the likely linguistic needs of Victorian gentlemen visiting France envisaged circumstances in which it would be necessary to say

*I believe I shall go mad with pleasure, the abomination has reached
its height* and that perennial tourists' favourite, *after so many mis-
fortunes, it only remains for me to die.*

Yet for all the supposed delights of travel, some will always
yearn for the familiar comforts of home. Such was the case of
George III's third son, Prince William (later William IV), who
wrote to his brother from Hanover on 23 July 1784, of being
'in this damnable country, smoaking, playing at twopenny whist
and wearing great thick boots. Oh, for England and the pretty
girls of Westminster; at least to such as would not clap or pox
me every time I fucked.'

A little thatch'd house is my principal joy

SINCE THE INVENTION OF THE PRINTING PRESS, there has
always been a market for publications which have ventured
where the easily offended fear to tread. The English song and
poem collection *Merry Drollery* (1661), for example, made the
following play on the similarity between the word *conny* or *coney*
(rabbit), and *cunny* (vagina) – indeed, the latter word was also
written as *cony* or *conney* in the 16th century:

> My Mistris is a Conny fine,
> She's of the softest skin,
> And if you please to open her,
> The best part lies within,
> And in her Conny-barrow may
> Two Tumblers and a Ferrit play, Fa, la, la.

If the common people of the 17th century were singing
ribald songs, the aristocracy were frequently a match for them.
Leading the charge was the dashing figure of John Wilmot, 2nd
Earl of Rochester, poet, war hero and favourite of King Charles

II, who offered this four-line verse about a daughter of the king's physician:

> Her father gave her dildoes six,
> Her mother made 'em up a score,
> But she loves nought but living pricks
> And swears by God she'll frig no more.

This may not have been as shocking to a 17th-century Londoner as it at first seems – indeed, Shakespeare himself had included talk of dildos in *The Winter's Tale* (1610/11), as did Ben Jonson in *The Alchemist* (1610) – and during his lifetime, most of Rochester's work was circulated only privately among friends. Similarly, throughout the following century, clandestine publications continued to print the kind of material which utilised the fullest range of current English words. *The Merry-Thought, Or the Glass Window and Bog-House Miscellany* (1731) collected together scurrilous rhymes originally written on lavatory walls and scratched into window panes, while the *Gentleman's Bottle-Companion* (1768) gave an authentic flavour of the bar-room ballads current in Dr Johnson's London. Among the many examples in the latter publication – all of which seem to centre on whoring, drinking or a combination of the two – can be found a song called 'The Stiff-Standing Member', part of which reads as follows:

> A member more humble you cannot employ;
> In a little thatch'd house is my principal joy,
> Which with raptures I enter, but quit with concern,
> And unless I can stand, naught avails my return.

The verses in some other collections might sound to our ears more like the products of the last couple of decades rather than those of a society which passed away a century or more ago. This is especially the case with a publication called *The Rakish*

Rhymer, Or Fancy Man's Own Songster and Reciter (1864), much of which was derived from then-current bawdy music-hall songs. In one ballad, 'Among the Leaves So Green, O', the male narrator employs slang words such as *gash*, *screw* and *twat*, claims to be *pretty fairly hung*, and speaks of making his lover *horney-hot*. Of course, there undoubtedly were examples of morally upright, repressed or puritanical people in Victorian times – as there tend to be in any age – but they were unlikely to be frequenting the halls of a Saturday night, singing along to songs like these.

There were gentlemen of that time whose preferred reading ran more to exclusive magazines such as *The Pearl* (1879–80), in whose stories fictional men encountered somewhat worldlier women than those usually found in Dickens. 'We awoke,' says one breathless narrator, 'to find Sophie, Polly, Emily, and Louisa all rolling on the floor in the delights of *gamahuching* [oral sex].' (The last word is first recorded in a clandestine publication from 1788 called *Venus School Mistress*, a flagellation volume credited to one R. Birch, and deriving from the French word *gamahucher*). *The Pearl* also ran a serial story called *Lady Pokingham – Or, They All Do It*, in which a gentleman comments, 'Her pussey was all wet with spendings'. For a very long time the word *pussy* served respectable society as a name for a cat, while at the same time conveying quite another meaning to many people. Today, however, even a naïve guest at the most dignified of vicarage tea parties would be unlikely to imagine that the Russian protest group Pussy Riot had named themselves after an uprising of four-legged household pets.

Numero uno

THE CONTENTS OF PUBLICATIONS such as *The Pearl* and *Cythera's Hymnal; Or, Flakes from the Foreskin* (1870) also included limericks – a literary form which has always concentrated heavily on the scurrilous and the obscene, despite the efforts of the likes of Edward Lear (1812–88), many of whose verses were aimed at children. Another man who felt that clean limericks were the way to go was Langford Reed, whose family-friendly *Complete Limerick Book* (1924) managed only to confirm Arnold Bennett's private opinion that 'the best ones are entirely unprintable'. The armed forces would appear to have concurred with this sentiment, since many of the finest 20th-century limericks were products of the troops of both world wars, in whose rhymes all manner of men, women, animals and inanimate objects were sexually employed in ways that would tax the most extravagant imagination. Reed, however, boasted in his introduction that he had 'examined several thousand Limericks' and then 'excluded a large number of "Rabelaisian" examples', which is the rough equivalent to a film censor declaring that Peckinpah's *The Wild Bunch* is a wonderful film, especially now we have removed all of that nasty shooting at the end. This approach left Reed with inoffensive fare such as:

> There was an old man of Sheerness,
> Who invited two friends to play chess,
> But he'd lent all the pieces
> To one of his nieces,
> And had stupidly lost the address.

Compare this with a limerick dated 1942–4, very likely of army origin:

> There was a young gaucho named Bruno

Who said, 'Screwing is one thing I *do* know.
A woman is fine,
And a sheep is divine,
But a llama is Numero Uno.'

Same rhyme scheme, different agenda.

Looking at the solemn faces in formal portrait photographs of men in uniform just about to be shipped out to the horrors of the First or Second World Wars, it is easy to imagine the serious side of their natures. However, another, more irreverent side of them is revealed in the survival of bawdy verses such as these, many of which have retained their bite and their wit, while decades-old jokes from magazines like *Punch* or the *New Yorker*, if viewed today, sometimes fail to raise even the ghost of a smile.

Thinking four-legged thoughts

OF COURSE, THERE ARE MANY WAYS of suggesting sexual intercourse without using the handful of words which have been prosecuted for obscenity in past times. Ernest Hemingway famously had his hero Robert Jordan in *For Whom the Bell Tolls* (1940) enquire directly after the act, 'But did thee feel the earth move?', although any attempt to use that particular phrase these days in such circumstances would probably not end well. Jordan is an American who has volunteered to fight in the Spanish Civil War, yet at times his manner of speech suggests that he has been transplanted whole from the 17th century:

> I love thee and thou art so lovely and so wonderful and so beautiful and it does such things to me to be with thee that I feel as though I wanted to die when I am loving thee.

Other male novelists in America in Hemingway's day, particularly crime writers, were taking a different approach. In

Dashiell Hammett's *The Thin Man* (1934), one character complains that her unfaithful husband is 'chasing everything that's hot and hollow', which is relatively explicit for the time. Perhaps even more so was the dialogue in the books of Ward Greene. In his novel *Death in the Deep South* (1934), whose action takes place in 1913, people say things like 'She was hot pants for him', and in *Ride the Nightmare (Life & Loves of a Modern Mister Bluebeard)* (1930), lines such as 'It was more fun than plain poontang' or 'then she'll be free to bang another guy, and before midnight I say she will' are bandied about, while a character named Dick Cheney (sic) exclaims 'There went a piece of hot stuff'.

These are familiar slang expressions, still in use today, but caution must sometimes be used when reading US pre-war crime fiction, since the word *shagging* to American private detectives at that time meant following or putting a tail on someone, rather than its UK meaning. ('Didn't you know we had been shaggin' you all night and morning?' a man is asked in Lester Dent's ultra-tough short story 'Sail', published in *Black Mask*, October 1936.)

The cops in hard-boiled crime fiction have generally seen it all and done it all, like the weary, methodical police chief in Hillary Waugh's superb 1952 procedural *Last Seen Wearing*, who asks a suspect, 'When did you first get laid, Mildred? Seventeen, eighteen, nineteen?' Waugh was a craftsman, whereas the various writers who toiled under the house name Hank Janson were probably thinking more of the deadline and the pay cheque than anything else. Even so, they had their way with an arresting image every so often, as in this description from the book *This Hood for Hire* (1960), of the convict Frank on his first day out of prison after a long sentence, eager for female company:

> I looked her over. Frank was looking her over, too. He had a

kinda look in his eyes that worried me. A look I'd never seen in his eyes before he went to jail, the kinda look that showed clearly what he was thinking. And he was thinking four-legged thoughts.

In the same year, Charles Williams summed up the aphrodisiac effects of wine on a character in his crime novel *Aground*, with the phrase 'he was inclined to get pretty goaty and unbuttoned among the grapes'. That was the start of the sixties. By the close of that decade, things had gone way, way out, as the black private eye Superspade in B. B. Johnson's novel *Death of a Blue-Eyed Soul Brother* (1970) would probably have been the first to tell you. Here he is casually glancing at the small ads in an underground paper:

> I opened the Free Press to the Personals. I was reading 'Swinging AC-DC couple would like to meet inclined pairs for funsies. Fags and dykes need not apply. Send photographs with phone number.'

Superspade was knowingly something of a caricature – indeed, the second part of his name employed a long-standing slang term for a black person, which by then was in use in counterculture circles. Chester Himes, however, for all that he had emigrated to Paris in 1953, brought an authentic whiff of Harlem street-life to his series of crime novels featuring detectives Coffin Ed and Grave Digger Jones. Here, in the 1969 novel *Blind Man with a Pistol*, a black woman is telling a black man that he's got no chance with another woman, because she's interested only in white men:

> 'You sniffing at the wrong tuft, Slick, baby,' said a sly female voice from somewhere up above. 'She like chalk.'

Talking about Uganda

BECAUSE THE USE IN CONVERSATION of the more graphic terms for the act can be problematic, there are all manner of slang ways of referring to sexual activity without causing great offence. In the mid-1980s British newspapers seized gleefully on the word *bonking* as a relatively family-friendly word for sex, safe even for headlines. 'MRS CAKE THE BAKER'S WIFE DRIVES 'EM BONKERS', shrieked the *Daily Mirror* in 1987, above a classic tabloid story about a housewife accused of annoying the neighbours by howling so much during sex. 'My friends do call me Lassie because I make such a racket when I'm bonking,' explained the lady in question. During Wimbledon fortnight that year, British journalists began referring to tennis player Boris Becker as 'Bonking Boris', because of his supposedly busy love-life. More recently, the name has been recycled and applied to London mayor Boris Johnson. It was of necessity very much a time of socially acceptable slang terms for sex. The rise of AIDS meant that the government had to find ways of encouraging people to use condoms, and one memorable television comedy sketch of that era featured a posh woman telling her boyfriend, 'If you want rumpy-pumpy, it's pop-it-in-a-bag time'.

Private Eye magazine is responsible for one of the most enduring euphemisms for the sex act, *discussing Uganda*. So famous has this become during the past four decades that when a website was launched some time ago devoted to showing every cover of the magazine since its inception, it was named Ugandan Discussions. The phrase owes its origin to a story which appeared in the Grovel column of *Private Eye* No. 293, 9 March 1973, concerning a couple allegedly having sex at a party while claiming to have been discussing the political situation in Uganda:

As I was sipping my Campari on the ground floor I was informed by my charming hostess that I was missing out on a meaningful confrontation upstairs where a former cabinet colleague of President Obote was 'talking about Uganda'.

At several points further down the page the words *'talking about Uganda' in a highly compromising manner, talk-in* and *dialogue* are used, but the surprise of reading the original article comes from the discovery that the word *discussion* is nowhere present.

Private Eye also contributed in no small way to the spread of various Australian slang terms in the UK, many of them concerned with sex, drinking and drunkenly having sex, courtesy of the *Barry McKenzie* comic strip, which appeared in the magazine from 1964 to 1974. Written by Barry Humphries and drawn by Nicholas Garland, it depicted the exploits of an Aussie who comes to London. McKenzie would announce a visit to the lavatory by saying 'I'm off to shake hands with the wife's best friend', or 'point percy at the porcelain', and remark of a sexual conquest that he was 'up her like a rat up a drainpipe'. In the first of two cinema adaptations, *The Adventures of Barry McKenzie* (1972), his idea of a smooth chat-up line to an air hostess on the plane is to ask for 'A Ned Kelly whiskey and a swift naughty in the dunny as soon as the No Smoking light goes out', and he laments his own bad luck with the phrase 'Jeez, if it was raining virgins I'd be washed down the gutter with a poofter'. All of which would presumably not have met with the approval of a journalist signing himself W.T.C., who wrote an article called 'The Slang Evil' for Melbourne newspaper *The Age* in 1923:

> The common parlance of our citizens evidences, sad be it to relate, that we Australians are travelling on a stream which, year by year, is being polluted by the alarming growth of the slang evil.

Can you keep it up for a week?

OFTEN, WORDS WHICH ARE NOT in themselves slang are combined together to make a slang phrase. For example, in the film *This Is Spinal Tap* (1984), Nigel Tufnel reveals the four-word title of the sensitive D-minor piano instrumental he has composed. Individually, none of the words involved would cause comment, and all could be found in any respectable dictionary. However, in many social situations, saying 'Lick My Love Pump' might prove problematic.

The flexibility of the English language has allowed for a vast range of expression over the years, with a wide scope for double meanings, most of which are routinely ignored in the course of everyday life. (To choose an obvious example, shops labelled *Family Butcher* are not generally taken to be establishments that butcher families.) People accept everyday phrases and clichés at face value – for instance, wishing you lots of luck, without considering that such a commodity comes in two shades, good and bad. Similarly, Barack Obama's much-praised campaign speeches during the 2009 US election called for 'Change we can believe in', yet change has no inherent merit. If your house burns down, that, too, is a change you can believe in – since the physical evidence is irrefutable – yet hardly one for the better, unless you are planning an insurance fraud.

However, it is precisely this ability of English phrases to be taken in various ways that gave the UK's soft-core sex film industry such enjoyment when titling their movies, often using ribald euphemisms for the sex act which might equally have come from the Two Ronnies. Innocuous everyday expressions were matched with lurid semi-nude artwork outside cinemas, soliciting an audience for the likes of *Can You Keep It Up for a Week?* (1974), *Penelope Pulls It Off* (1975), *I'm Not Feeling Myself*

Tonight! (1975), *Girls Come First* (1975) or *Under the Doctor* (1976).

These were certainly suggestive, but not nearly as blatant as the names which the Los Angeles porn industry would use around 1990 for their parodies of current Hollywood blockbusters, when they gave the world such deathless epics as *Edward Penishands* and *When Harry Ate Sally*. The British titles were following more in a tradition stretching back to the golden days of the risqué Donald McGill seaside postcard, and in particular the dying, post-war days of the music halls, which had turned to girly shows to bring in the crowds, with titles like *We Couldn't Wear Less* and *Strip, Strip, Hooray*.

Playing the crumpet voluntary

THE SEVENTIES WERE SOMETHING of a golden age for double-entendre wordplay. Christopher Wood wrote a series of best-selling paperback originals under the pseudonym Timothy Lea, beginning with *Confessions of a Window Cleaner* (1971), four of which were adapted into films. His hero Timmy advances through each book, sleeping with a selection of women, many of whom seduce him, rather than the reverse. A wide variety of slang terms for various sex acts are used, frequently cockney in origin, others of which are clearly the product of the author's inventive imagination. During the course of just one example in the series, *Confessions of a Private Dick* (1975), readers are treated to a formidable battery of sexual expressions, virtually all of them uttered with a knowing wink at the reader. Lustful desire is characterised as 'Hey presto! Open season for furtling the furburger' or 'these girls are obviously parched as far as contact with the one-eyed trouser snake is concerned', while intercourse itself is described by phrases like 'percy is flying blind' or talk of 'giving her pussy a protein injection'. There's oral sex for her ('it is clear that the lady is desirous of a grumble mumble'), and also for him ('Felicity is playing the crumpet voluntary on my hampton'). Exercising restraint at such times can be tricky, but as the narrator remarks, 'I can usually keep the cream of the British Empire in check until the time comes to send them in to No Man's Land'.

Hampton, Lea's most frequently used word for the male member, is venerable cockney rhyming slang (*hampton wick*, prick, immortalised in a 1970s television comedy sketch by the Carry On team in Tudor costume singing 'The Day Good King Harry Got His Hampton Court'). *Grumble* is also cockney slang of a similarly direct kind (*grumble and grunt*, cunt).

A sausage and doughnut situation

THE OBJECT OF THE CONFESSIONS books was clearly to entertain, using the uncensored language of the average bloke down the pub. A decade later, such speech was taken to extremes for comic effect by the writers of the *Viz* magazine character Sid the Sexist, a Geordie would-be Lothario, whose idea of a smooth chat-up line was 'Howay pet, me an' ye roond the back – a punch up the knickers', or, when suggesting mutual oral sex, 'I'll binge on yer minge if ye smoke the white owl, eh?' Sid's utter failure to find any takers for such defiantly un-PC advances was, of course, a surprise only to himself.

If Sid was clearly intent on raising the subject of sex at every opportunity, another *Viz* stalwart, Finbarr Saunders, managed to find a sea of double entendres in virtually every conversation he heard, prompting barely suppressed exclamations such as 'Fnarr, fnarr' and 'Arf, arf'. Mind you, it is easy to see why.

In a Christmas-themed story, when Mr Gimlet, a male 'friend' of Finbarr's mother, says 'I like a good hard shaft, don't I, Mrs Saunders. My balls always take a proper hammering', the accompanying pictures showed that he had just been given a present of a stainless steel golf putter.

The grand culmination of *Viz* magazine's explorations of the language of smut, lavatory humour and all-purpose swearing was the publication in 1998 of the book *Roger's Profanisaurus* – a heroic undertaking which has grown in subsequent editions into a vast compendium of expressions of dubious parentage. It ranges from phrases relating to desire ('She's a bit of a snake charmer. I'm pitching a trouser tent right here and now'), oral sex ('She knelt down in front of him and took him from flop to pop in three minutes flat'), masturbation both male ('strangle Kojak') and female ('play the invisible banjo'), to full intercourse ('a sausage and doughnut situation').

Of course, this kind of language might not be considered respectable in some quarters, yet the generally middle-class audiences who have listened in their millions to BBC Radio 4's long-running comedy panel show *I'm Sorry I Haven't A Clue* are also not averse to suggestive innuendo. Former chairman Humphrey Lyttelton was a supreme master at delivering lines about the supposed activities of non-existent scorer Samantha, such as her chance meeting with a nice gentleman at an ornithologists' convention, when 'she showed him her chough and he pulled out twelve finches'. All this was of course in the grand tradition of music hall performers such as Max Miller, all the way back to the likes of Marie Lloyd in the 19th century singing 'I Sits among the Cabbages and Peas'.

Me so horny

ALONGSIDE SUGGESTIVE INNUENDO, there has also been a strand of outright graphic expressions for sex, in which any concept of romance has been left straggling miles behind, winded, and prematurely retired from the race. Here, for instance, is a policeman interrogating a suspect in John Brown's crime novel *The Chancer* (1974):

> I'm not bluffing, moosh. She told me. She said you stuffed her on the front room carpet one o'clock this morning. She made a statement.

Similarly, the prison writings of Black Power leader Eldridge Cleaver, published in 1969 under the title *Soul on Ice*, often treat sex as something more like assault than affection:

> When I off a nigger bitch, I close my eyes and concentrate real hard, and pretty soon I get to believing that I'm riding one of them bucking blondes. I tell you the truth, that's the only way I can bust my nuts with a black bitch, to close my eyes and pretend that she is Jezebel.

Cleaver later became a born-again Christian and Bible-quoting member of the Republican Party, but such upfront language eventually fed into the mainstream of rap culture. In 1989, Miami group the 2 Live Crew had a significant hit with their shy, retiring song 'Me So Horny' – whose title derived from a phrase uttered by a prostitute in the film *Full Metal Jacket* (1987) – proving that sexual slang from 18th-century England was alive and well and living in the *Billboard* charts. Strangely appropriate, perhaps, given that Kubrick's film was shot in London's Docklands, doubling unconvincingly for Vietnam.

In recent years, of course, it has become increasingly more difficult to offend people with sexual phrases – religion, rather than rutting, is a far more contentious subject. You can call your band Fuck Buttons and – nearly four decades after the Sex Pistols' LP title *Never Mind the Bollocks* (1977) was prosecuted for obscenity – the music business and many other sections of society will not turn a hair. They have seen it all before.

Today, as the wonders of the internet allow previously unsayable words and phrases to be googled in seconds, or spread around the English-speaking world, hitherto arcane or regional expressions for sex acts become common international currency. In a 1965 *Daily Telegraph* style feature about hair fashions, the writers used the phrase 'short and curly like a Greek shepherd boy's', but anyone tapping that phrase into a computer search these days might find a wider range of subject matter than first intended. Your friendly electronic device will automatically seek out double meanings alongside innocent interpretations.

Technology, too, now has a dirty mind.

TWO

The Oldest Profession

The Bawd if it be a woman, a Pander
The Bawd, if a man, an Apple squire
The whoore, a Commoditie
The whoorehouse, a Trugging place

Robert Greene, *A Notable Discovery of Coosnage,*
Now daily practised by Sundry lewd persons, called
Connie-catchers, and Crosse-biters (1591)

Harlot, rare, notable harlot

AMONG THE MANY SLANG TERMS for sex, there has always been a distinct group of terms devoted to the business conducted by those who sell their favours for money, their facilitators, and their places of work. Of course, in certain eras or circles, even to admit the existence of such things was to risk an attack of the vapours. After the wild years of the 1920s, once the Hollywood moguls became born-again virgins under the stern lash of censor Will H. Hays – who acquired much stronger powers in 1934 – any slight hint in their screenplays about the activities of ladies of the night was forbidden. As the writer Peter Fryer once pointed out, the 'list of banned words, which might never be spoken in any motion picture, included *cocotte, courtesan, eunuch, harlot, madam* (for brothel-keeper), *slut, tart, trollop, wench, whore, son-of-a-bitch, sex* and *sexual*.

These were mere words that were being legislated against. Regardless of any picture content, it was enough of an offence if a fully dressed character in a drawing room even uttered one of them in conversation. This blushing attitude probably did not come easily to the film-makers, given the somewhat less-than-pure state of the private lives of numerous Hollywood actors, actresses, directors or writers at that time – but rules were rules, and money was money. In those days, if you spoke about John Ford, people generally thought of the Oscar-winning director who shot John Wayne westerns, not the English 17th-century playwright who wrote *'Tis Pity She's a Whore* (1633) – a title seemingly custom-made to give Will H. Hays a coronary. Still less could you quote certain of the lines from that play; for example:

> Come, strumpet, famous whoore! were every drop
> Of blood that runs in thy adulterous veynes
> A life, this sword – dost see't? – should in one blowe
> Confound them all. Harlot, rare, notable harlot,
> That with thy brazen face maintainst thy sinne,
> Was there no man in Parma to be bawd
> To your loose cunning whoredome else but I?
> Must your hot ytch and plurisie of lust,
> The heyday of your luxury, be fedd
> Up to a surfeite, and could none but I
> Be pickt out to be cloake to your close tricks,
> Your belly sports?

In this short speech, replete with sexual insults, delivered by the nobleman Soranzo, Ford rounded up several of the classic names for prostitutes. Yet Annabella, Soranzo's wife, at whom this tirade is directed, has not in fact been selling her body.

She has, however, just become pregnant after sleeping with her own brother. Incest, eye-gougings, stabbings, a poisoning and a burning at the stake: here was a play to make the censors of Hollywood three centuries later keel over in apoplexy. At the time, though, in the England of Charles I, mere whoredom was far more of a matter-of-fact business, and the varied words describing it often just a part of everyday speech. There had been talk of brothels in *King Lear* (1607) and *Much Ado about Nothing* (1600), and indeed the various words for the business of prostitution were bandied around in all manner of public spheres over the next two centuries without raising too many eyebrows.

One whore's town

IF THE POPULAR ASSUMPTION IS TRUE, and prostitution is genuinely the oldest profession – although that of hunter or warrior would very likely also be in the running for the title – then society has long needed names for those who follow it.

In Old English, the name for such people was *meretrix*, deriving from the identical Latin word for one who earns money by prostitution. The term, although antiquated, has survived among those who would understand classical allusions – for instance, *The Times*, in only its second year of publication (1786), felt confident enough of its readers to offer the following item of highbrow gossip involving a work of art:

> How came the *Venus Meretrix* into the collection of a late *Virtuoso Dowager*? Not sure as object of admiration, much less a *model!!*

Indeed, the word *meretricious*, which these days has acquired a wider meaning denoting something false and flashy, originally meant specifically that which was suggestive of prostitution.

Another Old English word, *hóre*, gave us the term *whore*, which itself was originally written without the 'w' – for instance, as *hore*, *hoor* or *hure* – and the Wycliff Bible of 1380 speaks of the activities of *horis*. It had acquired the extra letter by the end of the 16th century, and certainly carries the modern spelling by the time of Shakespeare's *First Folio*. Of course, in recent years, with the global popularity of rap music, the word has been shedding the 'w' and starting just with 'h' again, and is written and pronounced *ho*. As an unintended result, the street name for a prostitute in these circles has created a situation in which Father Christmas chuckling to himself runs the risk of appearing sex-obsessed, and the Devon coastal village, Westward Ho!, calls to mind an East Coast American pimp telling one of his stable to move to California. Such is life.

The business of writing *ho* as a way of mirroring black urban speech is a relatively new development. Iceberg Slim – who has been a significant influence on key figures in the rap world, not least Ice Cube and Ice T, generally wrote the word straightforwardly as *whore*:

> Goddamnit, Mr Murray, I was no trick baby. My mother was no whore. She married a white man. Do I have to pin her marriage license on my chest?

Given the freedom with which the word *bitch* is used in modern rap music as a blanket term for a woman – another trait also found in the 1960s writings of Black Panther leader Eldridge Cleaver – it is worth noting that in 18th-century London, where whores were numerous, the former term was apparently a greater insult. The second edition of Grose's *Classical Dictionary of the Vulgar Tongue* (1788) put it this way:

> BITCH. The most offensive appellation that can be given to an English woman, even more provoking than that of whore,

as may be gathered from the regular Billingsgate or St Giles's answer – 'I may be a whore, but can't be a bitch.'

Unsurprisingly, the various editions of Grose's dictionary are littered with terms describing prostitutes. There are the obvious inclusions, such as *punk* and *moll*, and then some names still in use today, but whose original 18th-century meaning time has softened: a *drab* Grose defines as 'a nasty, sluttish whore', while the posthumous 1811 edition has *bat*, meaning 'a low whore: so called from moving out like bats in the dusk of the evening'. A *hedge whore* is simply 'an itinerant harlot, who bilks the bagnios and bawdy houses, by disposing of her favours on the wayside, under a hedge', also known, for obvious reasons, as a *star gazer*. Other terms have fallen out of use, such as calling a whore a *buttock* or a *bunter* – indeed, the latter name would very likely surprise most readers of the school stories of Frank Richards (*Fifty Shades of Greyfriars*, anyone?).

Soiled doves and Winchester geese

IF CAPTAIN GROSE KNEW PLENTY of terms for whores, then he was merely following in a long English tradition. The word *prostitute* itself dates back only to the start of the 17th century, but the practitioners of this trade had been variously referred to prior to this by such names as *soiled dove* (1250), *common woman* (1362), *putain* (from the Anglo-Norman, 1425), *cat* (1535), *punk* (1575), *hackney*, because they hire themselves out (1579), *street-walker* (1591), *winchester goose*, because the brothels in Bankside were licensed by the Bishops of Winchester (1598), or *hell-moth*, apparently a corruption of hell's mouth (1602).

The anonymous compiler of the *Canting Crew* dictionary (1699) threw in numerous words for this occupation, such as *trull, curtezan* ('a gentile fine Miss or Quality Whore'), *draggle-tail, madam van* and *baggage*. As centuries passed, the latter name became something of an all-purpose term of affection – for instance, in Erle Stanley Gardner's crime novels of the 1930s and 1940s, *baggage* is the nickname Perry Mason gives to his private secretary Della Street – but what strikes perhaps the most disturbingly modern note in the *Canting Crew* is the following:

> *Crack.* A whore.

It has been a long journey from *crack* meaning *whore* to a time of crack whores, but nevertheless, some slang names would be instantly recognisable to the denizens of both worlds.

The Happy Hooker

ONE OF THE MOST FAMILIAR US slang names for a prostitute is *hooker*, a word also familiar to Elizabethan *conny catchers* and *vagabones*, but in those days it meant a thief who stole items such as clothes by means of hooked pole. In 19th-century Scotland, and early 20th-century America, if you asked for a *hooker* people would think you wanted a glass of whisky. However, in 1914 the word was listed in a short dictionary called *A Vocabulary of Criminal Slang*, published in Portland, Oregon, with the following definition:

> HOOKER, Noun. A prostitute.

Yet if you search in the same dictionary for another of the most common US slang terms, its meaning has shifted with the passing of time:

> HUSTLER, Noun. A grafter; a pimp who steals betimes. The genteel thief is designated a 'hustler'.

Other words in that volume that did refer to prostitutes included *dony* ('Current amongst pimps and free lovers chiefly. A female member of the demi-monde'), *tommy* ('a prostitute') and *flap* ('an opprobrious epithet for loose women. Also employed to designate the female sex organ'). The first is very close to the traditional English cant word for whore, *doxy*, but the middle example might well have raised eyebrows on this side of the Atlantic, being the established nickname for a British soldier.

As for the business of offering yourself in return for money, many 20th-century American blues and jazz musicians between the wars recorded songs which explored this theme, such as 'She Done Sold It Out' by the Memphis Jug Band (1934), or 'Anybody Here Want to Try My Cabbage?' by Maggie Jones (1924). A whore at that time in the US might also be known as a *hanky-panky* ('Helen wasn't no hanky-panky,' says a character in Dashiell Hammett's 1929 novel *Red Harvest*) or a *chippie*. 'My God! What did I ever think of to put in with a chippy like you?' asks someone in another landmark crime novel of that era, Raymond Chandler's *The High Window* (1943). Also commemorated in the jazz recording 'Chasin' Chippies' by Cootie Williams and His Rug Cutters (1938), the word was still current in post-war Harlem, seen here being used as the two detectives Coffin Ed and Grave Digger Jones interrogate a pimp in the 1960 novel *The Big Gold Dream*:

> 'I was watching out for my girls,' Dummy replied.
> 'Your girls?'
> 'He's got two chippie whores,' Grave Digger explained. 'He's trying to teach them how to hustle.'

Meanwhile, over in Scotland during the Swinging Sixties, such behaviour was allegedly not so common, according to the narrator of a crime novel by Jack Lang (Gordon Williams) called *The Hard Case* (1967):

Hoors, as he called them, were filthy old bauchles [worthless people] lurching about in Clyde Street... 'Hawking your mutton is what we say,' he grinned. 'It's not a major Scottish industry. You'd have to be perverted to pay for it up here. This is the land of knee-tremblers and wee bastards.'

Our worthy chairman has been running a knocking-shop

WHILE STREET WALKERS WALKED THE STREETS, and *star gazers* and *hedge whores* plied their trade al fresco, a great many women operated out of their own homes, or in brothels. The latter word for a house of ill repute has been common English currency since the end of the 16th century, but is itself something of a misnomer. The full term, dating to the 1530s, was *brothel-house*, being a place where you might expect to find *brothels*, or prostitutes. For instance, in 1535, the word was used in this sense by John Fisher, Bishop of Rochester, who complained, 'Why doeth a common brothel take no shame of hir abhomination?' Two centuries earlier, a *brothel* was simply a loose-living, disreputable man. In Old English, the establishment itself was simply a *house* – its meaning surviving intact through the centuries so that James Dean's character in *East of Eden* (1954) could remark contemptuously of his brothel-madam mother, 'She lives over in Monterey, she's got one of them *houses*.' In Chaucer's England, with the lingering influence of the Normans, the accepted term was the word *bordel*. To the Elizabethans, these were *bawdy-houses*, *trugging-places*, *nunneries*, *leaping-houses* or *vaulting-houses* – the last two being just the first in an ever-expanding list of names intended to conjure up the supposedly vigorous activities to be found within. Of these, perhaps the most durable has proved to be the deadpan expression *knocking shop*, which was known to the Victorians, and which is still regularly employed by the British tabloid press. In 2001, the *Daily Star* ran a story under the headline WHORE HOUSE HORROR, which said:

> Police are hunting the killers of a dad-of-six who plunged to his death from the window of a BROTHEL... He was inside the knocking shop in Middlesbrough, Teesside, when a gang of heavies burst in.

Like the phrase *bonking* as a shorthand for sex, *knocking shop* was another of those expressions which could be reliably used to evoke something near the knuckle, without prompting a shoal of outraged readers' letters of complaint. In 1973, a government sex scandal erupted featuring the call-girl Norma Levy, which led to the resignations of Air Force Minister Lord Lambton and Leader of the Lords Earl Jellicoe. The *Daily Mirror* reported that the two men were filmed in her Maida Vale flat via a hole drilled through a wall and the back of a wardrobe, while their conversations were recorded by means of 'a bugged teddy bear on a chair by Norma's bed. The bear had a microphone in its nose which was linked to a tape recorder.' All of which was prime fodder for the *Mirror*'s Keith Waterhouse, who devoted all of his column to a satirical piece imagining the conversation between a cabinet minister and his wife, which ran through a fair few slang terms for such behaviour:

> ...completely unknown to me, our worthy chairman has been running a knocking-shop. A knocking-shop, dear. A bordello. A brothel. A whorehouse. You may well ask what the world is coming to, old girl. I ask the same question myself. But what is more to the point, the P.M. is asking it too. Well, I mean to say, he can't have one of his most respected ministers consorting with a Soho brass, can he? A brass, dear. A strumpet. Whore. Prostitute.

Brass is cockney rhyming slang, usually given as *brass nail*, tail, although sometimes explained as *brass flute*, prostitute, or *brass door*, whore – although how many doors are completely made of brass?

A meer Dog-hole

BROTHELS, LIKE ANY OTHER KIND of accommodation, can obviously range in size and quality. At the lower end of the scale, you might find a *seraglietto*, which the *New Dictionary of the Terms Ancient and Modern of the Canting Crew* (1699) defined as 'a lowly, sorry Bawdy-house, a meer Dog-hole'. Others might be the last word in elegance, designed to attract a wealthy and titled clientele.

When the restoration of the monarchy under Charles II in 1660 ushered in a new era of sexual permissiveness, it was not just the theatre that took advantage of the situation. In that same year, an anonymous serial publication appeared that attempted to list many of London's prostitutes for the benefit of the well-heeled connoisseur. The presumed author and publisher was a man named John Garfield, and the title of his first issue employed a number of slang expressions:

> *The Wandring Whore* – A Dialogue Between Magdalena a Crafty Bawd, Julietta an Exquisite Whore, Francion a Lascivious Gallant, And Gusman a Pimping Hector. Discovering their diabolical Practises at the CHUCK OFFICE. With a LIST of all the Crafty Bawds, Common Whores, Decoys, Hectors, and Trappanners, and their usual Meetings.

To decode this by means of the *Canting Crew* dictionary, we find that a hector is 'a Vaporing, Swaggering Coward', and a *trapan* 'he that draws in or wheedles a *Cull* [fool] and *Bites* [cheats or robs] him' (a pimp, in this context). *Chuck*, meanwhile, was an old term for a whore and also for a *whoremonger* – one who frequents whores – and so the *chuck office* was a brothel. A *crafty bawd*, of course, was a madam.

Garfield's publication listed the names of a variety of people involved in London's prostitution trade at the time. Among the whores, there were 'Mrs Osbridges scolding daughter', 'Betty Lemon in Checquer-ally neer Bunhill', 'Mrs Smith a Bricklayers wife in whitechappel', and 'Mrs Bulls daughters'. Those wanting *crafty bawds* could seek out 'Mrs Eaton a Maiden-head-seller on the Ditch-side neer Hogsden', 'Mrs Pope in Petty France', 'Mrs Treely in Blomesbury', or perhaps 'Rachel War in Dog Yard'. As for *trapanners*, readers were advised to look out for a variety of upstanding citizens such as 'George Paskins, a Kid-catcher, at the Crooked-billet at the Armitage', 'Pimp Howard' – a certain clue in the name, perhaps – or even 'Ralph Asbington alias Shit-ten-arse, Grocer', who presumably adopted this trade once the public proved understandably reluctant to buy vegetables from him.

The other part of Garfield's *Wandring Whore*, consisting of dialogues between various fictitious members of the profession, provides a glimpse into the rough life and language of Restoration brothels. There are the everyday transactions:

> ...common Jades (such as *Mal. Savory, Honor Brooks* and *Nan. Jones,*) are numerous enough, and will sit with their leggs spread over the sides of a chair with their petticoates and smocks in their mouths, whilst their *Comrades* run a tilt at their *touch holes* in that posture, paying twelve pence a time for holing.

Then there are those who demand specialist services:

> ...she's hard put to please a young merchant in L----street, who will not be contented with doing the business, but will

have half a dozen Girles stand stark naked round about a Table whilst he lyes snarling underneath as if he would bite off their whibb-bobs [breasts], and eat them for his pains; … another who has brought rods in his pockets for that purpose, will needs be whip't to raise lechery and cause a standing P---- which has no understanding at all, and would quickly cool my courage.

The legal profession of that time had their own words for the activities taking place in brothels. When a suspected madam named Isabel Barker was tried at the Old Bailey in 1683, she was 'indicted, for that she did convert her dwelling house in More-Lane into a common Baudy house, suffering Lude Licentious people to commit carnal wickedness in a debauched way', which rather raises the question as to whether it is also possible to commit such wickedness in a refined, undebauched manner. This lady was acquitted, but ten years later Alice Randall was found guilty of a similar charge, after the court heard of her enticing a gentleman visitor and bringing him 'a brisk young Girl, who presently had the Impudence to pull up her Coats, and laying her hand upon her Belly said, Here's that that will do you good, a Commodity for you, if you'll pay for it you shall have enough of it'.

As the latter account demonstrates, such testimonies preserved in trial transcripts of proceedings at the Old Bailey down through the centuries record something of the everyday speech of the population, with an immediacy often missing in the literature and journalism of those times. Consider also this verbatim list of insults drawn from the trial of Mary Bolton in 1722, accused of killing her husband: '[He] called the prisoner poor beggarly Bitch, nasty draggle tail'd toad, ugly Puss, and stinking Punk'.

Fighting talk indeed.

The Linnen-lifting Tribe

THE IDEA OF A SEX-ORIENTED FORERUNNER of the telephone directory such as the *Wandring Whore*, for men-about-town seeking ladies of the town, proved popular. For instance, in 1691 a London printer based near Smithfield named R.W. published a two-page broadside pamphlet giving details of various local ladies, whose title says it all: *A Catalogue of Jilts, Cracks, Prostitutes, Night-walkers, Whores, She-friends, Kind Women, and Others of the Linnen-lifting Tribe, who are to be Seen Every Night in the Cloysters in Smithfield, from the Hours of Eight to Eleven, during the Time of the Fair.*

This, however, was but a flimsy thing, when compared to that landmark of 18th-century London publishing, *Harris's List of Covent Garden Ladies*, which appeared annually from 1757 to 1795. Credited to one Jack Harris, 'Pimp General of All England' (a pseudonym for John Harrison of the Shakespear's Head Tavern in Covent Garden), it has been suggested that it was in fact the work of the poet Samuel Derrick, although the *Oxford Dictionary of National Biography* does not credit him with authorship. Whatever the truth of the matter, Derrick certainly had the distinction of being dismissed by former acquaintance James Boswell in his *London Journal, 1762 – 63*, as a 'little blackguard pimping dog'.

Crucially, *Harris's List* did not just give the names of various London prostitutes, in the manner of the *Wandring Whore*, but also included a paragraph or two describing the appearance and likely specialities of the ladies in question. This involved the use of a wider variety of euphemisms and slang words, such as this entry from the 1789 edition concerning 'Miss W-ll-ms, No. 2, York Street, Queen Ann Street':

She is now of the pleasing age of nineteen, and has not hunted the Cyprian forest [*cyprian* – a whore] quite six months... we would advise the hero to lose no time, but immediately plunge the *carnal sword* into its *favourite scabbard*, and you will soon be convinced she has not lost the art of pleasing.

The same volume has this to say of 'Miss M-k-y, at Mrs. W-lp-ls, No. 1, Poland Street':

Her hands which were before employed as guards to that enticing spot, are now busy in making a *member* fit to *stand* in the *House of Commons*.

This humorous distortion of terms associated with politicians was then taken to extremes in the entry describing 'Mrs. Bu-e, No. 16, Union Street, Middlesex Hospital':

This spirited nymph... has shewn her patriotism, and liberality of sentiment, in opening her *port*, and exercising a *free trade* with all who chooses to bring their *commodities* to her *market*; when she, without reserve, unlocks her grand *reservoir* of natural productions, and *pours* out all her stores in *exchange*. She understands *loss* and *gain* exceedingly well, and the more her *imports* are, and the nearer they answer her *exports*, the greater her satisfaction.

This is a world in which the customer will go in search of 'the *sable coloured grot* below with its coral lipt *janitor*', seeking to place 'the *tree of life* into the *garden of Eden*', hoping afterwards that he has not 'proved himself a *bad horseman*'. As for the skill of the woman in question, it is said of one that 'she understands the up-and-down art of her posteriors as well as any lady of her profession', while another is 'always ready to obey standing orders' and has a 'charitable disposition... ready to relieve the naked and needy'. As for the ever-present threat of venereal disease, the 1793 edition employs nautical terms to remark of 'Mrs. Will-ms, No.

17, Pit-street' that this 'fine tall lady... has been in dock to have her bottom cleaned and fresh coppered, where she has washed away all the impurities of prostitution, and risen almost immaculate, like Venus, from the waves'.

Giving the ferret a run

OF COURSE, THE NAVY, not to mention the other branches of the armed services, have long had a wide selection of terms for prostitutes and their activities. During the 20th century, the Royal Navy on shore leave would traditionally be on the lookout for a *bag shanty* (brothel), in order to have a *pump up* (sexual intercourse) and *give the ferret a run* (ditto), thereby distributing some *population paste* (sperm). Foreign and home ports alike would be unofficially graded by sailors in terms of their facilities for drinking and whoring during a *run-ashore*. Portsmouth, the dockyard city on the south coast, has been a home for the navy since as far back as the 16th century, with a vast number of pubs and hostelries which even the heavy bombing during the Second World War failed to completely diminish. Yet its centuries-old reputation for catering to the demands of sailors clearly did not impress a British soldier interviewed during the Iraq war in 2003, in response to a comment by the Labour government's Defence Secretary Geoff Hoon that the Iraqi port of Umm Qasr was 'like the city of Southampton':

> He has either never been to Umm Qasr or he's never been to Southampton. There's no beer, no prostitutes and people are shooting at us. It's more like Portsmouth.

Spike Milligan recalled that, sixty years earlier, stationed further along the coast in the Royal Artillery, he had served alongside another gunner named Octavian Neat, who – aside from a fondness for stunts such as appearing in the barrack room stark naked and asking, 'Does anybody know a good tailor?' – would periodically disappear AWOL in search of seaside whores, telling his friends, 'I'm off sand-ratting.' The equivalent search in the RAF at that time, for any kind of female company, was known as going on *skirt patrol*, and the lady in question was also known as *one's target for tonight*.

Sometimes army slang derived from specific locations, such as the Second World War British troops' name *berker*, meaning brothel, derived from the red light district around Sharia el Berker Street in Cairo. A similar reputation clung to the entire Belgian city of Brussels in those days as far as British troops were concerned – they informally changed its name to *Brothels*.

Pimp my ride – ride my pimp

WHILE THE WORD *PIMP* itself dates back to the London of Shakespeare's time, perhaps the abiding image it conjures up today is of an early 1970s Blaxploitation character from Harlem in a long coat, velvet fedora, three tons of jewellery and a Cadillac Eldorado only slightly shorter than the George Washington Bridge. It is a testimony to the staying power of this particular word that it has managed to remain in current use while other terms for the same occupation have fallen by the wayside. For example, while John Camden Hotten's excellent mid-Victorian publication *A Dictionary of Modern Slang, Cant & Vulgar Words* (1859) lists the familiar *on the batter* as a term for someone walking the streets, few people these days when hearing the seemingly innocuous word *pensioner* would expect Hotten's definition – 'a man of the lowest morals who lives off the miserable earnings of prostitutes'.

Centuries before this, such a person would have been called a *pander* (c. 1450), a *bed-broker* (1594), a *fleshmonger* (1616) or a *mutton-broker* (1694). As ever, the good Captain Grose provides several expressive 18th-century terms for those following that particular profession, such as *brother of the gusset*, *she-napper* and *buttock-broker*. Over time, though, *pimp*, like *whore*, has become almost the default word. Iceberg Slim's 1967 book *Pimp* helped to crystallise the modern conception of how a pimp looks and behaves, and was followed by other books from the black perspective, such as A. S. Jackson's autobiography *Gentleman Pimp* (1973). Written in the slang of the street, it used plenty of remembered dialogue in order to tell the story of the author's early life running whores in the 1940s:

> I learned, during my time spent with the old pimps, that it was boag [unwise, bad news] for a cat to hang out where his rib [girl] did her gig [plied her trade], so I was about to split when my brother Willie walked up and said, 'Stoney, man, I'm hot [people are looking for me]. I gotta blow town, and I gotta blow quick, daddy...'

This is a rough world, full of money, drugs and casual violence:

> Chuck had two girls kicking mud [*mudkicker* – streetwalker, prostitute] around the city of Detroit. He was teethed on the street of broken dreams the same as I was. Me and Chuck sat around rapping and smoking and kicking whores in the ass all over Detroit.

Compare this to the sanitised view of up-market prostitution among the rich white areas of Manhattan in Bruce Manning's soft-core novel *Cafe Society Sinner* (1960) – 'A keyhole view of the call-girl business', according to the cover blurb – in which a madam gives the following advice to her male friend:

We aren't monsters. We don't enslave the girls. They're in it because they like the money. They come from all over the country, from all sorts of jobs. Most of them are working girls during the day, stenographers, sales girls, bit part actresses on TV. Clean, lovely girls, most of them.

Perhaps, but others writers tell a different story. In Stanley Jackson's non-fiction book *An Indiscreet Guide to Soho* (1946), when speaking of what he terms 'pimps, those heralds of the horizontal', he reports the following conversation with a local Italian wine waiter called Gabby:

> I got a room in Frith Street. Fifteen bob a week. It's in a flat run by a pal of mine. He's a waiter, like me, but lucky. Got a girl who goes out 'on the bash' for him. ... The poor cow thinks he's going to marry 'er when they've got enough dough!

Then, of course, there are the seen-it-all, done-it-all types like the short-order cook behind the counter of an American local diner in John Hersey's 1966 novel *Too Far to Walk*, responding to a local student who has asked for advice about where to find a prostitute:

> They got two kinds... You want a fi-buck or twenny-buck poontang? You fancy Shel bastids lookin for big-time hunnerd-buck stuff, you can't get it roun here. They only got homemade hair pie roun here. You know which one you want, Shel, five or twenny?

Who said romance was dead?

THREE

THIS BAG OF BONES

A separate television channel for cockneys?

IF YOU TELL PEOPLE that you are writing a history of English slang, my experience suggests that many of them will conclude that you are primarily exploring the cockney variety: *north and south*, mouth, *Gregory Peck*, neck, and so on. Would you *Adam and Eve* it?

Much quoted, and much misunderstood, cockney rhyming slang and its associated accent has had an international influence far greater than its traditional boundaries within the scope of the Bow Bells. Winston Churchill said in a 1944 speech to Parliament, 'I am still old-fashioned enough to consider Cockney London the heart of the Empire,' and there have been times over the years when members of both the Commons and the Lords have attempted to introduce cockney slang into debates, with varying degrees of success. In 1976, the Labour MP for Newham North West, Arthur Lewis, addressing a Scottish Nationalist colleague, commented, 'Perhaps I may put it in the Cockney vernacular and tell the honourable lady that if she will take a ball of chalk [walk] down the frog and toad [road] to have a butcher's hook [look], everyone will be happier. If she wants that translated I shall do so later.' Similarly, in a 1989 parliamentary debate which also straddled the English/Scottish border, Harry Greenaway (Conservative, Ealing North) responded to the proposal for a Gaelic TV channel by asking:

> Am I right in estimating mathematically, from what my honourable friend has said, that there are about 150,000 Gaelic speakers? That compares with several million Cockney speakers. What will he do to arrange for a separate television channel for Cockneys?

Should such a thing have ever materialised, there would presumably have to be a blanket ban on screenings of *Mary Poppins* (1964), featuring Dick Van Dyke's much-mocked accent as chirpy London geezer Bert. 'If someone from the UK sees me, they're on me like a pack of wolves,' Van Dyke told American chat-show host Conan O'Brien in 2012. 'I mean, it was the worst Cockney accent ever done. The guy who taught me was an Irishman.'

It is said that these days you are more likely to encounter genuine cockneys in Essex than in the East End of London, yet there is something about this particular slang that has survived through the changing years, despite many of its original reference points having faded into relative obscurity. Any talk of going for a *Ruby Murray* (curry) would still be intelligible to many these days, yet the number who remember her as a 1950s easy listening singer from Belfast would certainly be fewer.

In the death, i came to a kayf

NUMEROUS COCKNEY RHYMING SLANG DICTIONARIES have been published over the years. Ronnie Barker, after starring as hardened criminal Norman Stanley Fletcher in the television comedy series *Porridge* (1974–7), wrote a slim volume entitled

Fletcher's Book of Rhyming Slang (1979), in which he offered the following tongue-in-cheek etymology:

> 'Hello, me old cock!' Cock: cocksparrow = barrow: barrow of soil = boil: boil and bake = cake: cake and jam = ham: ham and pickle = tickle: tickle and touch = Dutch: Dutch plate = *mate*. Simple, isn't it?

Barker was playing a fictional prisoner, yet a cockney who was genuinely behind bars in Parkhurst Prison for murder also eventually weighed in with *Reg Kray's Book of Slang* (1984), which he compiled while *banged up* (incarcerated) doing *bird lime* (time). Some other works employing a fair slice of the cockney vernacular came complete with a handy glossary of phrases for the reader, such as Robin Cook's *The Crust on Its Uppers* (1962), Dougal Butler's memoirs of his time with the drummer from the Who (*Moon the Loon*, 1981), or that gem among Soho night-life books, Frank Norman's *Stand on Me* (1959), which consists almost entirely of passages such as 'In the death [eventually] I came to a kayf [café]. Feeling in my bin [pocket] I found that I had a tanner [sixpence].' The first of these expressions clearly had an influence on young Londoner David Jones, who later, as David Bowie, opened his 1974 LP *Diamond Dogs* with a spoken-word section beginning, 'And in the death...'

These books would undoubtedly have been of use to anyone applying for political refuge in the UK, had the government taken heed of a suggestion from Lord Campbell of Croy during a House of Lords debate about language testing for asylum seekers in 2002:

> My Lords, as foreigners often speak more correctly in English than we British do, might a relevant test be one of rhyming slang? For example, people could be asked how much of their journey had been made on their 'plates of meat'.

Indeed, as the *Daily Express* informed readers of its children's page back in 1932:

> A common expression for the feet is 'plates o'meat' and for the teeth, 'Hampstead Heath'. It is easy to see how obscure the slang becomes when only half the expression is retained and these become simply 'plates' for feet and 'Hampsteads' for teeth.

Individual parts of the body have always been well represented in cockney rhyming slang, some having multiple names. The head, for example, can be a *gingerbread*, an *uncle ned*, an *alive or dead*, a *lump of lead*, or a *crust* or *loaf of bread*. The last expression is probably the most common, usually shortened to *loaf*, as in 'use your loaf'. Back in the year 1900, the same newspaper had explained to its readers how this language could effectively conceal its meaning from outsiders:

> The professors of rhyming slang, which is now tolerably well known, have added a new terror to its study. Nowadays the adept subtly deletes the last and rhyming word of the phrase, to the confusion and despair of the novice. Below we print an abridged dictionary, the key phrase containing the rhyming word being given in brackets.

Inevitably, perhaps, they began with '*Apples (apples and pears)*, stairs', moving on to such staples as '*Daisies (daisy-roots)*, boots' and '*Elephants (elephant's trunk)*, drunk'. Unsurprisingly, a good proportion of their list had an anatomical theme, such as '*North an' (north and south)*, mouth', '*Mince (mince pies)*, eyes', '*Chevy (Chevy Chase)*, face' and '*Barnet (Barnet fair)*, hair'. Even less surprisingly, they failed to include some of the more risqué common examples, like *bristols* (Bristol City, titty), or the venerable *bottle* (bottle and glass, arse).

Arse longa, vita brevis

IN OCTOBER 2007, the then Labour prime minister Gordon Brown failed to call a snap election which might have consolidated his position. A little over a month later, events had overtaken him, his government was under siege, and the press crowed that he did not have the stomach for the fight. 'How he must regret that he lost his bottle when fate beckoned,' wrote Frederick Forsyth in the *Daily Express*, alluding to the term that many commentators used for the PM on this occasion, *Bottler Brown*. Yet, although the prime minister was widely said to have *bottled it*, few journalists bothered to spell out for the non-cockney-speaking reader the precise meaning of this expression, which is earthy and unambiguous. Someone whose *bottle and glass* has gone has lost all bowel control through fear. As Alan Lake's character says, taunting a nervous-looking Ian Hendry in a 1975 episode of *The Sweeney*, just before they're about to pull a criminal caper, 'Is your bottle twitching?' Since Lake was a friend of the Kray twins, this was effective casting.

The use of this particular slang term for the *nether regions* was hardly a first for the press. Whether it was the *Daily Mirror* in 1988 reporting a London policeman's comment that a recent armed robber was 'an amateur who lost his bottle', or the radio correspondent of the *Church Times* in 2002, reviewing a programme about the Cuban Missile Crisis, remarking that 'it was fascinating to hear how quickly Khrushchev lost his bottle', it has achieved a certain respectability over the years. Mind you, the word *arse* itself, while considered crude in many quarters, is hardly off limits in the media. For example, Peter Ackroyd, in a lengthy contemporary review in the *Spectator* of *Monty Python's Life of Brian* (1979), damned the film with very faint praise and complained of 'howls of laughter from the audience every time someone said "arse" or even, for one horrifying moment, showed one'.

Although dictionaries now categorise the word *arse* as vulgar, for almost a thousand years it was merely standard English, yet *bottom*, by contrast, dates only to the 1790s. Indeed, flag down a passing Anglo-Saxon in the run-up to the Norman Conquest, utter the word *arse*, and they would certainly have known what you were talking about, although if they belonged to that select minority of the population who could actually write, they would most likely spell it *ærs* or even *ears*. The latter rendering could, of course, lead to some confusion, especially among headphone manufacturers.

A woody word

THE LETTER R IN ARSE is crucial, and the link with other Germanic languages is crystal clear when you compare the venerable English *arse* with the modern German equivalent, *Arsch*. It is what the Monty Python team would have described as a *woody word* – one you can, ahem, get your teeth into – and can be spoken with all kinds of intonations, best exemplified by a character from another classic television comedy programme, Father Jack Hackett of *Father Ted*, who punctuated most episodes with regular cries of 'Drink! Feck! Arse!' Yet the *r* in this most expressive of words now seems in danger of dying out, despite its thousand-year lineage, owing to the increasing usage both in the media and the population at large of the US variant, *ass*.

The worldwide reach of popular music sung in English, of course, has helped the spread of American spellings, as has the long-time ability of US film companies to influence what is shown in cinemas and also to have a say in the selection of films that appear on television. In this way, the language of urban and suburban America becomes something of a default setting, crowding out other alternatives.

If you hear people say *ass* when they mean *arse* enough times, then that becomes the default setting. Consider the success of the Hollywood productions *Kick-Ass* (2010) and *Kick-Ass 2* (2013). Thirty years ago, these would have been films about donkey abuse.

His body of booty work

YET ASS HAS NOT ALWAYS been the default US spelling of the word. Here is the critic John Simon, from the American magazine *New York*, reviewing a new Broadway musical, *Celebration*, in 1969:

> Rich complains, 'I haven't had an erection in 25 years,' and sings about his lost youth, 'Where did it pass?' (Chorus echoes: 'Arse, arse, arse!')

More recently, a 2003 issue of the US supermarket tabloid *World Weekly News* took time off from its usual stories about mysterious sightings of a reanimated Elvis to inform its readers about a man from Richmond, Virginia, who painted pictures with his hindquarters: 'The arse artiste's specialty is nature, and a botanical theme is evident in his body of booty work.'

The variant *ass* meaning *arse* seems to derive from black American speech, popularised greatly through its use in music and film. A significant example would be the 1970 groundbreaking album *Free Your Mind... and Your Ass Will Follow* by Funkadelic, although Clarence Major's dictionary *Black Slang*, published the same year, lists only 'Ass: one's self or a dumb person'. However, the word was certainly in use among other sections of American society some time earlier than this. For instance, two years before Yoko Ono made her short film of various people's naked posteriors, *Bottoms* (1966), Andy Warhol produced a feature-length film at the Factory entitled *Taylor Mead's Ass* (1964), his camera trained unswervingly the whole time on the buttocks of his assistant. It was, as film historian J. J. Murphy wrote:

> ...made in direct response to a letter of complaint by film-maker Peter Emanuel Goldman in the *Village Voice* that he was tired of Jonas Mekas praising 'films focusing on Taylor Mead's ass for two hours.' Since no such film actually existed, Warhol and Mead playfully set about creating a film devoted to this premise.

All of which goes to show that in the right New York circles, an *arse* was an *ass* half a century ago, regardless of ethnic origin. However, if you reach back much further, to the 1920s, when the blues was first allowed into recording studios, the slang word *yas* was doing service as way of implying *ass* or *arse*, presumably a corruption of *your ass*. There is little in the way of ambiguity about the title 'The Duck's Yas Yas Yas' by James Stump Johnson (1929). In the same era, blues singer Merline Johnson was known as 'The Yas Yas Girl', but it was the great Peetie Wheatstraw – billed as 'The Devil's Son in Law' and 'The High Sheriff from Hell' – who really spelled it out in his song 'Shack Bully Stomp' (1938): 'I used to play slow but now I play it fast / Just to see the women shake their yas, yas, yas'.

A *booty*, of course, used to be an item of baby's footwear, but has now become an *arse*, rising to international fame in 1976 with the hit '(Shake Shake Shake) Shake Your Booty' by KC and the Sunshine Band. Despite this being swiftly mocked by Frank Zappa in the title of his 1979 LP *Sheik Yerbouti*, the lyrical tradition continued in the rap and R&B field in songs, such as the posthumous release 'Big Booty Hoes' by Notorious B.I.G. featuring Too Short (1999).

An Englishman might have asked you not to *butt in*, but it was an American who would tell you to *butt out*. Nowadays, though, the term *butt* – which in Britain was either the stock end of a rifle or the remaining part of a cigarette after it had been smoked – has gained ground. It even appears on the health advice pages of the NHS website, which not only includes exercises for what they call a *firm butt* ('Lose the droopy booty and get the perfectly toned posterior'), but also to combat that recent discovery, *bingo wings* ('Banish those flabby upper arms for good with this 10-minute bingo wings workout').

In the comedy series *The Fast Show*, which began in 1994, one of Arabella Weir's recurring characters was an insecure woman who continually asked, 'Does my bum look big in this?' Twenty years later, in a world where buttock-enhancement surgery has literally become a growth industry, the question in parts of the entertainment field had changed to 'Does my bum look big enough in this?' In 2014, as reality TV star Kim Kardashian's substantial rear end stared out from magazine and newspaper covers, rival hip-hop singers Meghan Trainor and Nicki Minaj each made a career of their rear, with the tunes 'All About That Bass' and 'Anaconda' fighting for supremacy in the singles charts in what the *Independent* described as 'the battle of the "booty songs"'.

Fanny by Gaslight

OF COURSE, THE CONTINUING UK/US struggle to find a proper slang name for the behind is even more complicated than it may at first appear. In 1933 Al Jolson sang the Rodgers and Hart song 'Hallelujah I'm A Bum' in the American film of the same name. It was also popular in the UK, despite the fact that it sounded to British listeners as if the vocalist was claiming to be a pair of buttocks. In public schools as far back as the 18th century, when a sound flogging on the posterior was an integral part of the *happiest days of your life*, an alternative name for a teacher was *bum-brusher*. In America, a *bum* is a hobo or tramp, and they call your *bum* a *fanny*, which is just one of the many transatlantic traps for the unwary. In England, the slang word *fanny* has always meant – as Farmer and Henley noted in their multi-volume, privately printed, late Victorian scholarly landmark *Slang and Its Analogues* (1890) – 'the female *pudendum*'. To take just one of many examples from a privately printed erotic magazine from Oxford, whose name was itself a slang word for the vagina (*The Pearl – A Journal of Facetiæ and Voluptuous Reading*, No. 5, 1879), here are a few lines of that old family chastisement favourite, 'The Spell of the Rod':

> She had been most naughty, and a bad rude girl
> Who presumed the hair on her fanny to curl;
> But the birch reached her quim as well as her bum
> The height of her agony was glorious fun.

A generation later, First World War tommies in the trenches nicknamed any woman in the First Aid Nursing Yeomanry (officially FANY) a *fanny*, doubtless aware of the double meaning, and the word duly shows up with two 'n's rather than one in Eric Partridge and John Brophy's *Songs and Slang of the British Soldier, 1914–1918* (1930).

In America, since at least the 1920s, they have it backwards, to coin a phrase. A *fanny* is an *arse* (or *ass*, as they would say, which is of course a donkey, or an idiot, but you follow the point). Hence, that magical item of waist apparel consisting of a belt with a hump-shaped zippered bag – which, perching above the buttocks, is guaranteed to reduce anyone's sex appeal by at least 85 per cent – is known in the UK as a *bum-bag*. In America, it is a *fanny-pack*, which sounds either like a pubic grooming kit or the Stateside equivalent of the group of ladies who used to assist Radio One DJ Annie Nightingale on her late-night shows, the *pussy posse*.

The English novelist Michael Sadleir raised a few eyebrows in 1940 with the publication of his novel *Fanny by Gaslight*, a melodrama set in Victorian times, with a heroine named Fanny, and prostitution among its themes. Filmed in London under the same title by the Gainsborough company in 1944 and released over here with a royal premiere attended by the Duchess of Kent, it fell foul of US censors – where its title suggested an illuminated posterior – and saw only a belated American release four years later, under the suitably vague name *Man of Evil*.

A typical late 20th-century instance of the British use of the word *fanny* occurs in *Jack's Return Home* by Ted Lewis (1970, usually reprinted these days under its film title, *Get Carter*), during a scene in which a woman deliberately leans over while wearing a very short skirt:

> As she poured, she swayed, allowing me to see right up to the maker's name. Cliff saw me looking.
>
> 'Glenda,' he said. 'Your fanny's in Jack's face.'
>
> Still leaning over, Glenda screwed her head round to look at me.
>
> 'I don't see him complaining,' she said.

Contrast this with an American usage of the same word from another great post-war crime writer, John D. MacDonald, one of whose characters is described as being 'thirty inches

round the fanny'. In the States, no problem; in England, see a
doctor immediately.

Merkin class heroes

FANNY IS OF COURSE JUST ONE of the many English slang words
for the female genitals. Perhaps the most controversial, *cunt*, is
also the oldest, with the *OED* citing around the year 1230 as the
earliest documented usage. Once again, for hundreds of years
this was not remotely a taboo or slang word, but merely everyday
speech. It was cognate with similar words in many European
languages, such as *kunt* in Middle High German, or *kunte* in
Danish and Norwegian. We have the Norman Conquest to
thank for the next-oldest appellation, *chose* (thing), as used by
Chaucer, who also employed the term *queynte*. This was followed
in turn by such names as *shell* – it may be fortunate that there
was no such thing as a petrol station in 1497 – and the even more
blankly descriptive *bearing-place* (1587).

These latter examples have long since fallen from use, but,
as is often the case with many time-honoured slang words, once
you start to approach the 17th century, the territory becomes
much more familiar: in relatively short order, *cunny* appears in
1593, then *quim*, *merkin* and *twat* (1613, 1656, and 1656 respectively, in this instance sounding oddly like a venerable legal firm.
These days, it is only *merkin*'s earlier variant meaning denoting a pubic wig that survives). Few today, except scholars of a
particular bent, would recognise *crinkum-crankum* (1670), but
before that century was over, it had given us another triumvirate
of favourites, all of which are still in regular use: *honeypot* (1673),
muff (1699) and the now ubiquitous *pussy* (1699).

Television viewers laughed knowingly during the

long-running series *Are You Being Served?* (1972–85) at middle-aged cat-owner Mrs Slocombe making repeated references to the condition of her pussy. Some of the ancestors of those same viewers may have been moved equally to laughter by the publication in 1854 of the English translation of popular French children's textbook *Le Grand-Père et Ses Quatre Petits-Fils*. Admittedly, its US editor saw fit to warn readers in his introduction of the 'necessity of expurgating [it] for American children', but the shameless depravity which had offended his puritan soul was simply that the young people in the original text 'engage on Sunday in labour and amusements'. In fact, it was not the mild contents of the book which encouraged sniggering in some quarters, but the name of its author, Madame Fuqueau de Pussy, who was clearly born a century and a half too early to fully exploit such a handle by becoming a cutting-edge rap artist or porn star.

About the Bush

ANTHONY BURGESS'S 1983 OBSERVER REVIEW of a dictionary of euphemisms – winningly headlined 'About the Bush' – noted the listings for 'terms like *box*, *Cape Horn*, the *golden doughnut*, *snatch* and *grumble*'. Most of these slang words for what Captain Grose two centuries earlier customarily referred to as the *monosyllable* would have been unfamiliar to the author of the *Classical Dictionary of the Vulgar Tongue*, but the latter contained some fine 18th-century examples which have since faded from use. Among these were *Eve's custom house* ('where Adam made his first entry'), *Miss Laycock*, the *mother of all saints*, the *bottomless pit*, the *black joke* and the *tuzzy-muzzy*. This, however, is nothing, compared to the encyclopaedic selection of English synonyms gathered together one hundred years later under the entry for *monosyllable* in Farmer and Henley's *Slang and Its Analogues* (1890). Here can be found terms such as the *Low Countries*, the *happy hunting-grounds*, the *manhole*, the *leading article*, *Cock Lane*, *Bluebeard's closet*, *standing-room for one*, *Hairyfordshire*, the *goatmilker*, the *doodle-sack*, the *bung-hole*, *County Down*, the *parsley-bed*, *home-sweet-home*, the *pulpit*, *Fumbler's Hall*, the *spit-fire*, the *pleasure ground*, *Sportsman's gap*, *Bushey Park*, the *oyster-catcher*, the *Midlands*, *rest-and-be-thankful*, *rattle-ballocks*, *nature's tufted treasure*, the *flower of chivalry* and *one of the agreeable ruts of life*.

The authors record that Sir Thomas Urquhart (1611–60) – the Royalist translator of Rabelais, rumoured to have died of laughter in exile when hearing the news of Charles II's restoration – had many ingenious names for that region. He variously referred to it as the *cunny-burrow*, the *skin-coat*, the *carnal trap*, the *justum*, the *solution of continuity*, the *intercrural trench*, the *contrapunctum*, the *hypogastrian cranny* and the *aphrodisiacal tennis court* – new balls, please? – but whether the ladies of his acquaintance had the first idea what he was talking about is open to question. Agatha Christie, meanwhile, may or may not have been aware that one of the other words listed by Farmer and Henley was the *mousetrap*, while Lemmy from Motörhead might have appreciated the fact that another name was the *ace of spades*.

Feline groovy

OTHER TERMS ANTICIPATE BY SOME DECADES the near-the-knuckle tendencies of some 1920s and 1930s American blues singers. Blind Boy Fuller's spirited 1938 recording, 'What's That Smells Like Fish?', finds an earlier echo in the synonyms *fish* and *fish-market* given by Farmer and Henley. Similarly, the expression *front-garden* – a forerunner of today's euphemism *lady garden* – also pre-dates one of the avalanche of superb double entendres in Ethel Waters's 'My Handy Man' (1928, lyrics by the great Andy Razaf), praising the titular gentleman's supposed horticultural skill at 'trimming the rough edges off my lawn'.

While the top-selling female blues singers of those days were capable of being as smutty as anyone – other fine contenders in this department include Hattie North's 'Honey Dripper Blues' (1938), and Sippie Wallace's 'I'm a Mighty Tight Woman' (1926) – the men could also hold their own, as the saying goes. One star performer in this respect was Bo Chatman, who recorded a great deal of risqué material under the name Bo Carter, and was seemingly never short of a good synonym for carnal activities or erogenous zones. On Thursday, 4 June 1931, he recorded the immortal 'Banana in Your Fruit Basket', and still found time for eleven more numbers, including 'Ram Rod Daddy', 'I Love That Thing', 'Pin in Your Cushion' and, the strain obviously showing, 'My Pencil Won't Write No More'.

However, it was not only in the black American blues market that such things occurred. Over in London that same year, Harry Roy co-wrote and sang a song that has since become something of a classic, and which still leaves most present-day listeners wondering how he got away with it. Despite one of the words in the title having long functioned as a pet name for a cat, and opening the performance with fake meowing sounds, Roy was perhaps going out on a limb in calling a song 'My Girl's Pussy' and singing lines like 'I stroke it every chance I get'.

Harry Roy, a mainstream bandleader, appearing regularly in the West End and on BBC radio, was in this particular instance operating very much in the music-hall tradition, where ribald songs could apparently have a perfectly innocent meaning. This was the argument put forward by Marie Lloyd (1870–1922), who once said, 'If I was to try to sing highly moral songs, they would fire ginger beer bottles and beer mugs at me. I can't help it if people want to turn and twist my meaning.' Indeed, anyone who read something smutty into her song about one woman's misadventures on the railway system, 'She'd Never Had Her Ticket Punched Before' (1897), or that tragic lament 'It Didn't Come Off, After All' (1902), clearly had a dirty mind to begin with. Indeed, in Harry's defence, he could have pointed to cat-care adverts in the national press around that time urging readers to 'Think of PUSSY' ('Pussy, too, needs a tonic to keep her in good condition').

This damn bust fetish

ALL THIS IS, OF COURSE, somewhat below the belt, and ignores the various slang names derived over the years for the breasts. In Richard Marsten's 1956 American novel *The Spiked Heel*, a woman and a man engage in the following conversation at a party, having already consumed their fair share of adult beverages:

> 'That's an indication of how far this damn bust fetish has gone in this country. Why, I bet I can think of a dozen words all by myself. Now, what's so special about breasts when you ask yourself the question? Fatty tissue, that's all.'
> 'Titty fassue,' Aaron corrected.
> 'See, there's one expression. And how about bubbles?'
> 'Or bubbies?'
> 'Or balloons?'
> 'Or coconuts?'
> 'Or mammaries?'
> 'Or headlights?'
> 'Or grapefruits?'
> 'Or bazooms?'
> 'Or balloons?'

'We said that one.'
'All right, how about knockers?'

Knockers, although sounding to English ears like a typical 1970s *Benny Hill Show* expression, is first recorded in that classic wartime dictionary of expressions heard at the lunch counters of America, Jack Smiley's *Hash House Lingo* (1941). Indeed, it even shows up a decade later in Salinger's *The Catcher in the Rye* (1951) – 'Her name was Lillian Simmons. My brother D.B. used to go around with her for a while. She had very big knockers' – but has long since crossed the Atlantic. In 1985, the *Daily Mirror* regaled their readers with this stirring tale of gallant nocturnal crime-fighters, under the heading 'The Too Blue Line':

> Police on night shifts used a new computerised telex system to send sexy messages to women colleagues at other stations. One said: 'Have you got big knockers?' Another asked: 'Do you do a turn?' And the girls sent replies that were just as steamy.

As much older English slang, a *knocker* was someone extremely good looking, very similar in meaning to the much more recent expression a *knockout*. It is used in this sense in Thomas Middleton's Jacobean comedy *A Chaste Maid in Cheapside* (1613) – 'They're pretty children both, but here's a wench will be a knocker'.

There are perhaps fewer slang names for the breasts down through the ages than one might expect. Poets such as Allan Ramsay (1684–1758) made heroic efforts to popularise the term *milky way* ('Behold her heav'nly face and heaving milky way'), while Jonathan Swift (1667–1745) offered the less-than-serious coinage *fore buttock* ('Her Fore Buttocks to the navel bare'). A century later, according to the anonymous author of the flash dictionary at the end of that indispensable early Victorian guide to the murkier aspects of the capital, *Sinks of London*

Laid Open (1848), breasts were known as *heavers*. None of these lasted, and in the main it has been a few tried-and-trusted expressions that have stayed the course. *Titties* (1746) became *tits* during the 20th century, and the word *bubbies*, known to Dr Johnson, became *boobies* in the hands, so to speak, of Henry Miller in the 1930s. This was then shortened to *boobs* round about the 1960s, thereby gradually subverting the latter's original slang meaning of a mistake. Indeed, the word *boob* shows up repeatedly in the UK press in the 1960s and 1970s, nearly always denoting an error, rather than a portion of anatomy, but here, for example, is Pamela Vandyke Price writing in the *Spectator* in 1973:

> Beneath the sexy sweater of today lie the dangling boobs of tomorrow. A girl who is not aware of this has demonstrated, at the very least, a lack of capacity for long-term planning.

Boob is also listed in drugs counsellor Eugene E. Landy's narco-centric compendium of hippie language, the *Underground Dictionary* (1971), alongside *jug, globe* and *bazoom*, together with more rarefied expressions such as *big brown eye* and *marshmallow*. The latter may have been current among the ageing flower children who Landy canvassed, but if he had turned at that time to members of the Royal Navy for examples, he could also have listed *jahooblies* and *BSH* (*British Standard Handfuls*).

Back in 1950s America, when falsies were a common trap for the unwary, the narrator in Sam S. Taylor's crime novel *Sleep No More* (1951) expressed his dilemma in these terms:

> As she stood there the rhythms of her body seemed in constant motion. I wondered if those two delightful ski jumps in black wool were real.

Venturing further back, before the invention of foam

rubber, we find the following entry by the ever-reliable Captain Grose, in his second edition, from 1788:

> DAIRY. A woman's breasts, particularly one that gives suck. She sported her dairy; she pulled out her breast.

All of which sounds somewhat reminiscent of what the *Guardian*'s reviewer termed the 'lascivious double entendre' inherent in the chorus of the 2003 song 'Milkshake' by female R&B singer Kelis. When asked what exactly the song meant, with its apparent suggestion that she was driving all the boys into a frenzy with her own particular dairy-based beverage, she took the Marie Lloyd approach of claiming that people could read into it anything that they wished. There are also references to milk in the subtly titled hip-hop song 'My Humps' (2006) by the Black Eyed Peas. Although *cameltoe* is one of the less appealing current synonyms for the female pudenda, this particular song was not, as it happens, a tale of body-positive dromedary empowerment, but rather a celebration of breasts and buttocks, with its talk of 'lovely lady lumps'. In this, there are echoes of one character's description of a female spy in Ian Fleming's first James Bond novel, *Casino Royale* (1953): 'She has black hair, blue eyes, and splendid... er... protuberances. Back and front.'

The man who utters this phrase is a Frenchman – René Mathis of the Deuxième Bureau – sadly living half a century too early to take advantage of the wealth of material available to students of the English language in *Viz* magazine's epic *Roger's Profanisaurus* (1998). Here, he could have taken his choice from *norks, charlies, headlamps, chebs, leisure facilities,* the *Bristol Channel* (for the cleavage) and, perhaps most descriptive of all, *dead-heat in a Zeppelin race.*

Be firm, my pecker

THE PENIS HAS BEEN EQUALLY WELL SERVED by the coiners of slang down the ages. Some names derive from its shape, others from its actions, while many are concerned with size (or the lack of it). Timothy Lea, in one of the *Confessions* books, offered some thoughtful words of advice for women on this subject:

> You can work wonders with a shy, sensitive lad if you give him a bit of admiration and encouragement. 'What an attractive spot to have a prick' or 'Goodness! I doubt if my slight frame will be able to withstand the onslaught of such a monster,' go down a lot better than 'Everything seems to be miniaturised these days doesn't it?' or 'OK, vole parts, let's be having you!'

With luck, those who have had the size of their sex organs compared to those of a small furry rodent are mercifully few in number, but the term *prick* – old enough to have been employed by Shakespeare – remains one of the most ubiquitous slang names for this organ. Not that it finds favour in all quarters; 1960s Black Panther leader Eldridge Cleaver saw this purely in terms of size and race (with just a hint of car mechanics thrown in):

> The black man's penis was the monkey wrench in the white man's perfect machine. ... Notice the puny image the white man has of his own penis. He calls it a 'prick,' a 'peter,' a 'pecker.'

This is all very well, but the oldest word for the penis listed by the *Oxford English Dictionary*, dating back just over a thousand years, is in fact *weapon* – hardly a shy or puny synonym to give to such a thing. Almost as long-standing, as they say, is the term *yard*, a usage which occurs in the Wycliff Bible of 1382. Mention of the word *yard*, these past hundred and fifty years, often conjures up images of Scotland Yard – an odd coincidence, since the word *dick* is a slang name for both a detective and a penis. The 1971 film *Shaft* exploited the double meaning behind the phrase *private dick* to the full, and indeed, the title character's surname was itself an English synonym for the penis dating back to 1772. As for the other two terms mentioned by Cleaver, both are relatively recent, and mostly used in the US: *peter* dates to 1870, and *pecker*, 1902. Mind you, just to confuse matters, in criminal circles for all of that time a *peter* has been a safe, and a *peterman* a safecracker, while in 19th-century Australia a *peter* was a prison cell. Then, of course, in the UK, to *keep your pecker up* has long meant to show resolve and be of good cheer. Hence, in Gilbert and Sullivan's comic opera *Trial by Jury* (1875), the character of the Defendant sings 'be firm, be firm my pecker', just after being led into the courtroom, which is certainly one way of making an impression.

Upstanding members of the community

THAT CONTROVERSY-HUNGRY American television programme *The Jerry Springer Show* (1991–present), when not tackling subjects like 'Gay Cousins in Love' or 'I Married a Horse', once broadcast an episode entitled 'I Cut Off My Manhood', thereby employing a term for the penis which had been around since 1640. Had the producers opted for other 17th-century variants – 'I Cut Off My Prependent' or 'I Cut Off My Runnion' – viewing figures might perhaps have been less impressive. Nevertheless, it was that century which also gave us one of the most enduring names, that of *cock* (1618).

It may be that there are few people these days who would refer to the organ in question as a *membrum virile* (1672), but the business of calling it a *member* is still quite prevalent, despite the fact that it dates back over seven hundred years – which, by an odd coincidence, is the same age as the House of Commons, whose occupants still refer to each other as *members* on a daily basis.

The term *meat* has an earthy and relatively modern air about it, typified in the classic 1936 salacious blues recording 'Take It Easy, Greasy' by Lil Johnson, off to see the butcher, looking for 'a piece of his good old meat'. Yet this, too, dates to the end of the 16th century, and can be found a century later being employed by the character Learcus in Sir John Vanbrugh's play *Æsop* (1697):

> Offspring of Venus. But I'll make you stay your stomach with meat of my chusing, you liquorish young baggage you.

Speaking of literary men, Sir Thomas Urquhart was just as adventurous when turning his attention to the correct names for male genitalia as he had been with the female, among which he numbered *Master John Goodfellow*, the *tickle-gizzard*, the *jolly member*, the *cunny-burrow ferret*, *Don Cypriano*, the *crimson chitterling*, the *nine-inch-knocker*, *split-rump* and the *live sausage*. If all this sounds rather conventional by Sir Thomas's usual standards, rest assured that he also referred to the organ in question at various times as *nilnisistando*, *bracmard* and *nudinnudo*. John Wilmot, 2nd Earl of Rochester (1647–80), by contrast, was a trifle more direct, preferring the expression *whore-pipe*.

Some of the highlights among the many rounded up by Farmer and Henley at the end of the 19th century include the *tent-peg*, *beard-splitter*, *crack-hunter*, *quim-stake*, *bald-headed-hermit*, *rolling-pin*, *middle leg*, *solicitor-general*, *bush-whacker*, *tool*, *eye-opener* and the *Member for Cockshire*. They also note some specifically Scottish examples, such as *dirk*, *cutty gun*, *Little Davy*, *mowdiwort* and *dibble* (the latter last seen holding down a job as a fireman in the 1967 animated series *Trumpton*). They note that *Irish root* was itself an English slang word for the penis, but Irish terms themselves are represented merely by *Langolee* and *jiggling-bone*.

Privates on Parade

IT HAS LONG BEEN TRADITIONAL among men in pubs, when rising to visit the lavatory, to announce to their mates that they are off to *shake hands with the wife's best friend*, to *shake hands with the unemployed*, *syphon the python* or *unleash the one-eyed trouser-snake*. In all-male societies such as the army, where men are thrown together in close proximity and showers and sleeping arrangements are communal, there will always be banter about people's *wedding tackle*, their *meat-and-two-veg*, or, in Royal Navy slang, their *toggle-and-two*. In the first volume of his Second World War memoirs, *Adolf Hitler – My Part in His Downfall* (1971), Spike Milligan recalled in particular the after-dark bar-rack-room performances put on by the prodigiously endowed Gunner 'Plunger' Bailey, who, by torchlight, 'manipulated his genitals to resemble "Sausage on a Plate", "The Last Turkey in the Shop", "Sack of Flour", "The Roaring of the Lions", and by using spectacles, "Groucho Marx". Finally for the National Anthem he made the member stand.'

When the playwright Peter Nichols used his own 1940s army days as the inspiration of a play in 1977– memorably described by Irving Wardle in *The Times* as 'altogether the kind of piece George Orwell might have turned out for the Carry On team' – he employed a winningly evocative double entendre as a title, *Privates on Parade*. The expression *private parts* had been around since 1623 as a way of referring to the genitals, which was itself a less judgemental version of what in earlier times had been variously called the *shameful parts* (Wycliff's *Bible*, 1382), or even the *filthy parts* (1553).

Filth was certainly much under discussion in 1977, when the title of the LP *Never Mind the Bollocks, Here's the Sex Pistols* caused it to be dragged through the courts on obscenity charges. In fact, while it may have been slang for much of its life, *bollocks* is actually the oldest word we have for the testicles, pre-dating *stones* (1154) and *balls* (1325). Captain Grose in the late 18th century listed expressions such as *nutmegs*, *bawbles* and *tallywags*, while *nuts* and *knackers* entered the language almost at the same time in the mid-1860s, but it took until the 1930s for the appearance of that evergreen item of rhyming slang, *cobblers* (*cobbler's awls* – balls).

Enveloping the pair in question, we have the bag of skin formerly known as the *cod* or *cods* (1398) – hence the term *codpiece*, that singular item of Tudor clothing, favoured in recent times by singers such as Ian Anderson from Jethro Tull and Larry Blackmon from Cameo. Another singer, the late, great Viv Stanshall of the Bonzo Dog Doo Dah Band, in his intermittent series of radio broadcasts for the John Peel Show about *Sir Henry at Rawlinson End* (1975–91), memorably named the character of the ancient butler Old Scrotum, since the man was a 'wrinkled old retainer'.

In the end, the album title chosen by the Sex Pistols was cleared of obscenity charges, and indeed was soon looking relatively quaint, in the light of subsequent LPs such as that perennial family singalong favourite, Flux of Pink Indians' *The Fucking Cunts Treat Us Like Pricks* (1984, also prosecuted for obscenity, also acquitted). The word *cunt*, of course, remains the term most likely to be censored with asterisks or bleeped out in the media, for fear of causing offence. This despite various campaigns to 'reclaim' the word, beginning, perhaps, with Germaine

Greer's winningly titled article 'Lady Love Your Cunt' (*Screw* magazine, 28 June 1971). In prosecuting the Sex Pistols' LP title, using a 19th-century obscenity law, no one seemed to be claiming that the word *bollocks* was offensive to men, the possessors of said body parts, nor is that argument advanced when people are variously insulted with names such as *dickhead, knob-end, old scrote* or *prick*, though few people would necessarily want these terms as a character reference. *Cunt*, it seems, has always been a tricky one. Indeed, in Captain Grose's first edition from 1785, he explains that even in those days it was possible to offend the police by placing the emphasis sharply on the first part of the word *constable*, a habit which has survived in some quarters to this day:

> THINGSTABLE. Mr Thingstable; Mr Constable: a ludicrous affectation of delicacy in avoiding the pronunciation of the first syllable in the title of that officer, which in sound has some similarity to an indecent monosyllable.

As for the *bollocks*, never mind.

Working your ground-smashers overtime

IT IS TEMPTING, AFTER THE FOREGOING SEA of erogenous zones, to conclude that the only parts of the body of interest to the coiners of slang are those of a sexual nature. They certainly account for a very large percentage of anatomical nicknames, but other limbs and extremities do occasionally get a look-in. Different societies and closed groups have all originated their own particular variants over the years, but to take one particular example as a case in point, imagine that you are a *hip-to-the-tip* American jazz musician, some time around 1942. What the cognoscenti would have called a *hep-cat*, a *solid-sender*, a *pressed stud* or, the new word of the day – whisper it quietly, because it has had a hard time of late – a *hipster*. Here is how things would shape up, from head to foot.

Your body generally was a *chassis*, covered in *enamel* (skin). As for your head, that was the *top storey, fusebox, knowledge-box* or *crust*. Covering that, unless you were bald, was your *moss, rug* or *wig*, and the face as a whole was your *puss*, or *pan* – hence the origin of the expression *deadpan*, when you deliver a message with a straight face. On either side of the head were your *lugs*, and right in the centre of that face you had a *smeller* (nose), below which was your *yap* or *piechopper*, containing a certain quantity of *crumb-crushers* or *biters*. You looked out at the world from a pair of *Edisons, baby blues* or *lamps*, maybe through a pair of *cheaters* (glasses). Your arms were pretty much just your arms – although if you were *on the sleeve*, that meant you were injecting drugs – but down at their furthest extremities it was a whole different story. Here could be found your *lunch-hooks, grabbers, biscuit-snatchers, flippers, mitts* or *paws*. The middle of your body would be somewhat vague – apart from your *pump* (heart), and the numerous words for what was in your underwear, front and back. Holding up the whole construction were *pegs* or *gams* (legs), and, if kneeling, you are on your *prayer-bones*. As for the feet, take your choice between *gondolas, dogs, pedal-extremities, crunchers, hooves, ground-smashers* or *roach-killers*.

If you could then transport this particular *righteously hep* individual in a time machine back to Covent Garden in the 18th century, they would mostly have to trade in their customary vocabulary for a whole new set of slang. To take just one example, the head becomes a *napper*, a *sconce*, a *costard*, the *crown office*, a *jobbernole*, a *poll*, a *jolly nob*, or the *idea pot*. Yet in among these terms that were unfamiliar to our jazz visitor could be found others such as *upper storey* and *knowledge-box*, which then managed to survive two centuries and a journey across the ocean basically intact in spelling and meaning.

The culture shock of such a journey, though, might well encourage our visitor to head for the nearest *hoofery* (dance hall), absorb some *tonsil paint* or *neck oil* (alcohol), *rest the weight* (sit down), and, being generally *cool, calm and a solid wig* (sensible), settle down and start whistling that old Lee Morse tune from 1930, 'T'aint No Sin to Take Off Your Skin, and Dance around in Your Bones'.

FOUR

Polari Missiles

The wrong pew

THERE IS NO SUCH THING as a gay slang dictionary published in the 18th century – or, indeed, any time before the late 20th century. This is hardly surprising, since for several hundred years the usual punishment for male homosexual activity in Britain was death, so those involved had little reason to draw attention to themselves, and indeed, a powerful incentive for disguising their meanings. As a result, their lives and language were mostly documented, when documented at all, in the law courts, and brief reports in the newspapers. Lesbianism was not illegal, but remained even more under the radar than its male equivalent.

Up until after the Second World War, when attitudes in some quarters began to shift, the prevailing view of homosexual relationships, and the language used to describe them, was not far removed from that expressed in this anonymous limerick from 1941:

> There was a young man from Purdue
> Who was only just learning to screw,
> But he hadn't the knack,
> And he got too far back –
> In the right church, but in the wrong pew.

Detestable and abominable

WHATEVER ENGLISH SOCIETY, and especially the Church, may have thought of homosexual relationships in the late Middle Ages, there were no laws against them. It was not until the year 1533, in the reign of Henry VIII, that a statute entitled An Acte for the punishment of the vice of Buggerie was introduced, which appears to have been directed as much at those who were romantically inclined towards our four-legged friends as at any potential same-sex liaisons:

> Forasmuch as there is not yet sufficient and condign punish-
> ment appointed and limited by the due course of the Laws of
> this realm for the detestable and abominable Vice of Buggery
> committed with mankind or beast...

Indeed, the difficulty involved in tracing the words *buggery* and *sodomy* is that, from medieval times until the 19th century, the legal definition of both in England was considerably wider than it later became. For instance, as far as the law was concerned, in former times, anything from cunnilingus and fellatio, up to and including the murky business of becoming overly intimate with a family pet or farmyard animal, all fell within the scope of the word *buggery*.

Nevertheless, it carried a death sentence, and could land you at the end of a noose up until 1861.

If his weapon be out

EVER SINCE THE PUBLICATION of *The Portrait of Mr W. H.* by Oscar Wilde in 1889 – inspired by a suggestion first made in the 18th century by the critic Thomas Tyrwhitt that Shakespeare's sonnets were addressed to a man – people have been searching the works of the Bard looking for clues to his sexuality. Yet, as the lexicographer Eric Partridge has pointed out, there are very few unambiguous references to homosexuality in Shakespeare's plays:

> Perhaps the clearest-cut passages are these two:— '*Thersites.* Thou art thought to be Achilles' male varlet! – *Patroclus.* Male varlet, you rogue, what's that? – *Thersites.* Why, his masculine whore' (*Troilus and Cressida*, V i 14–16); and the Hostess, concerning Falstaff, 'In good faith, 'a cares not what mischief he doth, if his weapon be out: he will foin like any devil; he will spare neither man, woman, nor child' (2 *Henry IV*, II i 14–17).

During the reign of Charles II, it was common for men to kiss each other by way of greeting. Indeed, in Richard Head's novel *The English Rogue* (1665), the narrator objects to the custom:

> For in my opinion, it is very unnatural, nay loathsome, for one man to kiss another, though of late too customary I know it is; yet I look on such as use it, inclining to Sodomy, and have had the unhappiness to be acquainted with severall, who using that unnatural action, found it onely the Preludium to a more beastly intention.

The word *lesbian* occurs relatively frequently in surviving 17th-century documents, but it generally referred to an architect's tool made of lead, known as a *lesbian rule*. At the close of that century, however, B.E.'s *A new dictionary of the terms ancient and modern of the canting crew, in its several tribes of gypsies, beggers, thieves, cheats &c.* (1699) contained the following:

> *Quean*, a Whore, or Slut.
> *A dirty Quean*, a very Puzzel or Slut.

However, these are heterosexual nicknames. Closer to the point is another slang expression in the same dictionary:

Tip the Velvet, c. [cant] to Tongue a Woman.

To many of today's readers and television viewers, this phrase will be familiar as the title of Sarah Waters's 1998 lesbian historical novel *Tipping the Velvet*, and its subsequent 2002 BBC drama adaptation by Andrew Davies. Much of the publicity surrounding both of these asserted that the title was based upon 'a Victorian slang word for cunnilingus', but it was a century and a half older than that, and not originally a lesbian-specific term. However, not far into the 18th century, a genuine coinage for this kind of relationship emerged. Women having sex with each other were said to be engaging in *the game of flats* – since *flats* was a slang name for playing cards, but also doubled as a colloquial term for the female genitals.

Ah ye little dear Toad!

IT WAS ALSO IN THE EARLY 1700s that the word *molly* as a name for homosexual men came into use, implying effeminacy. The first recorded use of the term occurs in Ned Ward's *Satyrical Reflections on Clubs* (1710). In it, he described a clandestine London club for homosexual men:

> There is a particular Gang of *Sodomitical* Wretches, in this Town, who call themselves the *Mollies*, and are so far degenerated from all masculine Deportment, or manly Exercises, that they rather fancy themselves Women, imitating all the little Vanities that Custom has reconcil'd to the Female Sex, affecting to Speak, Walk, Tattle, Cursy, Cry, Scold, and to mimick all Manner of Effeminacy...

The most famous establishment of this kind was brought to public notice during a series of Old Bailey trials in 1726, for offences said to have taken place at an establishment run by one

Margaret Clap in Holborn. This was the subject of Rictor Norton's book *Mother Clap's Molly House* (1992), which inspired the 2001 Mark Ravenhill play of the same name.

At one of the trials, Samuel Stephens, who had visited the establishment several times in order to investigate it with a view to potential prosecutions, testified that 'Mrs Clap's House was notorious for being a Molly-House'. Then, at Clap's own trial, Stephens described something of the scene he had encountered:

> I found near Men Fifty there, making Love to one another as they call'd it. Sometimes they'd sit in one anothers Laps, use their Hands indecently Dance and make Curtsies and mimick the Language of Women – O Sir! – Pray Sir! – dear Sir! Lord how can ye serve me so! – Ah ye little dear Toad! Then go by Couples, into a Room on the same Floor to be marry'd as they call'd it.

Satan's Harvest Home

A NOTABLE LONDON PUBLICATION in 1749 alluded to both male and female homosexuality in its contents, and in its extravagant title: *Satan's Harvest Home: or the Present State of Whorecraft, Adultery, Fornication, Procuring, Pimping, Sodomy, And the Game of Flatts (Illustrated by an Authentic and Entertaining Story) And other Satanic Works, daily propagated in this good Protestant Kingdom*.

The anonymous author claimed that 'some of our Tip top Beaus dress their Heads on quilted *Hair Caps*, to make 'em look more *Womanish*; so that Master Molly has nothing to do but slip on his *Head Cloaths* and he is an errant Woman'. In addition to the term *molly*, homosexual men are also referred to here as *ganymedes*, after the handsome young man in the Greek myths, said in some versions to have been the lover of Zeus.

While the term *lesbian* at that time would still either be

used in its earlier architectural sense, or else to denote a particular type of Greek wine, the writer made much of the legend of Sappho in a chapter devoted to the *game of flatts*, saying that she 'teaches the female World a new Sort of Sin, call'd the *Flats*, that was follow'd not only in Lucian's Time, but is practis'd frequently in *Turkey*, as well as at *Twickenham* at this Day'.

A few decades later, Captain Francis Grose's singular contribution to the lexicographer's art offered several expressions not to be found in Dr Johnson's *Dictionary*. Virtually all of his many sexual references were of the hetero variety, but he did manage to round up the following:

> BACK GAMMON PLAYER. A sodomite.
> BACK DOOR (USHER OR GENTLEMAN OF THE). The same.
> WINDWARD PASSAGE. One who uses or navigates the windward passage; a sodomite.

Thronged with margeries

THE 19TH CENTURY IN ITS TURN added surprisingly little to the slim roster of gay and lesbian slang words. On 11 April 1833, however, thanks to the testimony of someone giving evidence at the Old Bailey, the earliest recorded usage of the word *poof* was preserved. Three men were accused of having murdered a boy named Robert Paviour, who had gone missing from his home in East London. The witness said that one of the accused had told him that:

> ...there was a gentleman who gave a great deal of money for boys – that the gentleman lived somewhere in Horsemonger-lane; he said he was a captain – he said, there was a gentleman in the City, too, that was one of these poofs, as he called them... I had never heard the word poofs before.

Interestingly, he was not then questioned further about this term, which suggests that it was already familiar to some in the court.

The word reappeared as pouffs in a scurrilous guide to London's nightlife published anonymously in 1855, *The Yokel's Preceptor: More Sprees in London! Being a Regular and Curious Show-Up of all the Rigs and Doings of the Flash Cribs in this Great Metropolis etc.*, generally supposed to have been written by the pornographer William Dugdale. Its full title ran to roughly ten times that length, promising details of all manner of fleecing holes, dossing hotels and molly clubs. Dressed up as a terrible warning to unwary visitors from the shires, this in fact acted as a guide for the hedonist, gay as well as straight:

> The increase of these monsters in the shape of men, commonly designated Margeries, Pouffs, &c., of late years, in the great Metropolis, renders it necessary for the safety of the public, that they should be made known. ... Yes, the Quadrant, Fleet-street, Holborn, the Strand, &c., are actually thronged with them!

Across the Atlantic, dictionaries of slang and colloquial language had begun appearing with some regularity. John Russell Bartlett's *Dictionary of Americanisms – A Glossary of Words and Phrases Usually Regarded as Peculiar to the United States* first appeared in 1848. Any modern readers looking here for references to same-sex relationships will be disappointed, but one entry in the third edition (1860) now has an added resonance which the author had not intended:

> TO COME OUT. An expression used among certain religious enthusiasts, meaning to make an open profession of religion. 'I experienced religion at one of Brother Armstrong's protracted meetin's. Them special efforts is great things – ever since I *come out*, I've felt like a new critter.

Bona Parlare

THE MID-19TH CENTURY WAS A TIME of much investigative journalism, looking into the lives of the urban poor in England. In J. William Tweedie's *The Night Side of London* (1857), the author writes of having visited the Eagle Tavern – made famous in the nursery rhyme 'Pop Goes the Weasel' – and notes disapprovingly a group of heterosexual youths he describes as 'gay Lotharios, very disreputable and, to a certain extent, deliriously gay'.

Perhaps the best-known publication was Henry Mayhew's monumental series of studies, *London Labour and the London Poor* (1851 and 1861). In volume three, he examined the lives and language of itinerant Punch & Judy men, puppeteers first recorded two hundred years earlier in the diary of Samuel Pepys on 9 May 1662. Here, Mayhew gave details of a form of slang speech that, in the 1960s, would become closely associated in the public mind with homosexual men, owing to the great success of the Julian and Sandy characters on the BBC radio show *Round the Horne* (1965–8). In mid-Victorian England, however, this was simply the language of show people, with no particular same-sex associations.

One *punchman* explained the basics to Mayhew:

> 'Bona parlare' means language; name of patter. 'Yeute munjare' – no food. 'Yeute lente' – no bed. 'Yeute bivare' – no drink. I've 'yeute munjare,' and 'yeute bivare,' and, what's worse, 'yeute lente.' This is better than costers' talk, because that ain't no slang at all, and this is a broken Italian, and much higher than the costers' lingo. We know what o'clock it is, besides.

This hybrid language was often called *parlyaree*, but there are many other variant spellings, such as *parlare* and *pallary*, and the more modern spelling *polari*, all seemingly deriving from the

Italian word *parlare*, to speak. Paul Barker, in his book *Polari –
The Lost Language of Gay Men* (2002), distinguishes between
polari – the language of a certain section of the homosexual
community which had its heyday between the late 1940s and
the 1970s – and *parlyaree*, the much older language used by a
variety of itinerant groups for several centuries. That a great
many of the phrases which came to form part of *polari* were
drawn from earlier sources is clear in the dictionary which
forms the latter part of the book. To call a magistrate a *beak* is
hardly news – Sir John Fielding (1721–80), who presided over
Bow Street Magistrates' Court, was known to Londoners as the
blind beak. Similarly, calling the testicles *cods* would not have
surprised Henry VIII or any of his subjects. Kenneth Williams
used *polari* as a gay man in the 1940s, in his diary entry for 24
October 1947: 'went to the matelots' bar – met 2 marines –
very charming. Bonar shamshes [the latter probably meaning
smashers].'

All of which recalls the dialogue between two punchmen,
given by Mayhew in 1851:

> 'How are you getting on?' I might say to another punchman.
> 'Ultra cativa,' he'd say. If I was doing a little, I'd say, 'Bonar.' Let
> us have a 'shant a bivare' – pot o' beer... 'Fielia' is a child; 'Homa'
> is a man; 'Dona,' a female; 'Charfering-homa' – talking-man,
> policeman.

Afraid to palarie a dickie

SEPARATE FROM THE WORLD of the fairground grafters and
punchmen, the language of the real homosexual subculture of
the late 19th century surfaced rather in publications such as the
anonymous book *Sins of the Cities of the Plain, Or Confessions of
a Mary-Ann* (1881). The tale of a London rent boy named Saul, it

was issued in an edition of 250 copies by the publisher William Lazenby, and contained references to *margeries, mary anns* and *pouffs*. The word *homosexual* itself first surfaced as a coinage in the English language with the publication in 1892 of C. G. Craddock's translation of *Psychopathia Sexualis* by Richard Freiherr von Krafft-Ebing.

The 1890s also saw the advent of a variety of new slang expressions. This was the time of Oscar Wilde's public rise and fall, the latter triggered by his disastrous libel action aimed at the 9th Marquess of Queensberry, who had sent him a visiting card at the Albemarle Club in 1895 on which was scrawled 'For Oscar Wilde, posing as a somdomite [sic]'. The latter word never existed outside of Queensberry's imagination, but that decade provided a veritable embarrassment of possible alternatives, such as *urning* (1893), *queer* (1894), *Uranist* (1895), *fairy* (1895, originally US slang) and *invert* (1897).

Two years prior to the court cases that precipitated Wilde's downfall, his publisher, Leonard Smithers, issued the homo-erotic novel *Teleny, Or the Reverse of the Medal* (1893), often credited to a combination of Oscar and various collaborators, although the authorship is unestablished. The language veers between anatomical description and poetic declamations, yet gay slang is not present, and as for *parlare*, readers would have to turn rather to an entirely different book published that year, *Signor Lippo, Burnt-Cork Artiste, His Life and Adventures*, by P. H. Emerson. The latter showman's tale contained words such as *bona*, with a narrator much given to saying things like 'though they offered me lots of money to blow the gaff [confess], I felt afraid to palarie a dickey [say a word] for fear of being trapped'.

Making out extremely well

THE 20TH CENTURY BROUGHT GREATER AWARENESS of homo-sexuality among the public in general, and a proliferation of new slang words relating to it. A fair amount of this came from America, including the transformation of the word *gay* from one which had for centuries had multiple meanings, into the situation existing now in which they have virtually all given way to the one denoting same-sex orientation. In the 18th century, poetry was known as the *gay science*, and a worldly, hedonistic gentleman was termed a *gay man*, while the high spirits exhibited at the close of the 19th century caused them to be nicknamed the *Gay Nineties*.

In 1931, the American comic *Boy's Life* ran a serial about the adventures of a high-school student working at an amusement park, whose introduction would strike several conflicting notes if used today: 'Frank Madison... secures a job at Gay Acres, as a bathhouse attendant, and is making out extremely well...'. Meanwhile, back in England, readers were treated to the publi-cation of *Gay Agony* (1930) by one H. A. Manhood, 'The author of *Nightseed*'. Seemingly addicted to unwittingly suggestive titles, the same writer then put out a book of short stories called *Crack of Whips* (1934).

In a similar vein, while the Greek poet Sappho (and her home, the Isle of Lesbos) had for some time been associated in literary quarters with suggestions of female same-sex relation-ships, it was not until the 1890s that the word *lesbian* was first applied by psychologists to such behaviour. Among the general public, it took some decades for the word to gain recognition, so that, for instance, if you turn to the *Daily Mirror* for 16 January 1917, you will find a report of the sinking by a German U-boat of the British cargo steamer *Lesbian*, owned by the Liverpool-based company Ellerman Lines.

British newspaper readers during the First World War might have found nothing remarkable in this name, but when Louis E. Jackson and C. R. Hellyer compiled *A Vocabulary of Criminal Slang* in Portland, Oregon, in 1914, some of their examples seem to have come from a more modern-sounding, cynical world. In addition to entries such as 'SNOW – current chiefly among cocaine fiends', and 'JOINT… a business establishment, a hangout', can be found the following:

> DRAG… Amongst female impersonators on the stage and men of dual sex instincts 'drag' denotes female attire donned by a male. Example: 'All the fagots (sissies) will be dressed in drag at the ball tonight'.

Although in this instance written with one 'g' instead of two, this is the first recorded instance of the term *faggot*, an Americanism later commonly shortened to *fag* in the 1920s, giving rise ever since to a certain confusion in transatlantic conversations with British people asking for cigarettes.

The word *sissy* – usually denoting an effeminate man – was obviously felt to be well enough known at the time to help explain the word *faggot*. In the 19th century on both sides of the Atlantic, *sissy* was a common term of address for a woman, derived from the word sister, but by the 1890s had also acquired this extra meaning in the US. By the twenties, it was enough of an accepted slang word that it appeared, for instance, in the title of a song by blues vocalist Ma Rainey, who recorded the 'Sissy Blues' in Chicago in June 1926. Black American songs of that era pulled no punches, and played to an audience who had few illusions about life, so they provide a useful guide to the kind of slang words current in that community. Even so, not everyone went as far as Kokomo Arnold, with the openly bisexual lyrics to his song 'Sissy Man Blues' (Chicago, 15 January 1935), which not only speak of waking up with his 'pork-grinding business' [penis] in his hand, but ask the Lord if he can't send him a woman, then let him have a *sissy man*.

Steaming hot tea

IN ENGLAND IN THE FIRST DECADES of the 20th century, often the mere mention of Oscar Wilde's name stood as a shorthand for things which 'polite society' did not care to investigate, or, to use a phrase from the poem 'Two Loves', written in 1894 by Wilde's sometime lover Lord Alfred Douglas, 'the love that dare not speak its name'. Douglas himself later completely rejected the memory of his former friend, as a defence witness at a high-profile trial of the MP Noel Pemberton Billing, who claimed in his own magazine, *Vigilante*, that there was a vast German-backed hostile conspiracy involving 47,000 prominent homosexuals and lesbians. Supporting this view at the trial, Lord Alfred Douglas said of Wilde that 'he was the greatest force for evil in Europe for the last 350 years'. Yet to many younger readers of girls' boarding-school stories that year, Lesbia was simply the name of the heroine of Angela Brazil's new novel, *For the School Colours* (1918), who, as the narrator says, has 'a great sympathy for girls'.

As a schoolboy at Marlborough College in the early 1920s, future Poet Laureate John Betjeman entered into a correspondence with Lord Alfred Douglas, until Betjeman's father objected. Then, in 1930, John wrote home to a friend while on a trip to Berlin that 'I have drunk tea in my life, but never have I wanted to drink it so much as in this town', saying that it was 'obtainable' and 'steaming hot'. According to his biographer Bevis Hillier, *tea* was 'homosexual slang for boy trade'. Weimar Berlin at that time was known for its sexual tolerance across the spectrum.

However, over in New York, where matters were conducted somewhat more discreetly, clubs and bars where homosexual people could meet would often advertise in the newspapers using the coded phrase 'we cater to the Temperamental Set'.

Since 1927, a new term for anyone displaying such an orientation was the suitably vague *one of those*, yet this was obscure enough to not ring any bells with the Cincinnati publisher of the anonymous crime magazine *Confessions of a Stool Pigeon* (1931), whose subtitle simply said, *By One of Them*. Mind you, readers of the pulps at that time were generally thought to be aware of such things. Dashiell Hammett's *The Maltese Falcon* first appeared between September 1929 and January 1930 in *Black Mask* magazine. In it, the character of Joel Cairo – later immortalised by Peter Lorre in the 1941 film adaptation – is flamboyantly gay, and introduced as such to the reader in Hammett's opening description, after Sam Spade's secretary Effie Perine has forewarned him, 'This guy is queer' (later in the book he is described as 'the fairy'):

> He held a black derby hat in a chamois-gloved hand and came towards Spade with short, mincing, bobbing steps. The fragrance of chypre came with him.

Omee polones

PARLYAREE SURFACED PROMINENTLY in 1934 with the publication of the bestselling book *Cheapjack* by Philip Allingham, a memoir of his itinerant days working at fairs and markets up and down England as a 'fortune-teller, grafter, knocker-worker and mounted pitcher'. The brother of crime writer Margery Allingham, he worked his pitch wearing evening dress and a top hat.

Allingham's book came complete with a glossary, which

included the first recorded use of the word *polone*, meaning 'a girl'. Also present was *omee*, or *homey*, 'a man', which became familiar in post-war *polari*, although there was no sign of *omee polone*, meaning an effiminate man or homosexual. Other words here which eventually became part of gay slang were *nanty*, 'beware', and *bevvy* meaning 'drink'. These people used a reasonable selection of cockney rhyming slang – such as *daisy roots* for boots – as well as words from Romany, Yiddish and Italian sources, with a fair amount of criminal slang. Yet while there were a couple of characters who the author says 'had no use for women', this was not in itself a homosexual world.

The 1930s saw the appearance of the expressions *bent*, and, in America, *fruit*. Then the word *gay* first appeared with its new meaning at the start of the Second World War. It began as an American slang term for homosexual, just a few years after the latter term had been shortened in some circles to the word *homo*. The House of Lords in 1937 got into the act during a debate on whether homosexuality should be grounds for divorce, with Viscount Dawson of Penn saying that the word *sodomy* as a legal term had become 'inadequate and unsuitable', since it 'involves the question of a rather vulgar crime which is only open to the male', whereas 'homosexuality refers to both sexes'. This highlights the fact that there were still hardly any words for female same-sex relationships, although *sapphist* had gained currency during the previous decade.

Gay, however, certainly did not replace the existing terms overnight. Christopher Isherwood, who kept extensive diaries from the time of his emigration to America in 1939, was recording American slang words like *faggot* by the following year, and the word *sissy* also showed up occasionally. Mostly, however, he would use the word *queer*, and despite living in America, did not write *gay* until the 1950s.

However, George Melly, aged eighteen and conscripted into the Royal Navy in the closing years of the Second World War – where he said his open homosexuality was neither frowned upon nor uncommon – encountered this usage of the word *gay* some time around 1944. According to his memoir of those times, *Rum, Bum and Concertina* (1977), having written an article for a newspaper in which he said 'when on leave in London, I have a very gay time', he was cautioned by an older homosexual friend about the implied double meaning, as he recalled: 'I'd never heard the word "gay" at that time. "Queer" was in more general use among homosexuals.' Four years later, Gore Vidal was to note in his novel *The City and the Pillar* (1948) that in New York at that time the words *fairy* and *pansy* were no longer acceptable, and 'it was fashionable to say a person was "gay"'.

The Gay Bombardier

MANY YOUNG MEN HAD LATELY TRAVELLED the globe courtesy of the Second World War, which would certainly have helped spread such slang. Out in Singapore in 1947 with a touring concert party of the British armed forces, the young Kenneth Williams found an equally tolerant attitude among his fellow soldiers to his sexual orientation to that which George Melly had encountered in the navy. In addition to using *polari* words in his diary entries of that time, he wrote comments such as 'went round to the gay bar which wasn't in the least gay'. Williams also described something as 'so camp it wasn't true', using an expression that had first surfaced in Edwardian times, and which Quentin Crisp later recalled being used in that context in the 1920s. A fellow member of that concert party was future playwright Peter Nichols, who recalled in his superbly named autobiography *Feeling You're Behind* (1984) his first task upon joining the unit:

> I had more than enough to do mastering the new lingo. The vocabulary was of mostly familiar words with new meanings – camp, drag, chopper, gay and auntie. Some were from Romany or Parlyaree – vada, bona, roba.

The last term is of particular interest; a slang name for a woman dating back to Elizabethan times, being a shortened version of *bona-roba*, and defined by Dr Johnson as 'a showy wanton'.

As the forties became the fifties, even though laws punishing sodomy were still in force across America and in the UK, mainstream novels began to appear whose central characters were homosexual, often written by authors who were themselves gay. Angus Wilson, for instance, having used the slang expression *lizzie* for lesbian in his debut short story collection *The Wrong Set* (1949), then explored the life of a married man coming to terms with his homosexuality in the novel *Hemlock and After* (1952). The following year saw the publication of a very well-informed novel called *The Heart in Exile* by Rodney Garland (Adam de Hegedus), set squarely against a background of London's homosexual bars, clubs and parties, with a particular focus on Soho. Yet *polari* is nowhere to be seen. The activity which in more recent times has become known as *cruising* is often described, but the name used here is *hunting*. Sexual activity is mostly called *play*, while effeminate homosexuals are generally called *poufs* or *pansies*, and those less so are termed *inverts*, *queers* or, very occasionally, *homosexuals*. Much is made of the attractions of tough men of the working class, but they are not yet referred to by the later term of *rough trade*. No sign of the word *gay*, perhaps not surprising in the same year that the

Royal Navy still felt confident enough to proudly name its newly launched 75-foot motor torpedo boat *The Gay Bombardier*.

A variant American slang term for homosexual men appeared in *The Catcher in the Rye*, published in 1951, when Holden Caulfield says:

> The other end of the bar was full of flits. They weren't too flitty-looking – I mean they didn't have their hair long or any-thing – but you could tell they were flits anyway.

Mostly, though, the usual American expressions saw service in general conversation, such as this exchange in Alfred Bester's fine novel of the New York television industry, *Who He?* (1953):

> 'What about Charlie Hansel, the undercover queen? Trying to pass with that hoofer he married'.
> 'She's married? That fag?'

Familiar as these terms might have been to the average reader, Bester's story also included the more esoteric *cruising*, in its homosexual sense of trying to pick up a date – which was very different from the meaning intended by Gene Vincent two years later, when he and his Blue Caps recorded a track called 'Cruisin'', in which the singer was *cruising for a bruising*, looking to start a fight.

Taking the biscuit

IN THE MID-1950S, THE NEW USAGE of the word *gay* was brought to the attention of the general British public in the aftermath of a high-profile court case in which several men, including Lord Montagu of Beaulieu, were charged with having engaged in homosexual acts. One of the accused, the journalist Peter Wil-deblood, published a book about these events in 1955, entitled

Against the Law, in which he explained that the word *gay* was an American slang expression for homosexuality.

In 1957, a British government Committee on Homosexual Offences and Prostitution, headed by John Wolfenden – which had been set up in 1954 partly as a result of the publicity given to the prosecution of Lord Montagu – published its recommendations in a document generally known as the Wolfenden Report. During their investigations, they coined a pair of slang code words of their own, referring privately to their subjects as *huntleys* (gay men) or *palmers* (prostitutes), after the English biscuit manufacturer Huntley & Palmers. The far-reaching report recommended that homosexual sex should no longer be a crime in the eyes of the law, a suggestion which was often cited as an inspiration in America in the 1960s, and helped lead ten years later to the passing of the Sexual Offences Act 1967, which decriminalised such activities in England and Wales. The famous Stonewall riots in New York took place a full two years later, and in many American states homosexual sex was not only illegal then, but remained so until 2003.

The Wolfenden committee delivered their findings to a country in which you could regularly find large adverts on the front page of the *Daily Mirror* from a company called Go Deodorants for a product called Go Poof Body Powder. Indeed, on 9 April 1957, one appeared directly below another for Gor-Ray skirts, who were tempting their own customers with the slogan 'Come Out in Style'. Into this allegedly more innocent world where words could nevertheless mean several things at once stepped the benevolently laconic figure of comedian Kenneth Horne, whose radio show *Beyond Our Ken* began broadcasting in 1958. Its mid-1960s follow-up, *Round the Horne*, brought unreconstructed *polari* into the homes of the nation with the characters Julian and Sandy, played by Hugh Paddick and

Kenneth Williams respectively. *Beyond Our Ken* prefigured this with the same two actors appearing as a pair of camp characters named Rodney and Charles, and – although they did not use *polari* – their orientation was never seriously in doubt. Even when working in a coal mine, Kenneth has brought along his own 'special' miner's lamp:

> Williams: 'It is rather swish, isn't it? Don't you just adore the way it keeps changing colour?'
> Paddick: 'Yes. What a novel idea to have it set in a Chianti bottle.'

Three ways in front of the mirror

As FICTIONAL GAY MEN WERE APPEARING on national radio, lesbians made an appearance in one of the most successful series of novels of the 1950s, the James Bond books. Ian Fleming's *Goldfinger* (1959) pitted 007 against 'a Lesbian organisation which now calls itself "The Cement Mixers"', led by the subtly named Pussy Galore. Goldfinger himself claims that they are respected by the main mafia gangs, but, some time later, mobster Frank Midnight takes a more jaundiced view, as Pussy attempts to chat up Tilly Masterton:

> Cheezus how they bore me, the lizzies! You'll see, she'll soon have that frail parting her hair three ways in front of the mirror.

Frail was general 1920s jazz-era slang for a woman, but *lizzie* for lesbian was a more recent development. There still remained few specific slang words for female same-sex behaviour. Terms such as *muff-diver* had been around since the 1930s, while *dike*, spelled either with an 'i' or a 'y', appeared some time during the Second World War. Soho habitué and chronicler Frank Norman used various of these phrases in his book *Stand on Me*, published the same year as *Goldfinger*. In his regular hangout, a Soho café called the 86, he observes of the owner Gregorius:

> ...he was a bit kinkey about watching these birds dance together, but that is neither here nor there really because nearly every one is kinkey on dykes for some reason.

In an otherwise excellent book about cockney speech, *The Muvver Tongue* (1980), East Enders Robert Barltrop and Jim Wolveridge made the assertion that 'There is no Cockney word for homosexuality; it was virtually unknown before being publicised in recent years.' Both authors were born at the beginning of the 1920s, but their statement would very likely have surprised Frank Norman (born 1930), who wrote of his acquaintance in the fifties with a wide variety of what he termed *queers*, *lezzes* and *dykes*. In cockney rhyming slang, *ginger beer*, meaning *queer*, was certainly current at the end of the 1950s, as was *iron*, or *iron hoof* (poof), which dates back before the war, and appears as such in Jim Phelan's prison novel *Lifer* (1938).

Over in America as the sixties began, the word *gay* went public. In Christopher Isherwood's diary, he speaks of 'gay bar owners', while in Cothburn O'Neal's 1960 novel of San Francisco beatniks, *The Gods of Our Time*, one character says, 'It's just the gay boy coming out in Kurt. Fags are the most jealous-hearted creatures in the world.' The word *gay* could still refer to both sexes, however. Judson Grey's lurid slice of lesbian pulp, *Twilight Girls* (1962 – 'Down with men! That was the battle cry of the lascivious, lady-lusting League of Amazons'), although inexplicably overlooked by the Pulitzer Prize committee, certainly preserved a fair amount of current slang expressions in among the sleaze. One female character describes herself as a *gay girl*, while another is described as a *bull-dyke*, and an effeminate homosexual man is termed a *swish*. 'Your little Edie is a Mary-Jane,' says a lesbian. 'A chicken for some dyke.'

This was just one of hundreds of soft-core novels found at bookstalls, hardware stores and railway stations across America at that time, helping to educate the gentle reader about a supposed world of depravity outside their experience. Would-be bisexuals were targeted by books such as Carl Dodd's *The Switch Hitters* (1965), with the tagline 'Lesbians, Nymphos, Fags and what have you – they used him for an erotic yo-yo till he didn't know which way was which'. The novel's title derived from a baseball slang phrase that originally denoted a batsman who could use both left and right hands, which itself coincidentally prefigures a later term for a homosexual, someone who *bats for the other team.*

The reading public was certainly given many chances to pick up such phrases. Legendary book-length sex study *The Velvet Underground* (1963) by Michael Leigh – from which the pioneering New York band took their name – contained informative chapters on 'Women Who Want Other Women' and 'Men Who Want Other Men'. The former chapter gave details of a lesbian magazine published by an organisation called The Daughters of Bilitis, in whose pages could be found terms like *butch* and *femme*, as well as letters from women who wrote that they had been in the *gay life* for several years. Strangely, the chapter on men contained no slang whatever.

That's an in-joke, you know...

ONE OF THE MOST SUCCESSFUL FILMS at the box office in 1964 was the debut feature starring The Beatles, *A Hard Day's Night*, whose audience at that time included a great many schoolchildren, some of whom can be observed on screen, chasing the band from place to place. However, it also contained a knowing scene with the band in the make-up room of a TV theatre, in which Ringo is under the hairdryer reading a copy of *Queen* magazine. Lennon combs Ringo's hair, saying, 'Hey, he's reading the *Queen*,' then looks round and comments, 'That's an in-joke, you know,' to which Wilfrid Brambell – who in real life was gay – says, 'It's my considered opinion that you're a bunch of sissies.'

As it happened, if Ringo had been reading *Life* magazine that year instead, he might have chanced upon an article by Paul Welch in the 26 June issue entitled 'The "Gay" World Takes to the City Streets', which was an in-depth look at the homosexual scene in places like New York, Chicago and San Francisco. Even then, it referred to San Francisco as the nation's 'gay capital'. The piece explained terms like *queen, cruising, drag* and *S & M*, and gave an insight into the macho leather scene, courtesy of a bar owner in San Francisco's warehouse district: 'This is the anti-feminine side of homosexuality,' he explained. 'We throw out anyone who is too swishy.' By contrast, there was also a photograph of a decidedly straight Hollywood drinking establishment, with owner Barney Anthony standing in front of a sign he had hung up behind his bar, saying 'FAGOTS STAY OUT' (sic). 'I don't like 'em,' he told the author. 'They'll approach any nice-looking guy. Anybody does any recruiting, I say shoot him. Who cares?'

Whatever else Mr Anthony might have been reading that year, it is unlikely to have been Hubert Selby Jr's new book, *Last Exit to Brooklyn* (1964), whose self-contained second part is entitled *The Queen Is Dead* – inspiring the name of the 1986 LP by The Smiths – which begins with the words 'Georgette was a hip queer'. Written in a street-smart New York vernacular, the slang consists of the usual words like *fairy, punk, freak, queen* and *fag*.

In the UK from 1965, *polari* was being broadcast to the nation, courtesy of Kenneth Williams and Hugh Paddick as the camp duo Julian and Sandy, in the radio series *Round the Horne*, with scripts by Barry Took and Marty Feldman. The decriminalisation of homosexuality may still have been two years away, but these sketches were affectionately knowing and firmly let the audience in on the jokes. 'We've got a criminal practice that takes up most of our time,' they tell Kenneth Horne, who is visiting their legal firm, Bona Law, to which he replies, 'Yes, but apart from that, I need some legal advice.' Each week they plied their trade, so to speak, in a different setting, such as Bona Books in the King's Road ('Poe's *Raven*.' 'Is 'e?'), or the Bona Nature Clinic in Harley Street ('for your actual *homeo*-pathic practices'). When running a TV station – broadcasting, Horne suggests, to the Mincing Lane area – they have their own special version of popular series *Bonanza*, renamed *Bona-nanza*, as Julian explains, 'Yes, you know, that western about those four great butch *omees* trying to find themselves up the Ponderosa...'

While a large section of the adult population may have been tuning in, the idea that all gay men across the UK were speaking *polari* at that time is hard to support. For instance, the year 1966 saw the publication of a book by George Moor called *The Pole and Whistle*, set in an unnamed county not unlike Yorkshire, and – to judge from its music references – taking place in the very early sixties. 'Never before has a novel treated the contentious subject of homosexuality with such honesty and insight,' said the blurb – which is debatable, given precedents such as *The Heart in Exile* (1953) – but what is certain is that the book seems grounded in very authentic experience, yet contains little if any slang, and no *polari*. This contrasts somewhat starkly with the less serious approach taken by an American novel at that time, *The Intruders – The Explosive Story of One Man's Journey into a Homosexual Jungle* (1966) by Brad Riley, which concerned the efforts of a straight Los Angeles private eye to foil a gang of homosexual pickpockets who were apparently 'ruining the good name of the Hollywood homos'.

A tweedy butch?

As the sixties merged into the seventies, gay culture finally went mainstream. There were films and plays with lesbian themes or prominent lesbian characters: *The Group* (Sidney Lumet, 1966, based on the book by Mary McCarthy), *The Fox* (Mark Rydell, 1968, based on the novella by D. H. Lawrence), and, most famously, *The Killing of Sister George* (Robert Aldrich, 1968, based on the play by Frank Marcus). There were also homosexual-themed films, such as William Friedkin's *The Boys in the Band* (1970, based on the 1968 play by Mart Crowley). Even family listings magazine the *TV Times* treated its readers to a *polari* article ('The Walloper's Polari' by P. Gordino, October 1969, *walloper* being slang for a dancer), which has an added layer of irony, since *TV* is also a slang term meaning transvestite.

Not everyone was delighted with this turn of events. For instance, Black Panther leader Eldridge Cleaver had this to say in his 1969 book *Soul on Ice*:

> I, for one, do not think homosexuality is the latest advance over heterosexuality on the scale of human evolution. Homosexuality is a sickness, just as are baby-rape or wanting to become the head of General Motors.

As for the female of the species, he was equally blunt: 'If a lesbian is anything she is a frigid woman, a frozen cunt, with a warp and a crack in the wall of her ice.' Cleaver, who began writing this book while serving time in prison as a serial rapist, was given glowing notices in many quarters, including, of all places, *The Church Times* (21 February 1969), where, by a strange twist of fate, the reviewer was a man named Martin Fagg.

With the changing times came a new public awareness of formerly obscure slang words. In 1971, *Daily Mirror* columnist Marjorie Proops gave her readers the lesbian lowdown in a sympathetic article entitled 'Sad Little Gay Girl', which asked:

> What is a lesbian? Is she a mannish freak, a crew-cropped queer, a dyke in a collar and tie, a tweedy butch? Or is she, perhaps, the trendy dolly sitting beside you in the bus or the ordinary housewife doing her shopping in the supermarket?

Pop it in the toaster

AT THE SAME TIME IN AMERICA, *Life* magazine ran a lengthy article about the new Gay Liberation movement, under the title 'Homosexuals in Revolt', including a section about a lesbian couple, Barbara Love and Sidney Abbott, authors of a new book called *Sappho Was a Right-on Woman* (1972). This was also the year when what is thought to be the first specifically homosexual dictionary was published, *The Queens' Vernacular – A Gay Lexicon*, by Bruce Rodgers, lifting the lid on a world of gym-addicted *muscle queens*, and listing fifty types of *Miss*, from prudish (*Miss Priss*) to activist (*Miss Politics*). Compare this with a much later publication covering similar ground, *Gay-2-Zee – A Dictionary of Sex, Subtext and the Sublime*, by Donald F. Reuter (2006), which has just a handful, such as *Mister Sister* for a drag queen, but makes up for this with a great many of the esoteric terms which have evolved over the past few decades. Among these can be found such expressions as *pop it in the toaster* (sex at breakfast time), *cupcakes* ('a tasty set of bitesize buttocks'), *slut hut* ('a gay man's home') and *convertible* ('a bisexual').

Here, just as in the obscurely inventive terms for straight-sex practices listed in *Roger's Profanisaurus*, the creators of slang have reached for increasingly more specific ways of describing various activities, some of which are perhaps unknown to those engaged in them. However, the advent of AIDS in the 1980s eventually led to a greater general awareness of some expressions. While the *Sun* newspaper responded to the inclusion of a homosexual love story on the BBC's flagship soap *EastEnders* in 1987 with the typically sensitive headline 'NOW IT'S EASTBEND-ERS!', the UK government ran television adverts talking about safe sex and condom use. This shift in priorities eventually led, a decade later, to the following notable exchange in the House of Commons, as the MP for Ipswich, Jamie Cann, attempted to explain the terms *fisting* and *rimming* to his honourable friends during a debate on the Sexual Offences Amendment Bill (1999), backed up by a pamphlet issued by AIDS charity the Terrence Higgins Trust:

> Jamie Cann: For example, rimming—
> Stephen Pound (Ealing North): Oh God!
> Jamie Cann: It happens. Rimming, where one man licks out the rectum of another man, is not a practice that I would want my sons to get involved in; nor indeed is fisting, which is when one inserts the whole of one's fist and part of one's forearm up someone else's rectum.

In Canada around that time, if you bought a pint of milk, one of the leading brands was marketed in a white carton with the word HOMO written in large red block letters on the outside – short for homogenised – and café owners would ask you, when ordering a cup of tea, whether you wanted some homo with that. From there, it would seem just a short step to conversation about *teabags* (gay slang for the scrotum).

Since the 1990s, as a formal term, the acronym *LGBT* (standing for Lesbian, Gay, Bisexual and Transgender) has increasingly been favoured, rather than *gay* and *lesbian*, but many of the same core of slang terms which have seen service during the course of the last century are still very much in circulation. The word *queer* – at one time frequently an insult – has proved particularly durable, such as in the title of the American gay-makeover TV show *Queer Eye for the Straight Guy* (2003–7). Attempts have also been made in some quarters to revive *polari*, which had been largely dormant since the early 1970s, with notable exceptions in between, such as the Morrissey song 'Piccadilly Palare', which itself was on an album named *Bona Drag* (1990).

Exactly which word people now choose to use in order to define themselves varies enormously, and, like many other areas of life these days, has grown increasingly complicated. In March 2015, the *Guardian* reported the chief executive of lesbian dating app HER saying that it 'is about creating a space where lesbian, bi, queer, curious, flexisexual, pansexual and not-so-straight women can meet'. Still, as John Waters wrote in 2014, commenting on his sense of being a perennial outsider even in the gay community, not everyone fits the profile, no matter how many names may appear:

> Sorry, I also like Alvin and the Chipmunks better than the Beatles, Jayne Mansfield more than Marilyn Monroe, and, for me, the Three Stooges are way funnier than Charlie Chaplin.

FIVE

HERE'S TO CRIME

I want my vigourish, doll

EVER SINCE THOMAS HARMON published *A Caveat or Warening for Common Cursetors Vulgarely Called Vagabones* in 1567, a great many authors and journalists through the ages have attempted to inform the public about criminal slang. Exactly what any of them have known about the subject has varied enormously.

Harmon, of course, was a rich man addressing other wealthy property owners, advising them how to guard against burglars and recognise likely thieves. According to his own account, Harmon learned criminal slang at second hand, from talking to the beggars who called at his gate. By contrast, Dashiell Hammett, before he became the crime novelists' crime novelist, acquired his extensive background knowledge in a very direct fashion, working as a detective for the Pinkerton agency in Baltimore, and then in San Francisco between 1915 and 1922. Not many other crime writers will have had the dubious pleasure, as he did, of being beaten over the head with a house brick in an alley while tailing a suspect. Understandably, when Hammett employed the language of the underworld and those that investigated it, it carried the stamp of authenticity, for example in his short story 'Fly Paper' (*Black Mask* magazine, 1929):

The big man was a yegg [habitual criminal, also specifically a burglar]. San Francisco was on fire for him [he's a wanted man]. The yegg instinct would be to use a rattler [goods train] to get away from trouble. The freight yards were in this end of town. Maybe he would be shifty enough to lie low instead of trying to powder [*take a run-out powder*, escape].

At the other end of the scale, there are authors who seem to have learned everything they know about gangsters and criminals from reading other crime novels or watching television shows, while the actors who portray such people on screen may prove in real life to be about as hard boiled as one of the Teletubbies, and considerably less convincing.

The latter problem was eloquently portrayed in Alfred Bester's novel *Who He?* (1954), in which a well-heeled New York television director lays down the facts of the mobster life to an uncomprehending actor. When the thespian fails to put the proper authenticity into the line 'I want my vigourish, doll!', the director complains, 'You don't feel it like a gimpster':

> 'Vigourish,' he explained, 'is the thief talk for percentage. See? You're filing a beef about your cut in the caper. …. Make like you're pimping for the broad when you say that. You've got your hands up her skirt. You're naked but you're not catching any colds. Think about her naked and warm up. Then we'll try it again.'

Then there are the crime writers who knew the life from the inside, quite literally. Edward Bunker, for instance, had been sent to reform school at the age of twelve, was shot and wounded two years later while trying to rob a liquor store, then stabbed a guard while in youth prison aged fifteen, and eventually wound up doing hard time in San Quentin. This was just the beginning of two decades of life on the wrong side of the law, but he turned it all around in spectacular fashion with the publication of his first novel, *No Beast So Fierce* (1973), followed in 1977 by *The Animal Factory*, arguably the finest prison novel of them all. The stamp of authenticity is all over these books, in the motivations of the characters, the physical descriptions of the locale, and, of course, the slang, which is right for the time and place. The guards at San Quentin are *bulls*, knives are *shivs*, if things are going well then you are *shitting in tall cotton*, a criminal charge is a *beef*, and that ancient Shakespearean term for a whore, *punk*, is one of the worst insults you can throw at anyone. By contrast, Mario Puzo once said that when he created the unforgettable figure of Don Vito Corleone, he had never met any mafia god-fathers, and was basically imagining the way they might talk among themselves:

> I'm ashamed to admit that I wrote *The Godfather* entirely from research. I never met a real, honest-to-god gangster... After the book became 'famous,' I was introduced to a few gentlemen related to the material. They refused to believe that I had never been in the rackets.

Yet, whether this language came from personal experience, research or simply imagination, much of it then spread to the wider public through the medium of books, newspapers, films, plays, radio and television, so that people in quiet rural villages whose closest connection to a mob hit had been the buying of a Valentine's card were now able to talk like a wise guy, should they have the inclination. On the other hand, some crime language which might at first appear to be from the mean streets of Chicago or New York has another origin entirely. For instance, when a character in a novel speaks of a planned killing, saying that someone is 'booked... to hand in his checks on June 14th', this sounds as if it could be one of Capone's hit men or a member of Bugsy Siegel's Murder Incorporated talking. In fact, the quote is from an earlier era and the other side of the Atlantic; John Buchan's 1915 British espionage classic *The 39 Steps*.

Quick as a flash, right in the goolies

IT IS NOT ALWAYS ABOUT shooting or stabbing people. Knuckles and boots can cause a variety of unpleasant effects, and there are many fine phrases inspired by the business of basic physical violence. In 1968, country star Loretta Lynn called on one of the best, *going to fist city*, after another woman tried to move in on her husband. In reponse, Loretta wrote and sang the No. 1 hit song 'Fist City' as a warning, one she also backed up in person.

It is a staple of classic private eye fiction that the down-at-heel hero is roughed up several times in pursuit of a solution to their case. Cosh blows, punches and a variety of non-fatal physical abuse that would leave most ordinary people relaxing in hospital for several months are regularly absorbed and then shrugged off with disarming ease. A couple of rudimentary bandages, a slug of whiskey and then a wry explanation offered to concerned friends. 'Who's been kissin' your puss?' asks a character in Benjamin Appel's 1934 gangland novel *Brain Guy*. One of the nicer dismissive replies to such an enquiry about facial bruises can be found in Michael Avallone's *The Bedroom Bolero* (1963): 'I tried to carry a moose head through a revolving door'.

People have been engaging in what is sometimes known as *fist cuisine* ever since human beings first learned to walk, yet the self-appointed guardians of public morals in each generation have tended to claim that only in their era has a new low been reached. For instance, in 1970s Britain, the tabloids were greatly preoccupied with the activities of *boot boys*, who were said to be much given to causing *aggro* – a shortening of the word aggravation. This slang term was sometimes (mis)spelt out on the terraces in a football chant, as follows:

A – G,
A – G – R,
A – G – R – O,
AGGRO!

The teenage heroine of Richard Allen's novel *Knuckle Girls* (1977) notes disdainfully that some of the boys she knows were only 'all right when it came to having a bit of aggro, or going into Woolworths on a nicking spree'. Another popular seventies term for such people was *bovver boys*, yet the term itself belonged to an older generation. Frank Norman, working as a doorman at a Soho strip-joint, wrote in 1959 of someone threatening the owner with the words, 'If you ain't paid up by the end of the week you are in dead bovva!'

Similarly, anyone under the impression that life was quieter at that time in the provinces could find in the 1960 Anthony Burgess novel *The Right to an Answer* a comment from a pub landlord about one of his customers who hit someone 'quick as a flash, right in the goolies', thereby also employing in passing a pre-war slang word for the testicles, which has become less common since the 1970s. There are, of course, many other ways of expressing this, not least the more esoteric terms masterfully deployed by Rambling Syd Rumpo (Kenneth Williams) in his 1967 sea shanty 'What Shall We Do with the Drunken Nurker?', as various nautical punishments are devised for the aforesaid matelot. These mostly involved whacking the said gentleman variously in the *nadgers*, over the *grummit* or in the *moulies* – the results of which would apparently leave his *bogles* in a visibly altered condition. Of course, no further explanation was offered to the listener as to the exact meaning of such terms, but most people probably formed their own conclusions...

Newspapers have always enjoyed giving descriptions of violence, and in his 1909 dictionary *Passing English of the Victorian Era*, James Redding Ware quoted a choice late 19th-century English report of an attack upon a member of the police illustrating the slang London term for stomach, *bread basket*:

> Miss Selina Slops was invited before his Worship, on the charge of smearing the face of B.O. 44 with a flatiron, while hot, and also with jumping upon his bread-basket, while in the execution of his duty.

The expression was at least a century old, even then. Francis Grose listed it in his *Classical Dictionary of the Vulgar Tongue* as a term much used by boxers, giving as an example 'I took him a punch in his bread basket; i.e. I gave him a blow in the stomach'. He also recorded *bruiser* as a term for a boxer, which later became a more general slang word for a violent ruffian. In a fist-fight, Grose noted, the attacker might *plump* someone's *peepers* ('give him a blow in the eyes'). Alternatively, the assailant could also be said to have given someone 'a peg [punch] in the daylight [eye]', a 'click [blow] in the muns [face]' – which was also known as a 'wipe on the chops'. However, despite the many slang terms for individual acts of violence listed by Grose, some phrases encountered in 18th-century Covent Garden were not exactly what they seemed. If you overheard in a pub conversation that someone had 'suffered by a blow over the snout with a French faggot stick', the first assumption might be that they had been beaten in the face with a stout club. In fact, this was a way of observing that the man was suffering from the *French disease* or *French gout* (the pox, said to have been originally imported from our friends across the Channel), which had eaten away his nose.

As for the language used by street robbers at the time, when most items of clothing had a useful resale value, Grose gives the following example:

> The cull has rum rigging, let's ding him and mill him, and pike; the fellow has good clothes, let's knock him down, rob him, and scour off, i.e. run away.

To *mill* someone in this instance meant to rob them, but usually it was a long-established slang word for *kill*. In the *Canting Crew* dictionary of 1699, a *miller* is simply a killer.

Down through the centuries, this air of laconic under-statement when describing casual violence in slang terms has persisted. In commenting on someone's beaten-up appearance ('they lifted his face, huh?' – Dashiell Hammett, *The Thin Man* (1934), or 'who knitted *your* face and dropped a stitch?' – Laurence Payne, *Birds in the Belfry* (1966)) there have long been numerous ways of describing what cockneys would term *a bunch of fives, right up the bracket*. It is tempting to imagine George IV pausing over breakfast in 1825 when encountering some poetically inclined slang in *The Times*. It appeared in a report of the trial of three somewhat battered military men, accused of assaulting police officers while resisting arrest at Vauxhall Pleasure Garden in London. One told the magistrate that:

> ...the party, had they been inclined to contend with the police, were too far gone in wine to be able to make any resistance as had been stated; and as a proof that they (the defendants) had got the worst of it, one of them took a handkerchief from his face and exhibited his eyes, both of which, in the slang phrase, were in mourning.

An ill Knot or Gang

THERE ARE AMATEUR TROUBLE-MAKERS, and then there are professional criminals. For the former category, the word *yob* has long been deployed – a logical, if charmless, expression with an obvious origin, as the *Daily Express* informed readers of its children's page in 1932:

> A 'yob' is generally understood to be a slang term for an ill-mannered loafer. Actually, it is no more than the back-to-front of 'boy'.

Another favourite all-purpose word, dating back to late 19th-century London, is *hooligan*, said to be derived from the thuggish activities of a particular family gang from South London called O'Hoolihan or O'Hooligan. These were both reasonably common Irish surnames – indeed, in an unrelated case in Manchester, an Elisabeth Hooligan was sentenced to a year's imprisonment in 1880 for the theft of a jacket – but by the following decade, the word had passed into newspaper reports as a shorthand for a certain type of violent anti-social behaviour.

If there is one type of slang above all others that 18th-century England made a thorough job of exporting, it was criminal slang, by the very efficient process of transporting thousands of convicts to the American colonies, and then – after the revolution of 1776 put a spanner in the works – to Australia. This makes perfect sense. If you are a London house-breaker of Dr Johnson's era, and in the habit of referring to the basic act of burglary as *cracking a crib*, you are hardly likely to stop calling it that and invent a new term just because you have been unwillingly sent on a one-way pleasure cruise to a new land across the sea. Ever since the 17th century, people like you and your associates, when gathered together for criminal purposes, would be known as a *crew* – defined as 'an ill Knot or Gang', according to *A new dictionary of the terms ancient and modern of the canting crew* (1699), whose very title illustrates that use. Hence when the American rappers of today speak of *hanging out* with their *crew*, back at their *crib*, they are using slang phrases from London – the first of which dates back to the mid-19th century, the other two examples at least three hundred years – which mostly crossed the ocean as part of the vocabulary of criminals lucky enough to have escaped the noose at Tyburn or Newgate.

Ever since the dawn of newspapers in the late 17th century, and the concurrent appearance of eagerly devoured pamphlets and broadsides relating the exploits and final confessions of notorious recently executed prisoners, the lives and language of criminals have been publicised and discussed among the general population. Some 200,000 people are said to have turned out for the hanging of highwayman and serial jail-escaper Jack Sheppard at Tyburn in 1724. A huge figure, given that the population of London stood only at around three times that number. The story of Sheppard's life and death prompted an outpouring of publications, and directly inspired the character of Macheath in John Gay's enormously successful hit of the London stage, *The Beggar's Opera* (1728). Two centuries later, this figure emerged under the same name, but nicknamed Mackie Messer (Mack the Knife), in *Die Dreigroschenoper* (*The Threepenny Opera*) by Kurt Weill, Elisabeth Hauptmann and Bertolt Brecht.

Tip us your daddle

IN LIFE, AND POSTHUMOUSLY, Jack Sheppard was a classic example of the criminal as popular hero – at the time, unquestionably the most famous highwayman of the 18th century. Yet a strange thing happened over a hundred years after his death, when William Harrison Ainsworth published the novel *Rook-wood* (1834), which provided a lurid reimagining of the life of a lesser highwayman and sometime sheep-stealer of Epping Forest, Dick Turpin, hanged at York for horse theft in 1739. The book sold in prodigious quantities, and came complete with plenty of 'flash' language. Criminal speech patterns were a prime ingredient, and the *Spectator* remarked, when reviewing the fourth edition in 1836, that 'the present edition contains an Introduction, in which the author discourses learnedly on "flash songs" and slang phraseology'.

As a character, the romanticised Turpin of Ainsworth's book swiftly buried the grubbier reality of the historical original. Spurred on in the public mind by his fictitious horse Black Bess and his non-existent overnight ride to York, Turpin's transformation foreshadowed a similar case a century later, when the hit film *Bonnie and Clyde* (1967) took the story of two small-time 1930s thrill-killers and turned them into plastic folk heroes, brutally cut down in their photogenic prime. In popular culture, the myth generally trumps the facts: Clyde Barrow posthumously acquired movie-star good looks and morphed into Warren Beatty, while the pox-marked visage of the real Dick Turpin has been similarly airbrushed, and his name is now the first one people reach for when they think of highwaymen.

Ainsworth himself admitted soon after publication that 'Turpin, so far as he goes, is a pure invention of my own'. He was responding in particular to complaints published in the *Weekly Dispatch* that his book was 'of a mischievous tendency, as it invests a ruffianly murderer and robber with a chivalrous character, utterly undeserved, and in fact, entirely false'. The newspaper had also complained that it was degrading for anyone 'enlarging on the apocryphal exploits of a brutal wretch like this and to write flash songs too, full of cant phrases and vulgar slang, which thieves have invented for the purpose of concocting their schemes of depredation without being understood by any casual listener'.

Certainly, the reader was led to believe that the novel offered an insight into the way such highway robbers might talk among themselves. 'You pledge your word that all shall be on the square,' asks Turpin at one point. 'You will not mention to one of that canting crew who I have told you?' A little later, he says, 'Tip us your daddle, Sir Luke, and I am satisfied,' meaning, in this instance, give me your hand to seal the bargain. The latter expression had been listed, among many others advertised as 'Words not in Johnson – no fudge!', in a thoroughly entertaining volume by John Bee issued nine years before Ainsworth's novel, entitled *Sportsman's Slang; A New Dictionary of Terms Used in the Affairs of the Turf, the Ring, the Chase, and the Cock-Pit; With Those of Bon-Ton, and the Varieties of Life, etc.* (1825). Bee lists a nice variant of this expression which includes a suitably cynical euphemism for the hands, *tip us your thieving irons*, in an entry dealing with the word *tip*, some usages of which survive to this day. To *tip* was to give, and also to pay, and he also lists 'tip the wink, to hint'. Turning to criminal matters, he offers the following: '"Come, come, tip the bustle," said by a highwayman when he would rob the traveller'. *Bustle* was a slang term for money.

Clouting heaps and busting into a can

JUST AS THE EXPLOITS OF HIGHWAYMEN and then of 19th-century outlaws such as Butch Cassidy in the US or Ned Kelly in Australia were documented and deplored, yet simultaneously romanticised, so it was with the internationally famous

mobsters, bank robbers and gunmen who sprang up in Prohibition-era America. Gang life in Al Capone's Chicago was already
being fictionalised in books and motion pictures just as his iron
grip on the city was beginning to disintegrate, in films such as
Scarface (1932), and books like *Little Caesar* (1929), which was
itself adapted for the screen in 1931. W. R. Burnett, who wrote
the latter novel while living in Chicago, deliberately chose to use
a great deal of contemporary criminal slang in his book, prompting his later wry comment, 'It has been translated into twelve
languages, including English, as a witty friend of mine says.'

The mob world of those days mined a very rich seam of slang
– some of it surviving unchanged from earlier centuries, with
other words and sayings freshly minted – mostly shot through
with bone-dry gallows humour and the deadpan shrug of those
who, to borrow a title from a William P. McGivern crime novel,
might reasonably offer *Odds Against Tomorrow* (1957).

While the exploits of mafia gunmen understandably merited
a sizeable proportion of the headlines, a great deal of crime was
of a lower level, carried out by shoplifters (*boosters*), pickpockets
(*lifters*, *dippers*), muggers (*jack-rollers*), burglars (*porch-climbers*,
till-tappers), car thieves (*heap-clouters*) or fake-cheque-passers
(*paper-hangers*, *queer-shovers*). Those a little higher up the scale
who handled major robberies from institutions were said to be in
the *wholesale banking business*, and there were a variety of names
for any valuable specialist who could open safes. The latter was
known as a *peter man*, or *box worker*, adept at *busting into a can*.

On a general level, the kind of sharp operator who lived
on their wits by a variety of illegal, but non-violent, means
was known as a *grifter* – a term most famous as the title of
Jim Thompson's masterful novel of the scuffling life, *The Grifters* (1963). As for the various kinds of con games engaged in by
such people when attempting to separate the suckers from their

money, enough slang terms developed surrounding them to fill a book – a very fine one, as it turns out. Published in 1940, David W. Maurer's *The Big Con – The Story of the Confidence Man and the Confidence Trick*, laid bare the mysteries of the three classic large-scale con games, the *wire*, the *pay-off* and the *rag*, together with numerous smaller scams (*short cons*) like the *big mitt* (a crooked poker game), the *wipe* (a con with money supposedly concealed in a handkerchief) or the *slick box* (a fixed dice game). It came complete with a valuable glossary of terms – some of which, unsurprisingly, were old enough to have been familiar to Captain Francis Grose – and gave details of some of the contemporary masters of the trade, such as Yellow Kid Weil and Slobbering Bob.

This tradition of people engaged in life on the dubious side was perhaps best summed up in its English context by Robin Cook (later known as Derek Raymond) in his slang-rich landmark debut novel *The Crust on Its Uppers* (1962), whose narrator works very hard indeed at not having a job:

> I wasn't a layabout, I was a morrie [defined in Cook's glossary as 'reverse of slag', *slags* in this case being 'young, third class grafters, male or female, unwashed, useless'], and many was the time over our long association when I'd had a touch [acquired some money] and been handy to have around when it came to paying the duke ['duke of Kent, rent'] with my beehives ['beehive – five pounds'] down to a bit of archbishop ['Archbishop Laud, fraud'].

Considering that Archbishop Laud was around in the time of Charles I, it shows that rhyming slang can sometimes have a long memory (although to be fair, the fact that as Archbishop of Canterbury Laud was executed for treason in 1645 might have helped him remain in the public mind).

Urban gorillas

THIEVES AND GRIFTERS WERE ONE THING, whereas the gun-toting members of organised crime organisations were usually quite another. The much-mythologised figure of the *gangster* came to wide public attention during the Prohibition era in America, when the Volstead Act (1920–33) outlawing 'intoxicating beverages' inadvertently provided lucrative, albeit dangerous, business opportunities for a wide variety of underworld chancers. The term itself was of US origin, first recorded in the 1880s, but its usage then spread over to Britain, with a helping hand from the media. For instance, readers of the *Manchester Guardian* were treated to the following slice of life and death in the Big Apple:

> New York gunmen on the East Side yesterday killed their fifth man within four days. The name of the victim was Antonio Scamarino. The assassin used a shot gun, firing from the shadow of a doorway, and escaped. The four other recent murders include that of David Winzer, who was shot on Tuesday night by three gangsters on the Williamsburg Bridge over the East River.

While this story may appear to have all the hallmarks of the late-1920s heyday of mob violence, it actually dates from May 1913. After the First World War was over, the word appeared in *The Times*, in a favourable review of the motion picture *Skin Deep* (1923), whose star Milton Sills was described as 'a repulsively ugly New York criminal "gangster"'.

In the language of such men, and the people who wrote about them, the gangster and his associates became known as *wise guys*, *yeggs*, *hoodlums* or *hoods*. At the bottom of the mafia food chain, a common-or-garden thug was simply a *gorilla*, of the kind perhaps best summed up in this description from Carter Brown's novel *The Wayward Wahine* (1960):

He was shorter than I, around five-eight, but with wide shoulders out of proportion to his height. Except for a faint fuzz on the crown of his head, he was bald. His complexion was dark, swarthy – the kind of guy the razor ads dream about – and one eye turned slightly inward. If you showed him to little children, you'd do it gradually, a piece at a time.

Moving up a level in the skills department, a specialist gunman was called a *torpedo*, a *trigger-man*, *rod-merchant* or *hatchet-man*. He might also be known as a *plumber*, on call when someone had talked too freely, as W. R. Burnett explained in a later novel, *Little Men, Big World* (1951):

> The big boys just give a couple of the plumbers your address and that's it. If the first set of plumbers don't fix the leak, they send another set.

Tools of the trade like machine guns, pistols, knives, coshes and various types of explosive all acquired slang names. The Thompson sub-machine gun, patented in 1920, became an icon of the gangster era, peppering the soundtrack of films such as *The Public Enemy* (1931) and *Scarface* (1932). The exploits of Al Capone's mob when using this kind of hardware also gave rise to another popular expression, used here in the January 1932 edition of *Black Mask* magazine: 'If that louse makes a play for me, he'll get hit by Chicago lightning!' It was also sometimes known to mobsters, journalists and novelists by nicknames like *Chicago typewriter*, *Chicago piano*, *equaliser* or *chatterbox*, but mostly just called a *tommy*. Anyone on the receiving end of such a weapon was said to have been *hosed down*, *drilled* or *greased*.

A shotgun was a *crowd-pleaser* or *scatter-gun*, while most types of handgun were simply a *rod*, a *gat*, a *roscoe*, a *piece*, a *heater*, a *cannon* or just *iron*. A dirt-cheap weapon – sometimes home-made, and more likely to injure those using it rather than the intended victim – was a *Saturday night special*, or a *zip-gun*.

With the public fascination for tales of real and fictional gangsters, the spread of these terms internationally was swift. They surfaced in works like *Nighthawks* (1929), a tale of the Soho underworld by the prolific crime writer John G. Brandon, who was born in Australia but moved to England and wrote a dizzying number of London-based novels. The book's title employed a wide-ranging slang name which took in anyone from criminals, prostitutes and habitual party-goers to insomniacs and many other denizens of the night (over a decade before the most famous use of the term, as the title of a 1942 Edward Hopper painting). At one point in the novel, a relocated American mobster attempts to educate a French woman in Soho about crime-speak back home, after first asking her not to speak French, because 'I'm the horse's wish-bone [i.e. useless] when it comes to idle chatter in any other spiel [language] than English':

> Well, if I don't keep on forgettin' you ain't wise t' good li'l' ol' New York's language. Packin' a rod means carryin' a gun... I'm ain't [sic] a soft bimbo myself, babe; but I dunno I would be achin' t' carry the trouble to him on a tray [pick a fight with him].

There was certainly a significant transatlantic exchange of crime terms over the years. In a 1911 article entitled 'Slang of the Criminal', which appeared in the *Milwaukee Sentinel*, a lawyer is a *mouthpiece*, a shoplifter is a *booster*, while the average policeman is termed a *harness bull* – all terms which would later become familiar to readers of US pulp crime fiction. However, venerable survivals from the Old Country include *beak* for judge, *moll buzzer* for one who robs women, and *doss* meaning to sleep. The longevity of these expressions during the 20th century was perhaps aided by the publication of American books such as Herbert Asbury's non-fiction work *The Gangs of New York* (1928), which, although written during the era of the tommy gun, dealt with a fair number of 19th-century hoodlums and therefore contained an appendix of criminal slang drawn directly from George W. Matsell's *Vocabulum, Or the Rogue's Lexicon* (1859), which was itself full of 17th- and 18th-century London criminal words such as *ken* for house or *cove* for man.

Raymond Chandler's novels, rich in the slang of Los Angeles hoodlums, enjoyed great popularity in Britain, and it is a very short distance from some terms describing money in *Farewell My Lovely* (1940) – 'Fish, iron men, bucks to the number of one hundred' – to the following dialogue spoken by Jack Lang's London wide boys in his 1967 novel *The Hard Case*: 'Two hundred iron men will get you five that he's washed up.' However, *iron* itself was an all-purpose 18th-century English slang name for money, which could well have influenced the later American usage.

Indeed, anyone consulting that evergreen family favourite, *Reg Kray's Book of Slang* (1989), will find that this archetypal East End gangland villain rounded up pure cockney terms alongside others more associated with the days of Prohibition-era US mobsters such as Lucky Luciano or Meyer Lansky. This is not to say that the likes of Vincent 'Mad Dog' Coll would have been likely to remark that a friend was going 'on the hot cross' (*hot cross bun*, on the run) having robbed a *fish-and-tank* (bank). However, he would certainly have understood the term *knock-off gee* (mob hit man, assassin). Indeed, he followed that profession himself, until developing an acute case of *lead poisoning* when a Thompson sub-machine gun caught up with him in an 8th Avenue drugstore in 1932.

From wrong gee to O.G.

JUST AS A KNOCK-OFF GEE was a killer, an untrustworthy man was a *wrong gee* – both expressions employing *gee* (the letter G, short for guy, or indeed *geezer*, also common in the US at that time). *Gee* was originally American hobo slang, dating from before the First World War. In recent years, if you call someone an O. G., this is a hip-hop term, meaning *original gangsta* – which is slightly ironic, since organised gang crime came very late to the black community in America, compared with other groups. The *original* gangsters of the Prohibition era were either Jewish (such as Arnold Rothstein, Meyer Lansky, Bugsy Siegel), Italian (Al Capone, Lucky Luciano, Frank Costello) or Irish (Legs Diamond, Machine Gun Kelly), arising out of late 19th-century New York street gangs such as the Hudson Dusters or the Five Points Gang. This is not to suggest that there was a shortage of violence in black districts, a fact reflected in blues lyrics of the time, such as 'Brown Skin Woman Swing', recorded in Chicago in 1939 by Roosevelt Scott – a jaunty number urging a woman not to kill her errant boyfriend ('don't shoot him, don't cut him') – but this was not organised crime. Knife crime was common enough in those circles for the bloody wounds inflicted by edged weapons to be nicknamed *Harlem sunsets*. By contrast, the two most famous Los Angeles black gangs, the Crips and the Bloods, were not even formed until 1968 and 1972 respectively. In a 1999 episode of the *The Sopranos*, Tony's nephew Christopher encounters a rap record mogul named Massive Genius, some of whose crew are impressed to be meeting a real mafia member – 'So you is an OG?' one says, which Christopher brushes away disgustedly with, 'Yeah, whatever...'

In his second James Bond novel, *Live and Let Die* (1954), which was partially set in Harlem, Ian Fleming called attention to the historical lack of black organised crime, when 007 is sent to investigate a ghetto kingpin called Mr Big (a name which coincidentally foreshadows the one adopted by million-selling 1990s gangsta rapper Notorious BIG, killed in a drive-by shooting in 1997), although Bond's opinions are clearly those of his time and background:

> 'I don't think I've heard of a great negro criminal before,' said Bond, 'Chinamen, of course, the men behind the opium trade. There've been some big-time japs, mostly in pearls and drugs. Plenty of negroes mixed up in diamonds and gold in Africa, but always in a small way. They don't seem to take to big business. Pretty law-abiding chaps I should have thought except when they've drunk too much.'

The alternative spelling *gangsta* came to international notice with the 1988 release of the hip-hop album *Straight Outta Compton* by NWA – one of the founding statements of what was to become known as *gangsta rap* – which contained a track entitled 'Gangsta Gangsta'. Reviewing the record in *The Times* the following year, Robin Denselow commented that 'this is a report from the California the Beach Boys never told you about', and by the early 1990s a debate was raging in the media as to whether this sub-genre of hip hop was reporting or glorifying the criminal lifestyle, a controversy which has rumbled on ever since. Indeed, at the time of writing, the co-founder of rap label Death Row Records, Marion 'Suge' Knight, is in prison awaiting trial on murder charges arising from a fatality which occurred in South Central LA during the shooting of a film entitled *Straight Outta Compton*. In 2009, when Death Row auctioned off the contents of their offices after filing for bankruptcy, one of the top items under the hammer was an electric chair, which sold for $2,500.

Yet popular songs had always documented the exploits of

thieves and outlaws. For example, in the collection of centuries-old English and Scottish traditional songs known as the *Child Ballads* (published 1882–98), there are murders by the score, and a great many ballads devoted to the adventures of Robin Hood. Similarly, in late 19th-century Australia, there were songs depicting the exploits of Ned Kelly and his gang.

Oddly enough, popular songwriters failed to make much of the exploits of the famous gangsters of the 1920s and 1930s – although Woody Guthrie wrote a song called 'The Ballad of Pretty Boy Floyd' (1939), commemorating the deceased Georgia bank robber who became Public Enemy No. 1 after the death of John Dillinger. As for the music taste of the mob themselves, bar-room pianist and pulp author Jack Woodford – author of timeless gems such as *Indecent* (1934), *The Abortive Hussy* (1950) and *The Evangelical Cockroach* (1924) – recalled in his memoirs that the one tune which Al Capone requested him to play, time and again, was the sentimental British First World War song 'Roses of Picardy' (1916).

One gang that was singing, and also the subject of a song, was Billy Fullerton's 1920s Scottish Protestant outfit the Billy Boys, who composed their own lyrics to the tune 'Marching through Georgia', including a line about being 'up to our knees in Fenian blood'. Their activities are said to be the inspiration for the classic novel of the Glasgow razor gangs, *No Mean City*, by Alexander McArthur and H. Kingsley Long, published in 1935. In this book, a street fight is a *rammy*, the police are the *busies*, and the way to offer someone a drink is to say, 'I'm holding [i.e. I've got some money], what'll it be?'

However, the main group of musicians who developed a fascination with crime films and gangster mythology long before the gangsta rappers were those of the Jamaican reggae, ska and rock steady scene. From Prince Buster's landmark single 'Al

Capone' (1964), it was a short step from singing about mobsters to adopting their names, so that Lester Bullock began recording as Dillinger, and Dennis Smith became Dennis Alcapone. As for Toots Hibbert, of Toots and the Maytals, he commemorated his time in jail with the fine song '54-46 That's My Number' (1968). The pinnacle of this trend was the 1972 Jamaican crime film *The Harder They Come*, starring Jimmy Cliff as a gun-toting singer on the run from the police, whose hugely successful soundtrack album included the 1967 *rude boy* classic '007 (Shanty Town)' by Desmond Dekker & the Aces. One of its other highlights was a tale of the perils of the criminal lifestyle, 'Johnny Too Bad' by The Slickers, about a tooled-up young man walking around carrying a gun and a knife ('a ratchet in your waist'). As the author of the original LP's sleeve notes remarked of the group, 'they should know: when the lawyer was getting copyright clearance on that tune, one of the writers was underground. The other was on death row.'

Sadly, the other side of this fascination with gun culture has seen the violent deaths of fine Jamaican musicians such as Prince Far I, Winston Riley (who wrote and produced the 1971 Dave and Ansell Collins hit 'Double Barrel') and two of the Wailers, drummer Carlton Barrett and founding member Peter Tosh. Bob Marley himself was shot and wounded, along with his wife and manager, in 1976.

I smell of the bucket

Gaols and prisons have always loomed large in the mind and language of those whose activities were more than likely to land them in such an establishment. Appropriately enough, perhaps the oldest slang term for a prison derives its name from a real institution – London's the Clink, on the southern bank of the Thames, which entertained numerous malefactors from the 12th century up until its destruction in the Gordon Riots of 1780. The city's gaols had a rough time during that uprising, and among the others burnt down during a week of mayhem was the King's Bench prison. Standing near the present site of Waterloo Station, its formidable walls were topped with iron spiked defences known colloquially as *Lord Mansfield's teeth*, after the then Lord Chief Justice.

Francis Grose listed other slang names for prison which were in use at that time, such as the *iron doublet*, the *sheriff's hotel*, *lob's pound*, the *boarding school*, *limbo*, the *repository* and the *spring-ankle warehouse*. He also recorded that such a building was called a *queer ken*, and defined *queer birds* as 'rogues relieved from prison, and returned to their old trade', a usage which survived virtually intact into the 20th century, as in the classic 1936 London underworld novel *The Gilt Kid* by James Curtis, in which an ex-convict encounters an old friend in the street:

'Christ, Curly. I didn't recognize you.'
Curly laughed. It was a satisfied sound.
'Yes,' he said looking down on his striped suit with obvious pride, 'this whistle I got on's a bit different from the old grey one they dish you out with back in the queer place.'

In the same novel, prison warders are known as *screws* – a term also familiar in America at least thirty years earlier – yet this term also carries its older meaning of burglary, as when a character says 'I got nicked for screwing'. It had no sexual connotations in this context, and nor did another deceptively familiar phrase which occurs later in the same conversation, where to *have it off* is to commit a robbery:

'Had it off, since you come out?'

'For God's sake, Curly pal, give us a chance. I've only been
out just under a week.'

Curly nodded and took another pull on his beer.

'I had it off last week,' he said with a wink...

Of course, anyone now using such language in a television
costume drama would draw unintentional laughs from today's
audience – however historically accurate it may be – yet con-
versely, the BBC TV series *Peaky Blinders* felt able to have a
1920s Birmingham character remark that 'if the cops find us,
we're screwed', despite the fact that the *Oxford English Dictionary*'s earliest written example of *screwed* meaning *in trouble* dates
only from 1955.

That distinctive air which the recently released prisoner
seems to carry around when back in circulation can be summed
up in another phrase recorded by Raymond Chandler in his
1936 short story 'Goldfish', when a character fresh out of deten-
tion says, 'I smell of the bucket.' This term was one of many that
characterised prison as simply a dumping-ground for those that
society wanted to keep at arm's length. Other American terms,
many along the same lines, were *storage*, the *pen*, the *calaboose*,
the *can*, the *iron bungalow*, *pokey*, the *refrigerator* and the *cooler*,
while a women's prison was a *hen pen*. A fine old London word
for prison shows up in A. J. La Bern's superb novel of low life
in the capital, *It Always Rains on Sunday* (1945), in which it is
said of East End villain Tommy Swann, 'He joined up with the
Notting Hill boys, some of whom he had met in chokey.'

Satirical references to the supposed luxuriousness or educational benefits of this kind of establishment were inherent in
the names *county hotel* and *stone college*, where lucky individuals
might be said to be enjoying *breakfast uptown*. In America, Sing
Sing prison has long been the *big house* (or the *big house up the
river*, denoting its location in relation to New York City), a name

which itself echoes the British 19th-century habit of referring to the local workhouse as the *big house*. The name Sing Sing is of Native American origin, and translates, appropriately enough, as 'stone upon stone'. This is in marked contrast to the very earliest days of the colonial settlements in New Zealand, where the phrase describing the action of debtors who opted for a short prison sentence in lieu of payment was, according to an 1844 issue of the *Nelson Examiner and New Zealand Chronicle*, that 'he "takes it out in *wood*," as the slang phrase is – our gaols being wooden ones'.

A hot squat on the waffle iron

ONCE INCARCERATED, A PRISONER MIGHT be serving a life sentence with no remission – otherwise known as *doing the book*, or *sweating out the rest of it*. Habitual reoffenders were said to have *done more time than a clock*, and regular escapers thought to have *jack rabbit blood*.

Shorter prison sentences had various nicknames. In America, a very brief stay was simply *wino time*, while the slang expression for a five-year jail term was a *nickel*, after the five-cent coin, as in the 1977 Tom Waits song 'A Sight For Sore Eyes', where a character is described as being *up north* (i.e. in Sing Sing) doing a *nickel's worth*. A ten-year stretch was of course a *dime*. Longer sentences carried a certain status, as did certain criminal professions. When two black criminals meet in jail in *Trick Baby* (1967), the trivial charge one has been arrested for confuses the other:

> One thing puzzled me. How did a fast grifter like him wind up serving a chump's ten-day bit? One thing for sure, he knew the con game backward.

Describing a prison term as a *bit* dates back at least until the early 20th century, and appears in Jackson and Hellyer's *Vocabulary of Criminal Slang* (1914), which also gives such other long-standing variants as a *jolt* and a *stretch*. All of these have survived the last hundred years very well, but one prison slang word it lists is much less common, which is *tent*, meaning a cell: 'He's doing penance in a tent'.

These days it is a commonplace to picture life inside prisons being dominated by gang culture and inter-gang violence, especially in America, and usually divided along racial lines. Yet this is a surprisingly recent phenomenon. As the journalist Graeme Wood states, 'New York has had street gangs for well over a century, but its first major prison gang didn't form until the mid-1980s.' Currently the six main gangs in California prisons today are the Northern Structure, the Aryan Brotherhood, the Black Guerrilla Family, the Nazi Lowriders, the Mexican Mafia and Nuestra Familia. Still, long before the advent of such organisations, aside from the ever-present threat of being attacked with a *shank* (home-made prison knife), the principal danger which has occupied the coiners of prison slang is that found in the execution house.

Judicial hanging was long the method on both sides of the Atlantic, and in W. R. Burnett's *Little Caesar* (1929) one character makes the following laconic reference to someone else's likely sentence: 'Well, they're gonna put a necktie on Gus he won't take off.' One of the oldest terms for death by hanging is to *step off*, dating back to the business of being pushed off a cart on which you were standing at Tyburn by the hangman, which over the years has become a general slang phrase for dying. Something more 'modern' came along in 1924, when some US states began favouring the newly devised gas chamber over hanging. Arizona, which switched over to it in the 1930s, was still occasionally using this method as recently as 1999, which helps explain the old prison slang expression 'you'll be sniffing Arizona perfume'. Nevertheless, nothing seems to have stirred the slang imagination of the underworld quite like that frequently unreliable piece of hardware, the electric chair.

An invention of the late 1880s, which became known variously as the *sizzler*, the *waffle iron*, the *barbecue stool*, the *hot seat* or the *hot squat*, was first used for a spectacularly botched execution in 1890, in New York. The following year, an electric chair was first used at Sing Sing prison, and it eventually acquired a nickname, *Old Sparky*, which sounds more like a lovable character in a children's book than a repellent and inefficient machine for frying people. Other electric chairs in a fair number of states, including Kentucky, South Carolina and Pennsylvania, were also given this name. Such conformity looks a little uninspired, given that there never seems to have been a shortage of slang words for the device, most of them deriving from the same strain of pitch-black gallows humour. Dashiell Hammett used one in his novel *The Glass Key* (1931), when a character sarcastically asks another, 'Is there anything you haven't been through before? Ever been given the electric cure?' Other common ways of expressing such a fate included saying that someone has *a date with the fireless cooker*, is due for a *juice jolt*, or – in an ironic nod to electric hairtongs – *they're going to give him a permanent wave*. Sometimes old hands might simply say, 'He's gonna sit in the old rocking chair up at Sing Sing.'

Still, for every criminal whose career ended in the execution chamber, there were countless more whose life was simply a repeating cycle of offending, arrest, incarceration, release and then back to the start again, until prison became the only home they knew. Once they were thoroughly institutionalised, there was of course a slang phrase for the only thing left on the horizon to which they could look forward – *pine box parole*.

SIX

TAILS YOU BOOZE

Clipping the King's English

IN NOVEMBER 1770, THAT EMINENTLY RESPECTABLE London publication the *Gentleman's Magazine* entertained its readers by printing T. Norworth's list of eighty names for having over-indulged in drink. Founded in 1731, it was the first magazine to actually call itself a magazine, and the first to abbreviate the latter word to *mag* when referring to itself in print, which still sounds surprisingly modern.

The *Gentleman's Magazine* printed this collection of slang phrases for drunkenness without any suggestion that these were exclusively the province of the lower, or even criminal, classes. Indeed, the business of becoming thoroughly, incapably drunk was relatively normal in much of 18th-century society, and winding up unconscious beneath the dinner table at the end of an evening in agreeable company often considered unremark-able. As Mr Norworth explained, his list of words was intended merely '*to express the Condition of an* Honest Fellow, *and no* Flincher, *under the effects* of good Fellowship'. The obvious sus-pects are there – *drunk, intoxicated, tipsey, happy, boozey, in his cups, got his skin full, as drunk as a Lord* – alongside many which might fail to register these days, such as *overtaken, concerned* or *bosky*. It was also said that someone has *got his little hat on, been in the Crown Office*, or that he *clips the King's English*.

Drink, and ways of describing it, were enshrined in the culture of the time – unsurprising in an age when sources of fresh water in the capital were scarce. Water could kill you, and it was safer by far to stick to fluid that had been either brewed or distilled, beginning at breakfast with the *morning draught* so popular with Pepys, and floating through the day on a steady diet of red *fustian* or *kill priest* (port), *bingo* or *cool nants* (brandy), *rum guttlers* (canary wine), *bristol milk* (sherry), *knock me down* (strong ale), or, if you were unlucky, *balderdash* (adulterated wine). These slang terms are just a few of the blizzard of expressions relating to alcohol consumption recorded by Francis Grose in his *Classical Dictionary of the Vulgar Tongue* (1785). Interestingly, for everyone who thinks the term was probably invented in Kentucky, Grose also notes that 'the white brandy smuggled on the coasts of Kent and Sussex' was called *moonshine*, making it yet another in a long list of words which found their way across the Atlantic and have since come to be thought of as US coinages.

The 18th-century London which Grose observed was a world of seasoned and sustained imbibement. Pupils at public schools such as Christ's Hospital were served beer each afternoon, although of questionable quality. As an old boy of the time remarked, 'we used to call it "the washings of the brewers' aprons"'. Down at Winchester College, they drank a strong ale brewed at the school, known to the boys as *huff*, a local shortening of the wider 16th-century term *huff-cap*, meaning powerful liquor.

There is little if any sense in Grose's writings that drunkenness and its consequences carried any kind of social stigma; these things were noted more as a simple fact of life. Of the ruddy-faced intoxicated man, it was remarked that *the flag is out* ('signifying, the man is drunk, and alluding to the redness of his face') or *he has been out in the sun.* Alternatively, he might be called an *ensign bearer*, one who 'hoists his colours in his drink'. Someone *half seas over* was only partially intoxicated, and could also be said to have just *a little cut over the head*, since to be *cut* meant drunk – a term which survives to this day in the phrase *half-cut.* On the other hand, anyone who had made a more thorough job of *soaking, canting a slug into their bread room* or *bunging their eye* ('strictly speaking to drink until one's eye is bunged up or closed') might then be fairly described as *wrapt up in warm flannel,* or simply *mauled.*

Other plain terms for being drunk which appear in Grose include *cup shot, pogy, top heavy, flawd, groggy* or *grogified, corned* and *fuddled.* The latter was venerable even then, being first recorded in 1656. Addison and Steele used it in an article in *The Tatler,* 'From My Own Apartment', in 1709:

> I remember, when I was a young Fellow, we had a Companion of a very fearful Complexion, who, when we sat in to Drink, would desire us to take his Sword from him when he grew fuddled, for 'twas his Misfortune to be quarrelsome.

Cup shot, however, was even older, being a variation on the 14th-century expression *cup-shotten,* first recorded circa 1330, pre-dating the first surviving usage of the word *drunk* by roughly a decade. Pinning the blame for your inebriation on the drinking vessel or the bottle, rather than your own actions, seems to have been a popular theme, giving rise to such phrases as *pot-shotten* (1604), *in one's cups* (1611), *pot-sick* (1611), *jug-bitten* (1630) or *flagonal* (1635). A tankard was frequently called a *pot,* and so a habitual drunkard, fond of throwing drink down their own throat, had therefore been logically known as a *tosspot* since the late 16th century. This archetypal character was later satirised in a poem published in the *Morning Chronicle* in 1809, entitled 'Toby Tosspot', which complained:

> But there are swilling Wights, in London town,
> Term'd Jolly Dogs, – Choice Spirits, – *alias* Swine;
> Who pour, in midnight revel, bumpers down,
> Making their throats a thoroughfare for wine.

Dronke as a ratte

WHILE MANY OF THE FOREGOING WORDS for the activities of the *sons of Bacchus* (drinkers, 1640) have long since fallen out of use, others still sound surprisingly contemporary. During much of the past hundred years, it has been common to say that a person in a state of intoxication through drugs is *high*, yet this is merely adopting a 17th-century expression for drunkenness. Indeed, the first instance of *high* meaning *drunk* occurs in Ben Jonson's *Volpone* (1607). Francis Grose lists a nice variation on this, in which someone's companions might note that *the man is in his altitudes* ('the man is drunk'). Other venerable phrases which have yet to sound old-fashioned include *well-oiled* (1701), *stewed* (1737) and that perennial British favourite *pissed* (1812). By the same token, anyone these days using the common English expression *rat-arsed*, meaning drunk, is in some sense following in the fine tradition of the Lincolnshire writer Thomas Wilson, who employed the expression *as dronke as a ratte* in his work *The Arte of Rhetorique* (1553) – a book partly responsible for his later imprisonment and torture at the hands of the Catholic Inquisition in Italy.

Unsurprisingly, alcohol features regularly in the works of Shakespeare. For instance, in *Henry IV, Pt 1* (1598), Falstaff is referred to as 'that huge bombard of sacke' – a *bombard* being a leather bottle or jug, and *sacke* being the common term for dry white wine from Spain. In *The Merry Wives of Windsor* (1602), Bardolph speaks of someone being *fap* (drunk), while in *The Merchant of Venice* (published 1600), Portia tells Nerissa that she does not find the Duke of Saxony's nephew appealing as a suitor, because of his excessive drinking habits: 'I will do any thing, Nerissa, ere I'll be married to a sponge.'

Pour it back in the horse

HISTORICALLY, BEER IN ENGLAND was credited with being one of the only sources of nutrition the poor ever consumed. Wholesome British beer was a source of national pride, as when Hogarth in a pair of matched engravings contrasted the apparently orderly, contented life in *Beer Street* with the chaotic depravity of *Gin Lane*, never forgetting that gin had been introduced into the country from the continent. This belief in the health-giving properties of certain types of alcohol also prevailed when sixty-year-old writer Phillip Thicknesse published *The Valetudinarians Bath Guide, or, The Means of Obtaining Long Life and Health* (1780). In addition to extolling the benefits of 'having always partaken of the breath of young women whenever they lay in my way', he also thoroughly recommended regular alcohol consumption:

> Old Saunders, the well known landlord of the Angel at Abergavenny, who died lately at a very advanced age, seldom went to bed for the last forty years of his life, before he had swallowed some quarts of strong liquor, without any regard to the quality of it, nor much to the quantity, yet he died, I believe, a stranger to the gout.

Thicknesse was no shrinking violet when it came to

expressing his views – indeed, one biographer later commented that he could 'but marvel that nobody ever shot him or bludgeoned him to death' – but in this instance, as an 18th-century Briton, he was hardly being controversial in his praise for strong drink. Unless, of course, it was *rotgut*, a term first used by the playwright and clergyman Peter Hausted in his comedy *Rivall Friends* (1632), and later defined by Dr Johnson simply as *bad beer*. However, in 19th-century Kent, for instance, agricultural workers complained to a journalist that they were being partially paid with low-quality *rotgut cider*, while in Prohibition-era America, the term was generally applied to low-quality spirits. Not to be outdone, a 1937 *Daily Mirror* columnist even managed to apply the word to badly brewed cups of tea, but perhaps he had been having a trying day.

Of course, there have always been those who dislike one or another type of drink, regardless of the quality. 'Ugh, how I hate beer!' exclaims a character in one of Donald Hamilton's Matt Helm novels (*The Interlopers*, 1970); 'as the man said, they ought to pour it back in the horse.' While that series of books was generally quite hard boiled, Dean Martin, who played Matt Helm in the film adaptations, brought his own particular supremely relaxed air of *sun's over the yardarm* suavity to the role. As Dino's friend Frank Sinatra remarked during a 1966 live show at the Sands casino in Las Vegas, 'I would say, roughly, that Dean Martin has been stoned more often than the United States embassies' – thereby employing a slang phrase which for years generally meant simply *drunk*, but in the past fifty years has come to signify a state of drug intoxication. To be fair, Dean's own publicity people also played heavily on his amiable drunk persona, such as here in the brief sleeve notes to his 1968 LP, *Dean Martin's Greatest Hits, Volume 2*:

More sweet spice from the Potentate of Pop, guaranteed to hot your toddy, rum your collins, Cambridge your tea – and generally turn on aficionados from Mount Rushmore to Manhattan Beach.

For some public figures, being associated with a bar-room air is all part of the attraction. Visiting Forest Lawn cemetery in Glendale, California, some years ago, on passing Errol Flynn's grave, I was told that it is also supposed to contain six bottles of the finest whiskey. Whether true or not, this seems appropriate for a man who once shared a beach house with David Niven named Cirrhosis-by-the-Sea. Tom Waits, meanwhile, has said that around the time he recorded his superb 1976 LP *Small Change*, his alcohol consumption had become reasonably significant – as reflected in song titles such as 'Bad Liver & A Broken Heart' and 'The Piano Has Been Drinking'. The album opened with the ultimate touring musician's inebriated lament, 'Tom Traubert's Blues (Four Sheets To The Wind In Copenhagen)', its subtitle being a variation on a two-hundred-year-old British nautical term for being under the influence, *three sheets in the wind*. This latter expression was in turn based upon the centuries-older mariners' name *sheets*, meaning the ropes which control the action of sails on a ship – the implication being that an enthusiastic drinker would need to deploy several such ropes to keep them on a steady course after sinking a few. The term appeared, for example, in the following report in *The Times* in 1835:

> It is related of George III, that he once came down to Blackwall to review the troops previously to their embarkation... A 'jolly tar,' a little more than 'three sheets in the wind,' but 'brim full of loyalty,' and consequently regardless of all the rules of etiquette or decorum, designed to approach 'His Majesty's royal person' with a full quart of humble porter, which he had

just bought from a neighbouring alehouse. Jack 'tongued his quid' [chewing tobacco], 'unshipped his sky-scraper' [took off his tall hat], 'hitched up his canvass' [trousers], and hoped His Majesty would not refuse to drink with a 'true Blue.'

George III took this very much in his stride, but then he was a product of the 18th century. His later successor, Queen Victoria, is not usually associated with slang words for the demon drink, but one of the oldest of them all appears in a fine tale of the musical tastes of the lady in question, related by Clarence Winchester in his guidebook to the capital, *Let's Look at London* (1935):

> There is a story told of the late Queen Victoria who, it was said, once asked an official of Buckingham Palace to inquire the name of a tune that was being played by the Guards' band outside. The official made the inquiries and returned to Her Majesty not without some embarrassment, for her command demanded obedience and he was compelled to say: 'Madame, *Come where the booze is cheaper.*'

This song, set in a Regent Street hostelry, was written in the final decade of Victoria's reign, around 1890, by E. W. Rogers and A. E. Durandeau, and later featured briefly in James Joyce's *Ulysses* (1922). Of course, the concept of cheapness changes over time, and today, when a pint of beer in London is approaching the £5 mark, drink prices from bygone ages look enviably low. For instance, Alexander Warrack's *Scots Dialect Dictionary* (1911) records that the local term in those days for 'a very strong ale' was an *eightpence drink*. The word *booze*, meanwhile, can be traced back to the 14th century, generally at first rendered as *bouse, bouze, bowze* or *bowse* – the last being the spelling used in Thomas Harman's *A Caveat or Warening for Common Cursetors Vulgarely Called Vagabones* (1567).

As full as a pair of goats

THE WORD BOOZE SPREAD, like numerous other slang terms, from England over to America. It was defined simply in George W. Matsell's New York dictionary, *Vocabulum; or, The Rogue's Lexicon* (1859), as 'intoxicating drink', where it appeared sandwiched neatly between *booly-dog* ('an officer; a policeman') and *bordello* ('a house of ill-fame'). In June 1919, the powerful newspaper the *New York World* went so far as to refer to Wall Street as the 'Booze Exchange', but that was not because the financial traders were supposedly *in the grip of the grape, stewed to the gills,* or *boiled as owls.* The headline actually referred to an outbreak of stock movements in the brewing and distilling sectors in anticipation of the imminent legislation aimed at banning the manufacture, sale and importation of alcohol. Prohibition in America was in the offing, as the London *Times's* New York correspondent reported:

> By a vote of 55 against 11 the Senate yesterday extinguished the last hopes of the 'Wets'... At the convention of the American Neurological Society Dr L Pierce Clark, a well-known New York physician, entered an eloquent plea 'to save the bar-tender,' whom he described as a great social force and the genial friend of multitudes of light tipplers.

As it happened, the National Prohibition Act (1919–33) helped either create or popularise a vast quantity of alcohol-related slang, not to mention driving the majority of the US public into illegal activities, and giving organised crime a once-in-a-lifetime business opportunity. After drink became illegal, otherwise law-abiding citizens had no one else to turn to except criminals in order to secure their regular supply of *tonsil paint.* The majority of the government may have voted in favour of Prohibition, but the majority of the electorate voted with their feet, straight down to the nearest *speakeasy*, looking for a *liquid lunch*. The original impetus for this legislation came from a group called the Anti-Saloon League – the clue is in the name – and these measures also found great favour with those horse-back-riding stars of D. W. Griffith's *The Birth of a Nation* (1915), the Ku Klux Klan, who then enthusiastically enforced their pro-temperance views with violence in the 1920s. With friends like these, perhaps the only truly civilised response was to imitate a couple of characters in Dashiell Hammett's 1924 short story 'The Golden Horseshoe', and *hit the bottle high*: as one of them remarks, 'before long, we were as full as a pair of goats'.

It was not just the Ku Klux Klan who were in favour of banning alcohol. Millionaire industrialist Henry Ford was also – as with many other aspects of everyday life – outspoken on the subject. 'FORD SAYS HE'LL QUIT BUILDING CARS IF BOOZE EVER COMES BACK; COULDN'T TRUST DRINKING WORKERS', read one 1929 headline. This, however, would not have come as a surprise to anyone who had encountered the virulently anti-Semitic four-volume compen-dium Ford had published in 1920, *The International Jew*, a vast, paranoid, conspiracy-theory exercise which included sections entitled 'The Jewish Element in Bootlegging Evil' and 'How Jews Gained American Liquor Control'.

Originally, in 17th-century England, a *boot-leg* was simply that, the leg of a tall boot. However, in America at the close of the 19th century, the term *boot-legger* came to assume its modern, alcohol-related meaning. An 1890 edition of a New York publication called *The Voice* explained things as follows: 'The "boot-legger" is a grim spectre to the anti-Prohibitionist... He is a man who wears boots in whose tops are concealed a flask or two of liquor.' It was also around this time that the slang phrase *speakeasy* appeared – another American coinage

– meaning anywhere that engaged in the illegal sale of alcohol. Prohibition saw hundreds of thousands of such establishments opening across the US, which flourished despite the well-publicised efforts of the authorities to close them down, and the word was common currency in the post-First World War era, for instance in this 1930 headline from the *Pittsburgh Post-Gazette*, 'FEDERAL MEN HIT ELKS CLUB – Steel Door Bars Way Into Braddock Speakeasy'.

Nix on those lush heads

OF COURSE, IN THOSE DAYS, if you managed to find a joint that hadn't been raided, the quality of the liquor on sale could vary enormously. The colloquial expression *bathtub gin* was often a literal pointer to the beverage's origins, while some just cut to the chase and called it *embalming fluid*. In some of its rougher forms, the home-made product was pure poison, a hazard acknowledged among consumers even as they indulged. The hit song 'Button Up Your Overcoat' (1928), made popular by Ruth Etting, listed various potential dangers her lover should avoid, among them frozen ponds, peroxide blondes and, not least, *bootleg hooch*.

Song titles and lyrics from blues, jazz, hillbilly and rock'n'roll records of the first half of the 20th century were often shot through with the kind of slang familiar to their target audiences. Unsurprisingly, a fair amount of it was drink-related. For instance, when jazz combo The Charleston Chasers, led by prolific bandleader Red Nichols, cut a tune called 'Feelin' No Pain' for the Columbia label in 1927, they were not celebrating a successful visit to the dentist. Similarly, malleable art materials played little part in inspiring Chauncey Morehouse and His

Orchestra when they recorded 'Plastered in Paris' for the Brunswick label in 1938. The following year, New Orleans blues singer Blue Lu Barker, backed by her husband Danny Barker and his Fly Cats, recorded four songs one afternoon for the Decca company, two of which had drinking slang in their titles: 'Buy Me Some Juice' and 'Nix on Those Lush Heads'. While, to a toddler, the word *juice* might conjure up images of orange squash, as far as many adult Americans were concerned at that time it meant the hard stuff. Indeed, when Alabama sax player Cootie Williams recorded a number called 'Juice Head Baby' (1945), the subject of the song was no infant, and the liquid in question was unlikely to have been served at a kindergarten. Just as a *juice head* was a heavy drinker or alcoholic, so was a *lush head*, often shortened just to *lush* (such as in Orrie Hitt's 1960 pulp novel *The Lady Is a Lush*), so the title of that second Blue Lu Barker song was a five-word condemnation of *sloppy drunk* behaviour. The word *nix*, an American slang term of refusal or rejection, had been around since Edwardian times – perhaps its best-known usage worldwide occurs in the lyrics to Elvis Presley's 'Jailhouse Rock' (1957), when a character named Bugsy turns down the chance to escape in favour of dancing – while *lush*, as a term for drinking alcohol, has a venerable history, and was first recorded in the 1811 edition of Francis Grose's dictionary.

Of course, no discussion of music-related drink slang could possibly manage without a mention of Texas honky-tonk singer Bill Nettles and his landmark hymn to the joys of the inebriated hobo lifestyle, the 'Wine-O Boogie', recorded for the Starday label at Houston's Gold Star Studios in 1954 – a curiously uplifting tale of the hazards of swigging cheap alcohol within sight of a policeman, in a country where packing a pistol might be perfectly fine, but being a tramp and then drinking booze in public could merit jail time. One of the first recorded uses of the term *wino* appeared in the classic hobo memoir, Jack Black's *You Can't Win* (1926), in which the author described his fondness for the rough, largely ad hoc drinking joints favoured by the tramps of the West Coast, and also listed some of their slang names for wine:

> The wine dumps, where wine bums or 'winos' hung out, interested me. Long, dark, dirty rooms with rows of rickety tables and a long bar behind which were barrels of the deadly 'foot juice' or 'red ink,' as the winos called it.

In the early 1990s, when Johnny Depp was engaged to Winona Ryder, he had the words *Winona Forever* tattooed on his right arm. Forever turned out to be somewhere in the region of three years, after which they split, and he famously had it altered to read *Wino Forever*.

Here's lookin' up your address

PRIVATE EYES AND VILLAINS in pulp crime novels from the 1920s to the 1960s generally seemed to do a heroic amount of drinking, and the novelists responsible thereby preserved a fair slice of entertaining alcohol-related slang. To start things off, there were various phrases to be used by way of a toast. *Here's how* was one common salutation, as was the ever-popular *here's to crime*, which probably has its origins in the clandestine nature of alcohol buying in the bootlegging days. Consider this post-war example, from Bruce Manning's *Cafe Society Sinner* (1960):

> He got up and went into the kitchen again. He built the drinks strong. 'Jolt and a bolt,' he said as he handed her the glass. 'Here's to crime.'

Other toasts are sadly less well known, such as this fine example from John D. MacDonald's *Soft Touch* (1958):

'Here's lookin' up your address,' she said. She drank and sighed and said, 'I needed this one.'

As for stating your intent, here is a determined character in Erle Stanley Gardner's 1935 novel *This Is Murder*:

'I've changed my mind.'
    'About what?'
    'About getting crocked.'
    'You mean you're going to get crocked?'
    'Absolutely pie-eyed. Polluted. I'm going to celebrate.'

Or, if you prefer things more succinct, why not follow the example of someone in Richard Marsten's *The Spiked Heel* (1956), and observe that 'this is a good night to get pleasantly looped, don't you think?' For those requiring an excuse for such behaviour, *Esquire* magazine published a helpful list in their *Handbook for Hosts* (1954), entitled '365 Excuses for a Party', which included 25 August ('Independence Day in Uruguay'), 29 July (Mussolini's birthday'), 30 October ('Buy a Doughnut Day'), 7 April ('birthday of Fala, President Roosevelt's dog'), 24 July ('Mormon Pioneer Day') and 20 July (Anniversary of the National Shuffleboard Open Championship').

During the course of an evening's liquid entertainment, you could rely on your companions to let you know how things stand. Anyone showing signs of *running a temperature* – from the rosy alcoholic glow of the cheeks – might also be said to be *burning with a low blue flame, awash, tanked, soused, in the bag, unable to see a hole in a ladder, behind the cork, all gone, in a heap* or afflicted with the *blind staggers*, among many, many others. The idea of a body slowly filling up with drink from the feet upwards is reflected in a few expressions, such as saying that you're going to *get both your eyeballs wet*. One of my favourites occurs in Budd Schulberg's classic novel of a Hollywood get-rich-quick merchant, *What Makes Sammy Run?* (1941), in which someone remarks, 'You're drunk, Al. Your teeth are swimming.' Late at night in a New York bar in the book *Greenwich Killing Time* (1986), Kinky Friedman's detective alter-ego observes of his drinking buddy, 'He was pretty bombed and I was just about walking on my knuckles.' Meanwhile, Down South, you might just say that you had been *Dixie fried*, after the popular beer made by the Dixie Brewing Company of New Orleans, immortalised in the Carl Perkins rockabilly single 'Dixie Fried' (1956).

The following day, assuming you have made it that far, some stocktaking is perhaps in order. After knocking on the door of a log cabin in *The Lady in the Lake* (1943) Raymond Chandler's Philip Marlowe encounters a bad-tempered gent who then apologises for his temper. 'I was out on the roof last night,' he explains, 'and I've got a hangover like seven Swedes' – a variant on the expression *out on the tiles*, deriving from the supposedly wild exploits of cats roaming at night. Or, to employ another Chandler phrase, he had simply been *doing next week's drinking too soon*. A more direct way of saying much the same thing is employed by a character in the 1960 nautical crime novel *Aground*, by Charles Williams: 'I feel like hell, I theeeenk. And if I ever catch that lousy parrot that slept in my mouth...'

Booze heads, stay away

DESPITE THE CLAIMS OF POLITICIANS, religious leaders and temperance organisations, Prohibition came and went in

America, leaving behind a society just as partial to alcohol as before, perhaps even more so. In a 1949 edition of the US entertainments industry trade magazine *Billboard*, Arkansas carnival organisers the Crescent Amusement Company took out an advert looking for all manner of seasonal show people. As well as seeking 'Hanky Panks, Six Cats, Glass Pitch, Bumper, High Striker, Novelties, Jewelry Set, Custard, Fish Pond', and other specialists familiar in the trade, they also had need of drivers for articulated lorries who could restrain themselves from *drinking their lunch out of a bottle*:

> First Class Wheel Foreman and Second Men Truck Drivers for new No. 5; must be sober and drive semi trailers. Booze heads, stay away.

Despite the abject failure of Prohibition in America, there are many dry counties to this day across the US, including the one where the Jack Daniel's distillery is sited in Lynchburg, Tennessee, which means that the many thousands of visitors each year are able to buy all sorts of branded souvenirs there, but none of the district's most famous product.

While it is hard to imagine something like Prohibition ever making it onto the statute books in the UK, Cromwell's 17th-century parliamentarians certainly had an equivocal view of alcohol, and there were numerous prosecutions of alehouses and inns. The staunch puritan MP Major General Charles Worsley – who commanded the party of musketeers that entered the House of Commons and closed down the Rump Parliament on Cromwell's orders in 1653 – was certainly active in this field. The historian Bernard Capp notes that Worsley called alehouses 'the very womb, that brings forth all manner of wickedness', and that 'in January 1656 he and his commissioners ordered the suppression of over 200 in and around Blackburn alone'. As it happens, it was another puritan MP of those days, the writer William Prynne, who, in his book *The Soveraigne Power of Parliaments and Kingdomes* (1643), first used that venerable slang term for water long popular among the teetotal fraternity, *Adam's ale*.

Quite what Worsley would have made of Britain in more recent times is anyone's guess, particularly if given access to a selection of tabloid newspapers pursuing one of their favourite lines of enquiry – lurid tales of drunkenness. Perhaps especially disturbing to a man of his religious sensibilities would have been the alleged exploits of a senior London cleric in 2006, reported under the title 'HE MITRE HAD A PEW TOO MANY'. It was claimed that the man in question had climbed into the back seat of a stranger's car in a state of some inebriation, and, when asked by the owner what he was up to, replied, 'I'm the Bishop of Southwark, it's what I do.' These events then prompted a statement to the press from the bishop's spokesman, which included a down-to-earth slang term more reminiscent of a rugby club than the General Synod: 'He'd clearly had a glass of wine but does not recall being drunk as a skunk… That's the strongest denial you'll get.'

Opening up the sluices at both ends

IT WAS THE LONDON SATIRICAL MAGAZINE *Private Eye* which coined the famous expression *tired and emotional* – as a shorthand for *drunk* – in 1966, describing the bibulous condition of the then Labour cabinet minister George Brown. Two years earlier, they had begun publishing their *Barry McKenzie* cartoon strip, which helped cement the popular notion of the citizens of Australia being not averse to *sinking a few swift ones*. The cartoon provided an outlet for the Australian Barry Humphries to take numerous pot-shots at various targets he observed around him, as its artist Nicholas Garland later wrote:

> The author's attitude to Poms and their poor old country was quite clearly conveyed in casual asides and by the ludicrous and hypocritical behaviour of all Englishmen and women in the strip.

Having landed in Britain, McKenzie tells his fellow train passenger on the way to London that he wants to *celebrate my arrival with a skinful*. In the film adaptation, *The Adventures of Barry McKenzie* (1972), with a script co-written by Humphries, the titular hero then exclaims after drinking some beer, 'I really needed that. I was as dry as a dead dingo's donger.' Recalling his flight over from Australia, McKenzie observes that it had 'got a bit rough over the Hima-bloody-layas. One of the blokes starts chundering, y'know. Fella near me yodelling his jelly and ice cream.'

Barry Crocker, the actor who played McKenzie, later sang the theme tune for quintessential Aussie soap series *Neighbours* – a far cry, perhaps, from the songs he had performed in the original 1972 film, such as 'One Eyed Trouser Snake' and 'Chunder in the Old Pacific Sea', the second of which also rounded up another term for drink-induced vomiting, the *technicolor yawn*. Unsurprisingly, the lyrics to both were also written by Barry Humphries – indeed, the earliest citing of the latter phrase given by the *OED* comes from this song, so it seems to be one of his own coinages. The word *chunder*, by contrast, was not. It was brought into international usage by the McKenzie cartoon and films, and also by Eric Idle on the 1972 LP *Another Monty Python Record*, speaking knowledgeably about imaginary Australian table wines such as Chateau Chunder, 'an *appellation contrôllée* specially grown for those keen on regurgitation. A fine wine which really opens up the sluices at both ends.' However, in 1964, the year that *Private Eye* began publishing the cartoon, the word was clearly in common use in Australia, appearing, for example, in the newspaper *Woroni*, the journal of the Canberra University College Students Club:

> The long-awaited Chunder report has at last been released. The work of a commission appointed by the A.P.C. (Association for the Prevention of Chundering), it represents an analysis of data collected over a period of ten minutes. There has, in the past, been much speculation as to the cause of chundering, a disease which half-kills more than 100,000 people in Australia every year, most of whom are students in the 17 to 22 age group.

The *OED* gives the first written appearance of the word *chunder* in Nevil Shute's novel *A Town Like Alice* (1950), but New Zealand pilots were certainly using the word as a slang term meaning 'air-sick' a decade earlier, as a 1941 report in the *Auckland Star* makes clear. Interestingly, Shute himself had previously enjoyed a very distinguished career as an aeronautical engineer and pilot. He was also what the locals would have called a *pommy*, having arrived from England only that same year, aged fifty-one. The origins of the word *pommy* or *pom* are often disputed, but the earliest citings from Australian newspapers in 1912 give it as a shortening of *pomegranate*, a tortuous play on the word *immigrant*: 'Now they call 'em "Pommygranates,"' said the Sydney newspaper *The Truth* in 1912, 'and the Jimmygrants don't like it.' Poms, therefore, are not strictly the English at all, but newly minted Australians – a breed who two decades earlier might have been referred to by a different Australian slang name, *squatters* – people who had arrived in the country but were unable to gain permission to buy land outright. This term appears in what is often regarded as the earliest home-grown Australian detective novel, Fergus W. Hume's *The Mystery of a Hansom Cab*, published in Melbourne in 1886. It is a fascinating book, yet anyone expecting it to be full of choice Aussie slang would be sorely disappointed. Moving forward half a century to another landmark Australian crime novel, Arthur Upfield's *The Mystery of Swordfish Reef* (1939), set among the coastal fishermen of Bermagui, New South Wales, there is also surprisingly little indigenous slang in evidence. People are occasionally feeling *crook* (ill), and at one point someone says *Day* as a greeting (though not *g'day*). However, some of the slang which seems today to be most typical of Australia feels more like a post-Second World War development.

Bring on the breathalyser bag

IN 1967, WHEN CHURCHILL'S former wartime chauffeur appeared in court charged with being under the influence, one newspaper headline read: 'SIR WINSTON'S DRIVER TOLD P.C.: I'M SLOSHED'. The person in question was then said to have exclaimed, 'Bring on the breathalyser bag,' and later, when taken into custody, allegedly declared, 'I'm drunk, drunk as an owl.' Some years afterwards, in 1981, it was Sir Winston's twenty-one-year-old grandson who, as an Oxford University student and member of the Bullingdon Club, was interviewed by Peter McKay of the *Daily Mirror* about his use of a more recent upper-class term for inebriation, *hog-whimperingly drunk*. However, he stressed that 'in fact, I used the expression to describe another club here who are a load of silly prats'.

Four years later, a book of supposed *Upper Class Rhyming Slang* appeared, designed to be filed under 'humour', although the contents offered precious little of that: *mont blanc*, meaning *plonk*, or *cabin cruiser* for *boozer*, and so on. In the main, it served only to highlight the fact that most slang seems to originate lower down the social scale, although it often travels upwards. For example, in 2003, Prince William, when celebrating his twenty-first birthday in the company of Prince Charles – and within earshot of the press – asked his father after a number of drinks, 'Are you trying to get me pissed?' The *Daily Mirror* immediately weighed in with the results of a reader survey into this momentous event, which found that '80 per cent of people thought Prince William was right to use a swear word'. Meanwhile, the *Daily Star* offered a helpful list of fifty alternative slang terms for drunkenness – some obvious, some not – that he might have chosen instead, including *wasted, banjaxed, ankled, paralytic, trollied, blotto, squiffy, plastered, mashed* and *legless*. In some ways, times had changed very little since the *Gentleman's Magazine* published their own, even longer, roll-call of such words back in 1770.

In America, of course, if you say that you are *pissed*, it means angry – a shortening of *pissed off* – rather than drunk; however, its British usage dates back two centuries, whereas the earliest listings in the *OED* for the US variant are post-Second World War. On the face of it, the word *paralytic*, for *incapably drunk*, might sound equally modern, but it is first recorded in 1843, and of Australian origin. It appeared in an irreverent four-page publication from Sydney called the *Satirist and Sporting Chronicle*, under the slight variant *paraletic*, in a short paragraph strewn with sexual innuendo suggesting that a gentleman named Brook had been seen too often in this condition coming home from 'the little house under the hill', having been 'fishing for salmon out of season'. Other gossip items in the same publication give a picture of free-spirited life in the city at the time, with seemingly relaxed attitudes to alcohol and sex, such as the following cryptic entry:

The Pitt-Street Auctioneers – These gentlemen had better attend to their business, and knock-'em-down, than to visit Biddy's, at twelve o'clock at night, to take their *ball* – it's no go *long nose*; Hannah says she's engaged, and that you had better attend to *Cavanagh's bar maid*, who will in all probability meet you.

Yet there was another side of Australia with quite a different attitude to strong drink, as seen in another newspaper from the same year, the *Teetotal Advocate* – published in Launceston, the second-largest city in the penal colony Van Diemen's Land (now Tasmania) – whose correspondents described spirits as *distilled damnation* and *liquid fire*. However, despite the resistance to alcohol of some sections of Australian society, it is worth remembering that there, as in England, your friendly neighbourhood apothecary of those days was happy to supply a wide variety of other substances quite legally over the counter. Among the items listed for sale in an advert from the firm of W. Paxton on the front page of an 1841 edition of another temperance-friendly newspaper, the *Adelaide Independent and Cabinet of Amusement*, were sulphuric acid, opium and arsenic. Each to their own.

Pumping ship in the used beer department

ONE INEVITABLE RESULT OF ALL THIS INGESTION of fluids is the eventual need to expel it, and there have always been slang ways of describing the process. Touring musicians in cheap tour vans are well used to requesting that the driver pull over at the next available stopping point for that purpose, and, among those of my acquaintance, one common phrase is to say you need a quick *guns n' roses*, since that band have a guitarist called Slash, which in England obviously has other connotations. In Philip Atlee's 1963 American spy novel *The Green Wound*, the lavatory in a bar is referred to as the *used beer department*, while Anthony Burgess described the use of the equivalent facilities in a provincial British pub in his novel *The Right to an Answer* (1960) as follows:

> The ladies, in sororities, made excursions to the toilet. The men went out to pump ship.

In employing the latter expression, Burgess was probably well aware that it dated back to the late 18th century, and is of nautical origin – indeed, this is yet another phrase that was rounded up by Francis Grose in his *Classical Dictionary of the Vulgar Tongue*. Another slang term which has lasted down through the centuries is *leak*, which was used by Shakespeare in *Henry VI, Pt I* (1598), and later by Jonathan Swift in his satirical poem about a honeymoon couple, 'Strephon and Chloe' (1734), although here the cause was non-alcoholic:

> Twelve Cups of Tea, (with Grief I speak)
> Had now constrain'd the Nymph to leak.
> This point must needs be settled first;
> The Bride must either void or burst.

Although there are slang terms for drinks that are brewed, distilled or even alcohol-free, perhaps it is fitting to leave the last words to the drinkers of spirits. First, a salutation, from the title character in Francis Grierson's entertaining novel of West End low life, *The Buddha of Fleet Street* (1950): 'May you never go ragged to mass'. To conclude, an expression which occurs in John Le Carré's 1968 espionage novel *A Small Town in Germany*, as two characters are drinking whisky:

> 'Do you like water?' he asked, and added a little to each of their glasses, but it was no more than a tear shed for the sober.

SEVEN

HIGH AS A KITE

Portable ecstasies corked up in a pint bottle

PRIOR TO THE 20TH CENTURY, many of the drugs on which the governments of our own time have declared 'war' were legally available. Indeed, as Thomas De Quincey pointed out in the introduction to his pioneering narcotic memoir, *Confessions of an English Opium-Eater* (1822), his daily doses of opium were purchased over the counter from 'respectable London druggists'. They assured him that he was not alone in his habit, and that, as he later put it, 'the number of amateur opium-eaters (as I may term them) was, at this time, immense'. However, despite this level of popular narcotic use, the cant and slang dictionaries of the time, so rich in terms for alcohol and drunkenness, remained virtually empty of drug-related phrases. Indeed, the vast range of colloquial names which exists today for drugs and their effects is almost entirely a product of the years since 1900. As a broad generalisation, before that date, drugs were usually known only under the straightforward names used by chemists and apothecaries. Opium was simply opium, rather than *hop, tar, midnight oil, fireflower, God's medicine, skee, gong* or *Chinese molasses*, as the 20th century variously called it.

De Quincey has sometimes been accused of making the

whole subject of drug addiction too attractive in his book – and it is easy to see why, given the following, which appeared under the forthright subheading 'The Pleasures of Opium':

> Here was a panacea… for all human woes: here was the secret of happiness, about which philosophers had disputed for so many ages, at once discovered: happiness might now be bought for a penny, and carried in the waistcoat pocket: portable ecstasies might be had corked up in a pint bottle: and peace of mind could be sent down in gallons by the mail coach.

It is tempting to think that the shade of De Quincey might be amused to know that roughly 160 years after he coined the term 'portable ecstasies', some people in early 1980s Texas rebranded the drug MDMA – first synthesised as far back as 1912 – with the self-consciously trendy name *ecstasy*.

Opium in De Quincey's day was hardly new to the capital, having long been traded by the East India Company in a complex web of arrangements between the UK, India and China. Looking back to the 17th century, it can be found openly listed for sale in a newspaper broadsheet entitled *The Prices of Merchandise in London* (1674). Gathered together with various items labelled 'Drugs' – although the others would not now be considered so – it cost eight shillings a pound, as opposed to 'Rubarb of Turky' at twelve shillings, 'Quicksilver' at four shillings, and 'Turmerick' at a whopping 52 shillings a pound. A decade later London apothecary Thomas Pritchard, at the Pestle and Mortar in Watling Street, advertised 'fine Coffee-Powder from 2 s. 6 d. to 3 s. per Pound', as well as 'Tea and other Drugs at reasonable rates', which serves to show that the word *drug* – which dates as far back as Langland's *Piers Plowman* (1378) – was applied rather more loosely in Restoration England than in our own time. Imagine, if you will, if one of the even older names for such a substance had instead been the one which had taken hold, and the politicians of our own day had to speak in stern tones of the need to clamp down on dealers selling that evil substance *treacle* (1340).

The only narcotic reference in that fine slang compendium *A new dictionary of the terms ancient and modern of the canting crew* (1699) is to an alcoholic beverage drink called *China ale*, so called 'from the well known East-Indian Drug of that Name'. The substance in question was *china root* – used, for example, in the 16th century when treating syphilis – and the diction-ary compiler's only complaint was that there was not nearly enough of it in his beer, blaming landlords for 'making it sweet only and adding a little spice'. Meanwhile, although the indig-enous peoples of South America had by this time been chewing coca leaves for centuries owing to the latter's narcotic properties, cocaine as such was not isolated as a substance until the 1850s, and so the appearance in the *Canting Crew* of the slang word *coker* signified not an enthusiastic *snowman* or *coke fiend*, but simply a bare-faced lie. Even as late as Farmer and Henley's all-inclusive compendium *Slang and Its Analogues* (1890), when they quote the colloquial insult 'Go and eat coke', the suggestion refers simply to the hard fuel substance derived from coal, which even the most spaced-out 1970s Laurel Canyon musician would have difficulty hoovering up their nose.

Slinge like a dope

THERE ARE FURTHER TRAPS when seeking historical antecedents for today's drug slang. On 20 March 1661, Samuel Pepys recorded in his diary some new ecclesiastical appointments to the House of Lords, at which the crowd in Westminster Hall shouted 'No Bishops! No Bishops', which prompted him to comment that 'indeed the bishops are so high, that very few do love them'. In this case, *high* meant an elevated station, and giving youself airs and graces, although even at that time it could also be a term denoting alcoholic intoxication, three hundred years before it was applied to the effects of drugs.

Opium may have been openly sold at auction in the capital in those days, but its dangers were evident, as reflected in this London newspaper report from the year 1700:

> Christened this week 313, buried 411, decreased [sic] 6. Casu-alties, one drown'd in the Thames, one hanged himself being Lunatick, 4 killed, one by a fall, one by a Coach, one by a Dose of Opium, and the 4th by the biting of Dogs.

Despite this, however, opium was many 18th-century Lon-doners' first port of call when afflicted with gout, although a 1773 edition of the *London Chronicle or Universal Evening Post* noted that the pain relief it afforded in such cases was 'dearly paid for, by the disagreeable effects of that languid and enervated state into which the poor patient is plunged by the use of this drug'. Self-medication by means of opium, or laudanum (tincture of opium), led a great many law-abiding people into accidental addiction, sometimes with fatal results. In contrast to the image of drug addicts as young, lawless, borderline criminals which developed in the 20th century, the following typical example from an 1850 issue of the *Illustrated London News* shows how the profile was very different in Victorian times, for example:

> On Saturday, an old woman named Elizabeth Draper, aged 82, resident at Donington, Lincolnshire, who was an habitual opium-eater, poisoned herself with an accidental over-dose.

In addition, as journalists, MPs and De Quincey himself noted, in the harsh working conditions of the Industrial

Revolution, drug use was endemic, not just among employees, but also their dependants. Speaking in a parliamentary debate on factory conditions in 1844, Lord Ashley commented that hours were so long that it denied mothers 'the possibility of them attending to their natural duties, and thus their children were drugged with laudanum until it became almost a necessary of existence'. Furthermore, in a different debate on taxation some forty years earlier, a Mr Vansittart had informed the House of Commons that 'with respect to opium, it was also intended to increase the duty, as great quantities, he understood, were used in adulteration of beer'.

Yet despite these bastions of the British Empire being seemingly awash with dangerous narcotics, the colloquial terms to descibe them had not yet arisen. For instance, the earliest use of the word *dope*, in any context, occurs in an anonymous nineteen-page pamphlet entitled *A Glossary of Provincial Words Used in the County of Cumberland*, issued in an edition of just sixty copies in London in 1851. The word was defined as 'a simpleton', and appeared alongside other indispensable stand-bys of the English north-west such as *wantle* ('to fondle'), *slinge* ('to go creepingly away, as ashamed'), *glop* ('to stare'), *cobbs* ('testicles') and *dadge* ('to walk danglingly'). It is, of course, tempting to wonder if the last two expressions are in any way connected.

A rare example of a drug reference surfacing in a slang dictionary of those days can be found in that very fine book from 1823 compiled by a man signing himself John Bee (John Badcock), whose title very much does justice to its contents: *Slang. A Dictionary of the Turf, the Ring, the Chase, the Pit, of Bon-Ton, and the Varieties of Life, Forming the Completest and Most Authentic Lexicon Balatronicum Hitherto Offered to the Notice of the Sporting World, etc.* Badcock was a man with a deep knowledge of the sporting and gambling worlds. This makes it less surprising that he included the following term, which could apply equally to humans or animals, since the illegal use of drugs on racehorses was a matter of serious concern to those with money riding on the outcome:

> *Hocus,* or *hocus-pocus* – A deleterious drug mixed with wine, &c. which enfeebles the person acted upon. Horses, too, are *hocussed,* at times: Dawson was hanged for *hocussing* Sailor, because it died.

Rosy cheeks, plumpness and health

In the main, the average 19th-century drug user called these substances by their proper names, with little recourse to slang. Consider the opening chapter of Sir Arthur Conan Doyle's second Sherlock Holmes novel, *The Sign of Four* (1890):

> Sherlock Holmes took his bottle from the corner of the mantelpiece, and his hypodermic syringe from its neat morocco case. With his long, white, nervous fingers he adjusted the delicate needle, and rolled back his left shirt cuff.

A similar scene in any 1950s pulp crime or juvenile delinquent novel would have gone to great lengths to play up the horror, degradation and also the illegality of such a scene, but this is late Victorian England, no law is being broken, and the narrator, Dr Watson, blithely poses the following question:

> 'Which is it to-day,' I asked, 'morphine or cocaine?'
> He raised his eyes languidly from the old black-letter volume which he had opened.
> 'It is cocaine,' he said, 'a seven-per-cent solution. Would you care to try it?'

In the language of today's authorities, this would make Holmes not just a *user* but also a would-be *pusher*. At that time, some people could trace the origins of their addiction to a simple visit to the dentist. In 1897, the *South Eastern Gazette*, from Kent, drew attention to the drawbacks involved in the common use of cocaine during treatment, 'and the craving developed by the patient after a few applications for its use habitually afterwards'. They further stated that 'in the United States it was found that the almost general application, by dentists, of cocaine had led to the development of a new form of disease, especially among society women in need of an artificial stimulant'.

Of course, if you were not having your teeth fixed, you could always buy that invigorating new beverage, Coca-Cola, which, from its beginnings in the 1880s until 1903, featured cocaine as one of its ingredients. However, non-narcotic salvation was at hand, according to an advert in an 1896 edition of the *Illustrated London News*:

DRUGS WON'T DO
Free Trial Of Something That Will Do
Now, strength and muscular activity, rosy cheeks, plumpness,
and health can be obtained without medicine.

The name of this miracle product – 'a perfect, flesh-forming, palatable, and agreeable Food beverage' – was *Dr Tibbles' Vi-Cocoa*.

If only someone had informed Mr Holmes.

Worse than a crime like murder

IT WAS THAT WELL-KNOWN UPHOLDER of law and order, President Richard M. Nixon, who is usually said to have launched the expression *war on drugs* – which probably sounded dynamic to whatever overpaid focus group dreamt it up, but also conjures up visions of heavily armed troops breaking into your friendly

neighbourhood chemists and machine-gunning boxes of haem-
orrhoid suppositories. (Back in 1930, the *Illustrated London News*
had published an article about the destruction of heroin and
opium supplies in Cairo, entitled 'Egypt's War Against Traffic
in Dangerous Drugs', which was undoubtedly more precise, but
clearly inferior as a soundbite.) Vague it may have been, but
Nixon's slogan was still somewhat better than the one later used
by George W. Bush, who in 2001 declared a *war on terror*, thus
no doubt striking fear into a word which had been happily existing as a noun since around 1480.

'NIXON CALLS FOR A WAR ON DRUGS', said the
headline in the *Palm Beach Post* on 21 March 1972, quoting a
phrase he had first employed the year before. The president told
reporters that 'I consider this to be the No.1 domestic problem
that concerns the American people'. He also called drug traffick-
ing 'the most reprehensible of all crimes. It is worse than a crime
like murder, a crime like robbery, a crime like burglary.' Clearly, in
the intervening three-quarters of a century, the world had moved
a long way from simple domestic chit-chat such as 'Which is it
today, morphine or cocaine?' As for 'a crime like burglary', this
was something much closer to home as far as Nixon was concerned. Three months after he made that statement, five burglars
paid by Nixon's own staff broke into the Watergate building in
Washington, DC, looking for compromising material about his
political opponents. This eventually cost him the presidency, but
Nixon's war on drugs is still with us.

Just as Prohibition in 1920s America drove millions of
otherwise law-abiding people into the hands of the mob when
looking to buy alcohol, the gradual criminalisation of formerly
legal drugs during the 20th century has been a colossal business opportunity for the underworld. As Mike Jay points out in
his fine book *High Society: Mind-Altering Drugs in History and*

Culture (2010), 'Today's illicit drugs trade, estimated by the UN at $350 billion USD a year, now constitutes one of the three largest international markets on the planet, along with arms and oil.' As far as wars go, it seems pretty clear who is losing.

Up tight? Cool it man

NIXON LAUNCHED HIS ANTI-DRUG CRUSADE shortly after the close of a decade in which – if you believed the media – recreational narcotic use was, shall we say, *mushrooming* to unprecedented levels. Indeed, even if you were a teetotal octo-genarian living in the Louisiana swamps or the Outer Hebrides, newspapers, television programmes and popular music could easily have kept you aware of a bewildering range of current and past drug slang. The same goes for the young and impres-sionable: if you were somehow unaware of then current terms such as *leapers* (amphetamines), *miss emma* (morphine), *giggle weed* (marijuana), *red devils* (the barbiturate seconal) or *chunks* (hashish), there was often a handy journalist or media-savvy swinger to spell things out for you. 'Twenty years ago few young people had even heard of marijuana and other such drugs, much less experienced them,' claimed the *Spokane Daily Chronicle* in 1969. 'Today, "pot," "grass" and "Acid" are part of most teenagers' vocabulary.' Indeed they were, and it was articles like this which helped them learn.

Of course, the youngsters themselves might not be reading the local newspapers delivered to their parents' homes, perhaps favouring instead the underground press, such as *Oz* and *International Times* in London, the *Berkeley Barb* in San Francisco or the *East Village Other* in New York, which covered the subject from – as they would have seen it – the *freak's* point of view.

A 1970 copy of the *East Village Other* ran an article for users simply entitled 'Cocaine', while in among the small ads for wife-swapping clubs and 'assisted' relaxation services ('Up tight? Cool it man. Climax your day with a mind-blowing massage') could also be found the following:

> TAKE A TRIP. Turn on with the 'FAMOUS TRIP-OUT BOOK.' Sure fire chemicals. Make peyote, DMT, cannabis, LSD, etc. Do it NOW! Send $2.00 to: TRIPS UNLIMITED Box 36347-EV Hollywood 90036.

This was an era in which some were advocating putting LSD into the water supply, to *turn on* the whole population, whether they liked it or not. Jerry Rubin, co-founder with Abbie Hoffman and others of the Youth International Party (Yippies), said in his book *Do It! – Scenarios of the Revolution* (1970), 'Get high and you want to turn on the world.' In this work he set out his incoherent plan for a brave new era of blitzed-out grooviness:

> Millions of young people will surge into the streets of every city, dancing, singing, smoking pot, fucking in the streets, tripping, burning draft cards, stopping traffic... Clerical workers will axe their computers and put chewing gum into the machines... Yippie helicopter pilots will bomb police stations with LSD-gas... Kids will lock their parents out of their suburban homes and turn them into guerrilla bases, storing arms. We'll break into banks and join the bank tellers in taking all the money and burning it in giant bonfires in the middle of the city.

Ten years later, Rubin was a millionaire stockbroker working on Wall Street, having made a killing investing in a fledgling company named Apple Computers, presumably having first run out of chewing gum.

Papers for your head

OF COURSE, RUBIN'S LANGUAGE has to be measured against the backdrop of the times. These were days when a large company such as mail-order giant the Record Club of America would send out flyers to its 3.5 million members advertising not only LPs and cassettes, but also a range of drug-related products they named *pyschedelicacies*, as Florida journalist Jack Anderson pointed out in 1972:

> The handsome circular also advertises a 'candlestick stash' for hiding 'goodies from unannounced intruders.' 'Stash' in drug slang is a narcotics supply. Also available from the club are 'mind-blowing' lights, 'papers for your head,' a 'stash bag' and a 'toker' pipe for smokers who want to 'take off.' All are marijuana terms. The 'toker' pipe, for instance, refers to a 'toke' which is a drag from a marijuana pipe. The ad says the 'toker' cools the smoke so a smoker can 'hold it longer.'

How much of this language was a surprise to the target audience is debatable, but any readers of an older generation who then heard the following year's American hit single, 'The Joker' by the Steve Miller Band, would at least have known what the singer meant when he called himself a *toker*.

Of course, since the mid-1960s rock music had been awash with more or less overt drug references. To take one well-known example, on their 1967 debut LP The Velvet Underground used junkie slang such as *spike* (needle) in the song 'Heroin', while on their follow-up album, *White Light/White Heat* (1968), the title song was all about amphetamines, and 'Sister Ray' was an eighteen-minute ode to the joys of looking for a *mainline* (vein). Similarly, the single by British mod band John's Children 'Smashed! Blocked!' (1966) was named after two slang terms common in the London club scene at the time for being under the influence of drugs.

While those releases of the Velvets and John's Children were hardly million-sellers at the time, you did not have to look far among the chart-topping singles to find drug slang, whether it was the Small Faces using the word *speed* on the amphetamine song 'Here Come the Nice' (1967), and getting *high* in 'Itchycoo Park' (1967), The Beatles wanting to *turn you on* in the song 'A Day in the Life' (1967), or Jefferson Airplane taking pills – and an unspecified type of *mushroom* – in 'White Rabbit' (1967). Clearly, by the time the summer of love rolled around, the implication seemed to be that the whole world had *tuned in, turned on, and dropped out*. Except, of course, many people hadn't. For some, the idea of trying to keep up with the mythical ideal of the newly liberated cosmopolitan drug aficionados was later exemplified by Woody Allen's character Alvy Singer in the film *Annie Hall* (1977). At one point, he inadvertently sneezes a fortune in someone else's chopped-out cocaine all over the coffee table, while elsewhere he explains to Diane Keaton as Annie his troubled relationship with drugs, turning down the joint she has just offered him:

> No, no, I, uh, I don't use any major hallucinogenics, because I took a puff five years ago at a party and tried to take my pants off over my head…

Coke Ennyday

NOT EVERYONE TURNED ON, lit up or had their hair cut by Vidal Sassoon – indeed, on the average 1960s UK high street, many hairstyles owed more to Ena Sharples than Edie Sedgwick – while in local libraries, filed under 'Burroughs', you were more likely to encounter Edgar Rice than William. Still, in the same way that many television drama series from our own time which are set in 1960s Britain have a tendency to pretend that everyone was driving a brand-new Mini or E-Type Jag – despite the fact that numerous cars on the roads in those days were clapped-out old bangers fully twenty or thirty years older than that – the rewriting of history from a modern perspective would sometimes have you believe that until the psychedelic hippie free-love explosion came along circa 1967, few people had ever experimented with anything stronger than a pint of beer or a cup of tea.

Consider this: a Hollywood film in which the famous star plays a drug-fuelled detective named Coke Ennyday, who wears a belt full of hypodermic syringes, shoots up every two or three minutes, and has a huge container on his desk simply marked 'Cocaine', from which he gleefully snorts an entire handful, blowing a cloud of it all over the room. A clock on the wall divides the day into four sections, *dope, drinks, sleep, eats*. On the trail of a gang of opium smugglers, he follows them to the knowingly titled Sum Hop laundry in Chinatown. Finding a sample, he takes an exploratory taste, then another, and another. Suitably hopped up, our hero defeats the criminals by either injecting them with drugs or blowing a blizzard of coke up their noses.

The Swinging Sixties? The decadent seventies? No, Hollywood made this during the First World War. The film was *The Mystery of the Leaping Fish* (1916), starring Douglas Fairbanks as the coke addict in question. This was intended as a broad comedy, partly satirising Sherlock Holmes. The previous year, Hollywood had made a slightly more serious attempt at portraying drug use in John W. Noble's film *Black Fear* (1915). Upon its London release the *Daily Express* noted that 'the terrible effects of the cocaine habit play an important part in the thrilling new Metro film drama'.

Sackloads of beak

THE WORD COKE HAS BEEN SENDING out mixed messages for years, some of them knowingly under the radar. For instance, when the Beatles made their debut feature film, *A Hard Day's Night* (1964), as noted earlier, many of their audience were screaming schoolchildren, of the kind seen chasing them through Marylebone Station during the credit sequence. However, a few minutes later, while on the train, John Lennon pretends to snort from a Pepsi bottle, one nostril after another, presumably as a veiled joke about coke sniffing, which would very likely have been lost on most of their younger fans.

The adult world, however straight, had long been informed about cocaine through a variety of mediums. In 1921, the *Observer* treated its readers to an examination of the supposed popularity of the drug in Rome, employing a fine collective noun for addicts into the bargain, speaking of cocaine 'or "lift" as it is called in the slang of the sunken fraternity'.

Simply referring to the drug as *coke* dates back to the start of the 20th century, with the first written record appearing in Ray Stannard Baker's *Following the Color Line – An Account of Negro Citizenship in the American Democracy*, published in New York in 1908. Under the heading 'Negro Cocaine Victims', the author described the scene as various poor people from both sides of the colour line appeared in front of a judge at a court in Atlanta:

> Not a few of the cases both black and white showed evidences of cocaine or morphine poisoning – the blear eyes, the unsteady nerves. ... They buy the 'coke' in the form of a powder and snuff it up the nose; a certain patent catarrh medicine which is nearly all cocaine is sometimes used; ten cents will purchase enough to make a man wholly irresponsible for his acts, and capable of any crime.

Over a century later, the slang word is still common currency, and was plastered all over the front pages of British tabloids once again in July 2015 when the Deputy Speaker of the House of Lords was photographed allegedly taking the drug. The *Sun on Sunday* broke the story under the headline 'LORD COKE – Top peer's drug binges with £200 prostitutes', while a leader in its weekday counterpart the *Sun*, entitled 'Lord A-Leaping', referred to him as a 'low-life coke-head', and the *Daily Star* called him Lord Snorty. The satirists at the *Daily Mash* then offered the following friendly advice in their 'Psychic Bob' horoscope section:

> Aries (21 MAR–19 APRIL)
> Sometimes, treating yourself might be something as simple as a nice bath or a takeaway. Other times it's sackloads of beak and a room full of saucy doxies.

The assumed blithe familiarity of the general public these days with drug terminology is now such that Netflix announced their 2015 series about notorious Colombian drug overlord Pablo Escobar with the slogan 'There's No Business Like Blow Business'. Similarly, in 2001, Hollywood released a Johnny Depp film about the cocaine trade simply entitled *Blow*, safe in the knowledge that its target audience would conclude that the subject matter would be cocaine, rather than what the *OED* defines as 'a firm stroke; a violent application of the fist'.

The bread to score weight

'COCAINE,' SAID A 1983 ARTICLE in the *Montreal Gazette*. 'It goes by many names: Snow, blow, toot, nose candy, ego food...' The term *nose candy* fits perfectly with the atmosphere laid down a decade earlier in the first great Blaxploitation film, *Super Fly*

(1972), in which the lead character Priest is the man with the best supply, as described in the novel of the script:

> Priest was no pimp. He was a dealer, a high-class dealer of the best cocaine in the city, a pusher-man of the nose candy. Not a street dealer; he had lieutenants for that action. Priest himself handled only the richest clientele, those who had the bread to score weight. And in Harlem, that's high society, all the way.

Yet just as the word *fly*, describing someone who is knowing or aware, dates back to 18th-century England, *nose candy* originally appeared long before the days of purple felt fedoras and stack-heeled boots, being first recorded in a crime story by Dashiell Hammett entitled 'Dead Yellow Women', in the magazine *Black Mask* (November 1925). Similarly, referring to cocaine as *snow* has a relatively venerable history, and since the 1940s the slang words *snowbird* or *snowman* have generally denoted someone who sells, or is addicted to, cocaine. In Francis Grierson's entertaining novel of West End low life *The Buddha of Fleet Street* (1950), he included a translation in brackets for the benefit of his less-worldly readers:

> Did you know that Prudence was a snow [cocaine] taker?...
> There was a snow bird who used to supply the stuff to members of a small gambling club.

The term has endured, and in 1980 the manager of customer services for the Oregon State Motor Vehicles Division told the press about certain number plates which were not permitted because of their drug associations: 'One man wanted SNOMAN on his plates. We turned him down. Snowman is drug slang for cocaine dealer.' However, as far back as 1926, a play opened in London's West End entitled *The Snow Man*, in which the title character sells drugs, although in this case the word referred to morphine. All of which highlights the fact that slang terms in the drug world, as elsewhere, can often be applied to several different things at the same time. In the early 20th century, various drugs capable of being inhaled were originally called *nose candy*, while virtually any drug you can name was at one time or another referred to by perhaps the most flexible term of all: *dope*.

Ixnay on the opeday

IN 1906 THE *MANCHESTER GUARDIAN* helpfully informed its readers about the meaning and etymology of a new American term for a drug addict:

> Mr Thaw, the American millionaire murderer, is reported to have been described by one of his friends as a 'dope fiend'. The expression does not quite speak for itself to English readers. It means the slave of a drug habit, and might be translated as 'drug-maniac'. 'Dope' is purely American English. ... The New English Dictionary recognises it in two senses, both American. The first is 'any thick liquid or semi-fluid used as an article of food or as a lubricant'... The second sense is 'an absorbent material used to hold a liquid'.

The phrase *dope fiend* certainly had staying power. In the William Burroughs novel *Dead Fingers Talk* (1963) – handily illustrated by one London paperback publisher at the end of the sixties with a fisheye-lens cover photo of someone leaning into the camera and fixing up with a hypodermic – it was clearly still in fashion more than half a century after being explained to Edwardian newspaper readers:

> I tied up for a shot, my hand trembling with eagerness, an archetype dope fiend. 'Just an old junky, boys, a harmless old shaking wreck of a junky.'

In the US in the 1870s, the slang word *dope* originally signified opium. Across in England, twenty years later, Farmer and Henley offered the following definition in their dictionary *Slang and Its Analogues* (1890):

DOPE, verb (American) – To drug with tobacco. Also DOPING = the practice.

For many years after this, the word *dope* became simply a shorthand way of describing a variety of drugs. For instance, in Herbert Asbury's 1928 *The Gangs of New York*, he described how underworld leader Monk Eastman, shot dead in 1920, 'had been bootlegging and selling dope'. A decade later, in Los Angeles, when Groucho Marx appeared as the somewhat unconventional doctor Hugo Z. Hackenbush – a qualified vet, but treating humans – in *A Day at the Races* (1937), he also used the word, but this time in back-slang:

MRS UPJOHN : Oh, doctor, I think it's time for my pill
GROUCHO: Ixnay on the opeday [nix on the dope]

Back-slang – the reversing of a word so that it is pronounced backwards – was listed by John Camden Hotten in his 1860 work *A Dictionary of Modern Slang, Cant, and Vulgar Words, Used at the Present Day in the Streets of London* as 'the secret language of costermongers', in which 'sometimes, for the sake of harmony, an extra syllable is prefixed, or annexed'. He gave examples such as *elrig* (a girl), *mottab* (bottom) and *erif* (fire). In recent years, a similar kind of back-slang has developed among young people in France, in which the word for eating, *manger*, becomes *géman*.

By the late 20th century, *dope* had mostly settled down to its narrower use as a term for marijuana. However, as late as the seventies, the word could still be applied to cocaine, such as in the novel *Super Fly* (1972), in which the main Harlem dealer's partner asks him:

> You gonna give all this up? We got eight-track stereo, a colour TV in every room. We can snort up half a piece of dope every day. Now, nigger, that's the *American Dream*, ain't it? Ain't it?

Even so, *dope* sometimes has a different meaning. For instance, when a couple of teenage American girls are ordering soft drinks in Ward Greene's novel *Death in the Deep South* – published in 1936 but set during the First World War – the exchange goes like this:

> 'What'll it be ladies?'
> 'Dope and cherry, Fred,' said the taller girl.

This conversation was, of course, taking place in a *drugstore*, but *dope* for them was a word meaning a Coke, not cocaine.

Feeling a little horse this morning

TO MANY, ESPECIALLY THOSE in the armed forces, *dope* was simply slang for information. For instance, in Agatha Christie's second novel, *The Murder on the Links* (1923), when Hercule Poirot asks an old-school London theatrical agent for some details about a music hall performer's schedule, the man replies, 'You go home, and I'll send you round the dope in the morning.'

However, American radio listeners were left in no doubt about the narcotic implications of the word one night in 1951, with the national broadcast of a pioneering documentary show, *The Nation's Nightmare*, exploring the drug underworld, as *Billboard* magazine reported:

> Via tape, the aural magic carpet, the show roamed the United States to bring listeners such unique material as the sounds a

crazed New Orleans dope addict makes while being driven into a frenzy for lack of the drug, a purchase of dope being made by radio reporters in Chicago, kids in Central Park showing off their vocabulary of narcotic slang (horse, mainliner, reefer, pusher) and the entry of an addict into the government hospital at Lexington, Ky., for treatment.

These were early days for the use of the word *horse* for heroin – the *OED*'s first recorded entry is from the previous summer – but it caught on fast. A June 1951 report in *Life* magazine about drug-taking in schools informed its readers that 'horse… is traded and sniffed in some classrooms under the eyes of lecturing teachers', and later that decade it could be found, for example, in hard-boiled crime novels such as Ross Macdonald's *The Doomsters* (1959), which also employed the term *cold turkey* to describe heroin withdrawal. A year later, his near-namesake, John D. MacDonald, included this description of a girl and boy heading off from school to a teenage drug party in his crime novel *The Neon Jungle*:

> 'I got some sticks [reefers],' he said softly.
>   'How many?'
>   'Enough. Ginny's got some caps [capsules of heroin]. A hell of a lot of them. Bucky is all set with the car. How about it?'
>   'They want us along?'
>   'So why not? They want to pop. They want company. Ginny got the sticks and the horse. She says they're both real george [OK].'

It was not for nothing that the heroin-addicted Puerto Rican gang in John Frankenheimer's film of New York turf wars, *The Young Savages* (1961), were called The Horsemen, or that Len Deighton's follow-up to his best-selling debut novel *The Ipcress File* (1962) was named *Horse Under Water* (1963), which told the murky tale of a heroin-packed U-boat wreck submerged off the coast of Portugal.

Here comes the man with the jive

OF COURSE, WHETHER ANY of this esoteric vocabulary came as a surprise to those who were not narcotics users might well depend on their taste in music, since blues and jazz musicians had been including slang drug terms in songs for several decades by that stage. The Storyville district in New Orleans, where many jazz pioneers worked in the early years of the 20th century, was a free-living legalised brothel district of thirty-eight city blocks, established by official edict in 1897, in which drugs were an everyday fact of life. Pianist Jelly Roll Morton, who began playing at *sporting houses* around the district at the start of his teens, later recalled the variety of addicts found in those circles in 1902:

> …some were habitual drunkards and some were dope fiends as follows: opium, heroin, cocaine, laudanum, morphine, et cetera. I was personally sent to Chinatown many times with a sealed note and a small amount of money and would bring back several cards of hop. There was no slipping and dodging. All you had to do was walk in to be served.

One supposed explanation of the origins of the jazz term *hip* was that it derived from the practice of lying around on your side all day in opium dens, so that your hip joint eventually deteriorated over time. Thereafter, the story goes, other regular users could tell you from the uneven way you walked – 'He's *on the hip*, he's a *hip guy*'. For all its appeal, it may just be a fanciful explanation nailed on after the fact.

In 1917, Storyville was closed down on the insistence of the military authorities on the grounds that it might have a corrupting influence on the delicate flowers of the armed forces before they marched off to the joys of the First World War, but many of its services simply went underground.

The release of Mamie Smith's 78 rpm single 'That Thing Called Love/You Can't Keep a Good Man Down', and in particular her 'Crazy Blues' (both 1920), signified that the US phonograph industry had finally caved in after three decades and deigned to allow African–Americans into studios to record the music which had been developing in honky-tonks, gin joints and brothels since the late 19th century. In the blues and jazz boom which followed, especially during the 1930s, lyrical references to drugs, along with sex and alcohol, were a regular feature in the vast number of songs recorded. For instance, in the summer of 1927, Luke Jordan wrote and sang a song in Charlotte, North Carolina, with the admirably direct title 'Cocaine Blues'. Three months later, up in New York City, Victoria Spivey cut a number of her own called 'Dope Head Blues', and it is a fair bet that its target audience would have been aware that the substance under discussion was probably not the 'preparation of pitch, tallow, and other ingredients' which 19th-century Americans had applied to the undersides of snow shoes in cold weather.

Among many other examples, there followed the Harlem Hamfats with 'Weed Smoker's Dream' (1936), and the same year also brought 'Here Comes the Man with the Jive' by Stuff Smith & His Onyx Club Boys, in which the singer urges his companion to *light up* and *get real high*. The word *weed* – which dates back over a thousand years to Anglo-Saxon times in its original sense denoting a wild plant of no value or benefit, and then also served as a way of referring to tobacco from the start of the 17th century onwards – had been used in US blues and jazz circles as a term for marijuana since the mid-1920s. When Bea Foote cut her succinctly titled 'Weed' (1938), she sang that she was going to *send* herself, and claimed to be the queen of all *vipers*, the latter being a term for a drug smoker probably best remembered from the Fats Waller tune, 'Viper's Drag' (1934). Waller's recording was an instrumental, but Fats later made things abundantly clear in 'The Reefer Song' (1944), in which he dreams 'about a reefer five feet long' and also uses the phrase *bust your conk*, signifying getting high.

Jive, meanwhile, in the black community, had signified a way of talking since just after the First World War, probably deriving from the English word *jibe*, and in the 1930s also came to be an alternative name for *swing* music. However, in the Stuff Smith song, it specifically means marijuana, as it also did when Andy Kirk and His Twelve Clouds of Joy recorded 'All The Jive Is Gone' in 1936, the tale of a party when there's only booze left, but no reefer. 'Hit That Jive, Jack' (1941), by the Nat Cole Trio, was all about a dealer on the corner who 'wants to make you high', in which the narrator is off 'to see a man', anticipating the basic scenario of Lou Reed's classic Velvet Underground song 'I'm Waiting For My Man' (1967) by a quarter of a century.

Other then-current drug slang words appeared in songs like Trixie Smith's superb 'Jack, I'm Mellow' (1938), in which she sings of having *blown some gage* (smoked marijuana), or 'Wacky Dust' (1938) by Ella Fitzgerald with the Chick Webb Orchestra (1938), a homage to cocaine, thinly disguised as a song about the uplifting effects of music, which has the singer 'kickin' the ceiling apart'. Buck Washington, meanwhile, informed his listeners in 'Save the Roach for Me' (1940) that he had been in his backyard smoking *tea* (marijuana), and also threw in references to *gage* and *jive*, in case anyone required further clarification. Calling the remaining end of a reefer itself a *roach* probably sounds to modern ears like a quintessentially 1960s word, but it was actually a product of the US jazz scene of the 1930s. Mind you, in terms of smoking something, *gage* goes all the way back to the *Canting Crew* dictionary of 1699:

> *Gage*, a Pot or Pipe. *Tip me a Gage*, give me a Pot or Pipe

The righteous bush

IN CASE IT MIGHT BE THOUGHT that such records with drug references were somehow under the radar, and reaching only the black community, it is worth noting that Cab Calloway and His Orchestra could be seen performing their 1932 single 'Reefer Man' in the Paramount Pictures film *International House* (1933), which starred a winning combination of W. C. Fields and Bela Lugosi. The lyrics, written by the great Andy Razaf, include references to being *high*, and its variant, *sailing*. On Broadway that year, the musical revue *Flying Colors*, which ran for 188 performances at the Imperial Theatre, included a song written by Arthur Schwartz and Howard Dietz entitled 'Smokin' Reefers'. An entirely different view of such behaviour was later taken by the makers of the defiantly low-budget anti-marijuana film *Reefer Madness* (1936), originally released under the slang-free title *Tell Your Children*, which in later decades became an unintended hit with the *turned-on* generation. Conceived, as the foreword at the start put it, as a warning for concerned citizens about the 'new drug menace which is destroying the youth of America in alarmingly increasing numbers', it issued a handy – if eccentrically punctuated – description of the inevitable effects of smoking this 'unspeakable scourge':

> Its first effect is sudden, violent, uncontrollable laughter; then come dangerous hallucinations – space expands – time slows down, almost stands still... fixed ideas come next, conjuring

up monstrous extravagances – followed by emotional disturbances, the total inability to direct thoughts, the loss of all
power to resist physical emotions... leading finally to acts of
shocking violence... ending often in incurable insanity.

One man who was blithely ignoring all such warnings at
the time was white jazz player Milton 'Mezz' Mezzrow, whose
hugely enjoyable 1946 autobiography *Really the Blues* was hardly
coy about his drug-related activities, as the back cover blurb of
the original paperback edition boasted:

> Call it the modern Odyssey of an old-time jail-happy jazzman
> who spiked beer for Al Capone, smoked opium with the
> Purple Gang, peddled marijuana in Harlem (the law got him
> for that), played clarinet in dives high and low, married across
> the colour line, today heads a jazz record company!

The book included an extensive slang glossary, listing *weed*,
hay, *tea*, *grass*, *grefa*, the *righteous bush* and *muta* for marijuana,
hop for opium, *snow* for cocaine, and *white stuff* as a general term
for cocaine, morphine and heroin, while a *junkie* was defined as
a 'dope fiend'. J. K. Rowling enthusiasts might like to note that
muggles were 'cigarettes of marijuana', while Mezzrow's own name
and activities as a drug seller gave rise to a slang term denoting
marijuana of the finest quality, *mezz*.

The close association in the public mind between jazz
players and drug taking as a source of inspiration and day-to-
day lifestyle choice was perhaps best summed up in John Clellon
Holmes's Beat Generation novel *The Horn* (1958), whose musician character Edgar was partly based on the life of sax man
Charlie Parker:

> ...everyone repeated with awe Edgar's famous remark, deliv-
> ered with a Promethean sigh: 'Man, I got to get high before I
> can have a *hair*cut. I got to get *lifted* before I can *face* it!'

Joss Ackland's spunky backpack

ALTHOUGH SOME SLANG WORDS in the drug lexicon inevitably fell out of fashion, many of the ones popular in the hippie era were already in place before or during the Second World War, and remain common today. Newly synthesised or developed drugs, of course, require new names, while in other instances specialist slang has travelled to the UK and US from other English-speaking countries, such as those of the Caribbean. For example, the word *spliff* for a marijuana cigarette appeared in the Jamaican newspaper the *Daily Gleaner* alongside another local term for the weed: 'Here is a hot-bed of ganja smoking... and even the children may be seen at times taking what is better known as their "spliff"'. With the initial wave of Caribbean immigration to the UK, and the early popularity of Jamaican music in the form of ska, blue beat and rock steady, such words spread along with them, appearing, for instance, in the novels of Colin MacInnes. Spliffs are smoked in *Absolute Beginners*, while in *City of Spades* the boxer Jimmy Cannibal has a greenhouse for growing marijuana: 'my greatest enjoyment', he says at one point, 'ever since when a boy, is in charging with weed'. Later, with the global popularity of reggae music in the 1970s, the formerly local words *ganja* and *spliff* travelled with it.

The problem for anyone wishing to keep up with the street expressions for drugs, as with slang generally, is of course that new words appear all the time, sometimes made up by users, or invented as a marketing tool by the people trying to sell them. There are literally hundreds of slang terms for long-standing staples of the drug market like heroin and cocaine, while even the more recent entrants to the marketplace have multiple names. Drug users attempting to buy PCP, popularly known as *angel dust*, might also ask for it under a wide variety of names including *k-blast, amoeba, snorts* or *gorilla biscuits,* while those with a *crack* habit would be looking for some *fish scales, bonecrusher* or *kanga-roo,* and then be said to be smoking the *devil's dick* (crack pipe). Rave-culture ketamine users might know it as *kit-kat* or *vitamin k,* and the drug's frequent legal use in veterinary surgery for anaesthetising horses gave rise to a popular UK T-shirt slogan aimed at clubbers with a sense of irony:

KETAMINE – JUST SAY NEIGH

Films, music, television and now the internet all help spread the ever-expanding lexicon of drug terms, yet despite the ease with which their meanings can be checked, there remain ever-present pitfalls for public figures who either wish to campaign against some new drug horror or simply appear *down with the kids,* who are usually far enough away from street level that they are unable to distinguish genuine contemporary slang from made-up nonsense. This situation was exploited magnificently by the satirist Chris Morris in an episode of his 1997 TV series *Brass Eye,* simply entitled 'Drugs', in which he lured a selection of public figures into making statements about the supposed dangers of wholly imaginary new substances which he claimed were terrorising British youth. Initially, Morris is shown late at night asking a confused dealer if they have any *yellow bentines,* explaining, 'I don't want something that makes you go really blooty,' and that he didn't want his arms to feel 'like a couple of fortnights in a bad balloon'.

Later, the likes of Bernard Manning, Rolf Harris and Noel Edmonds are seen looking suitably concerned as they warn of an alleged 'new legal drug from Czechoslovakia called *cake*' – 'made from chemicals, by sick bastards', as Manning helpfully puts it. Harris speaks of a side effect called *Czech neck,* in which the throat swells, leading to asphyxiation, and warns that it might be offered under alternative names, such as *Joss Ackland's spunky backpack*, while Noel Edmonds helpfully advises listeners that an active ingredient in the drug 'stimulates a part of the brain called *Shatner's bassoon*'. The icing on the *cake* was perhaps the contribution of the then MP for Basildon, David Amess, who – in addition to informing viewers that dealers refer to *cake* buyers as *custard gannets* – outside the confines of the programme, went on to raise a question about this fictitious drug in the House of Commons, which received the following answer, as recorded in *Hansard*:

> We are not aware of any reports of misuse in the United Kingdom of the substance known as 'cake' but the advisory council nevertheless has under review the question whether this and a number of similar substances should be brought within the scope of the act.

Names may change as the decades pass, but, it appears, the war on (non-existent) drugs never sleeps...

EIGHT

Dig That Sound

Bowsing and nigling in the Old Kent Road

SLANG AND POPULAR MUSIC are inextricably linked – indeed, imagine the opening lines of the Rolling Stones song 'Honky Tonk Women' (1969), if rendered in the more formal language of earlier times: 'I met a Memphis lady of questionable virtue, much given to imbibing juniper-based spirits / Who attempted to persuade me to visit her chamber for the purposes of fornication'. Not only does it fail to scan; without the street phraseology, it also dies on its feet. Of course, many musical genres have names which began as slang terms in the first place: *jazz, punk rock, heavy metal, rock'n'roll, the blues*. The lyrics and titles of songs, centuries before the advent of recorded music, employed slang, and through live and eventually studio performances, that language has spread worldwide.

For example, the Victorian music hall performer Albert Chevalier had great success on the London stage in the character of a costermonger, with his self-penned songs full of Cockney rhyming slang such as 'My Old Dutch' (1892) and 'Wot Cher!' (1891, later known as 'Knocked 'Em in the Old Kent Road'). As a result, generations of people who had not been born within a hundred miles of the Bow Bells learned from the former that *old dutch* meant wife, and that someone talking a lot was *a-jawin'*. The latter song was even more awash with London vernacular, with its talk of *coves* and *toffs*, and other expressions such as *popped off* (died), but that did not stop Californian child star Shirley Temple performing it on two separate occasions during the film *The Little Princess* (1939), tap-dancing as she went.

Chevalier's 'Wot Cher!' was rounded up soon after its composition by John S. Farmer for inclusion in the pioneering work *Musa Pedestris – Three Centuries of Canting Songs and Slang Rhymes, 1536 – 1896* (1896), placing it firmly in the tradition of 17th-century songs such as 'The Beggar's Curse', which began with some fine vagabond argot:

> The Ruffin cly the nab of the Harmanbeck
> [The devil take the constable's head]

This song first appeared in Thomas Dekker's pamphlet *Lanthorne and Candle-light* (1608), which dealt thoroughly with cant language and vagabond speech. A few decades later, a fine slang-heavy ballad was sung on the London stage, in Richard Brome's comedy *A Jovial Crew, Or the Merry Beggars* (1641). It was entitled 'A Mort's Drinking Song' (1641) – *mort* being the word for a woman used among the itinerant poor. Brome introduced the tune by means of the following stage directions: 'Enter Patrico with his old wife with a wooden bowle of drink. She is drunk. She sings:–

> 'This bowse [ale] is better than rum-bowse [wine],
> It sets the gan [mouth] a-gigling,
> The autum-mort [wife] finds better sport
> In bowsing than in nigling [fornicating].'

Having sung this touching rhyme, her exit is then signalled by the author as follows: 'she tosses off her bowle, falls back and is carried out'.

None of this kind of behaviour would have been likely to impress the puritan killjoys in Parliament at the time. The play ran at the Cockpit in Drury Lane until 2 September 1642, when the government closed all theatres by decree, just a month after Charles I raised his standard at Nottingham at the beginning of the English Civil War, effectively killing off Brome's career as a dramatist. The theatres would not reopen until the Restoration, eighteen years later – too late for Brome, who died in poverty in 1652, or indeed for that humble man of the people Oliver Cromwell, whose salary of £100,000 a year as Lord Protector (roughly £7.5 million in today's money) barely kept the wolf from the door of his various palaces until his own demise in 1658.

Here's a damn'd funk

SHEET MUSIC PLAYED AN IMPORTANT PART in the dissemination of slang terms, but it was the coming of recorded sound in the last decades of the 19th century which enabled songs to reach out across the world in a way which would have been unthinkable in earlier times. Even before the dawn of the 78 rpm disc, wax cylinder recordings helped spread the word, although much of their content consisted of classical or brass band music. The actor Russell Hunting, from West Roxbury, Massachusetts, performed humorous monologues on a series of cylinders in the character of an Irishman named Michael Casey, one of which was called 'Casey as the Dude in a Street Car' (early 1890s). The word *dude*, whose use has multiplied over the years, first surfaced in America in the second half of the 19th century as a term for a dandified man, and there was a teenage gang in New York during the 1870s called the Baxter Street Dudes.

However, it was the dawn of jazz which really opened the

floodgates. 'This is a loose, fast age,' exclaimed humorist Kin Hubbard at the time, 'an' at the rate we're goin' jazz'll soon run its course, an' then watch th' demand fer decent, unscuffed girls.' Ultra-modern young women with a taste for jazz and nightlife were famously known as *flappers*, but the term is actually from the 19th century. James Redding Ware's *Passing English of the Victorian Era* (1909) defined a *flapper* as 'a very immoral young girl in her early "teens"', and quoted in turn an 1892 edition of the magazine *Notes and Queries*, which wrote 'about the use of the slang word "flapper" as applied to young girls'. They ventured the explanation that 'a "flapper" is a young wild duck which is unable to fly, hence a little duck of any description, human or otherwise'. Just as England's Teddy boys pre-dated the arrival of rock'n'roll in the country by several years, the word *flapper* was in existence long before its starring role in the mythology of the 1920s, a decade which came to be known as the 'Jazz Age'.

Jazz music had been around in its very earliest forms in the Storyville district of New Orleans since the end of the 19th century, but the name came later, and the music played at that time by pioneers such as cornet player Buddy Bolden was never recorded, so while the exact nature of what they were playing is hard to establish, some of their language survives. For instance, in the year 1900, Bolden frequently performed at Kenna's Hall, at 1319 Perdido Street, New Orleans, which was known to the regulars as 'Funky Butt' Hall, or F B Hall for short, because Bolden's band had a song entitled 'Funky Butt', alongside others of an equally direct persuasion such as 'If You Don't Shake, You Don't Get No Cake'. So, more than half a century before *funk* became associated with a particular strand of black music, or *Life* magazine in 1963 could describe renowned black author James Baldwin as occasionally speaking in 'the funky argot of Harlem', the word was already known to the gig-going cognoscenti of

New Orleans. In the glossary of his influential jazz memoir, *Really the Blues* (1946), Mezz Mezzrow defined the word *funky* as 'smelly, obnoxious', which is also how it was understood in England in the 17th century, appearing as follows in *A new dictionary of the terms ancient and modern of the canting crew* (1699):

> *Funk*, Tobacco Smoak; also a strong Smell or Stink. *What a Funk here is!* What a thick Smoak of Tobacco is here! *Here's a damn'd Funk*, here's a great Stink.

Funky music, therefore, was down and dirty, the sound of people working up a sweat – either in a smoky club, or else in bed. Of course, anyone sweating through fear has for centuries in England been said to be in a state of *funk*, as, for example, in Samuel Naylor's 1845 rhyming translation of Goethe's version of 'Reynard the Fox', which now looks somewhat odd to modern eyes:

> Quoth Malkin, 'Is it quite safe, nunky?
> Because I do feel somewhat funky!'

Plant you now, dig you later

EARLY PROTO-JAZZ WAS NOT CONFINED to halls, however. Guitarist 'Sweet Lovin'' Charlie Galloway, who led one of the earliest bands on the scene and who first employed Buddy Bolden as a sideman, apparently also played in the streets, sometimes in what were known as *skiffle* bands – a term which would later be revived in 1950s Britain. The Razzy Dazzy Spasm Band, led by Emile 'Stalebread' Lacoume, who were active in New Orleans from the mid-1890s, often played outdoors, working in front of brothels, stores and theatres – anywhere they could gain attention. The band were boys rather than men, seemingly aged ten or eleven in early photographs, and they were also white. Jazz historian Daniel Hardie notes that they 'inserted yells of hotcha and hi de di or ho de ho, expressions apparently used in songs of the river, into their performances'. All three of these terms survived into the swing era of the 1930s, when jazz went mainstream and could be heard in Hollywood films and on national radio, helped in no small measure by a man who did more than his share to publicise and explain the jazz argot – bandleader, songwriter, vocalist and all-round force of nature Cab Calloway.

Cab performed slang-rich songs such as 'Minnie the Moocher' (1931), with its talk of *frails* (women) *kicking the gong around* (smoking opium) and a rousing chorus of *hi de hi* and *ho de ho*, which prompted his publicists to bill him thereafter as 'His Hi-de-Hiness of Ho-de-Ho'. Other songs such as '(Hep-hep!) The Jumping Jive' (1939) and 'We the Cats Shall Hep Ya' (1945) – the last of which he performed in a 1947 feature film, itself named *Hi De Ho* – helped place the slang word *hep* firmly in the jazz public's consciousness. (By 1955, the word was so familiar to the general public that the writer of the William Hickey gossip column in the *Daily Express* wrote an article about a jiving cellar which had opened at his old Oxford college, alma mater of various 19th-century politicians, entitled 'I Can't See Old Gladstone Getting "Hep"'.)

For those who wanted to delve deeper, Cab Calloway also published his own very popular booklet of slang, *The Hepster's Dictionary* (1938), which, as the following year's revised edition explained, gave the lowdown on 'words and expressions employed by the "hep cats" when they talk their "jive", as Harlemese is called on Lenox Avenue'. As a result, if you were a *square* ('an un-hip person'), an *ofay* ('white person') or even an *icky* ('one who is not hip, a stupid person, can't collar the jive'), salvation was at hand, and you, too, could astonish your equally *cubistic* friends with your newly acquired language skills. If hungry, you could say 'I'm gonna knock me [obtain] some food', when sleepy, 'I think I'll cop a nod', and when leaving a friend, 'Plant you now, dig you later'. Admittedly, several expressions were hardly jazz coinages – *So help me* ('it's the truth, that's a fact') had been used in solemn oaths for centuries at this point – while *hep* itself pre-dates Calloway by a generation, first surfacing in that jive-talking bastion of middle-class American respectability, the *Saturday Evening Post*, in 1908 ('What puzzles me is how you can find anybody left in the world who isn't hep'). Six years later, over in Portland, Oregon, Jackson and Hellyer's *A Vocabulary of Criminal Slang* (1914) gave the following explanation of the origins of the term:

> HEP, Noun – Sapiency, understanding... Derived from the name of a fabulous detective who operated in Cincinnati, the legend has it, who knew so much about criminality and criminals that his patronymic became a byword for the last thing in wisdom of illicit possibilities.

Whether the history of law enforcement from Ohio was in the mind of a British comic novelist from Guildford at that time is hard to say, but P. G. Wodehouse certainly included the word *hep* in a novel he wrote around that time, *Piccadilly Jim* (1917), in which the title character has the following exchange with a woman called Ann:

> '...Jerry Mitchell has told me all!'
>> Ann was startled.
>> 'What do you mean?'
>> 'The word "all,"' said Jimmy, 'is slang for "everything."'
>> You see in me a confidant. In a word, I am hep.'

On the face of it, such a usage by the author whose most famous characters, Jeeves and Wooster, are both in their divergent ways archetypal examples of Englishmen might seem unlikely. However, Wodehouse was at that time living in New York, writing Broadway musicals with the likes of Jerome Kern and Guy Bolton (including one, in 1917, which took its name from a slang term, *Oh Boy!*, as admirers of Buddy Holly might be interested to learn). His Jeeves stories made their debut appearance in 1915 in the same magazine which first gave the world *hep*, the *Saturday Evening Post*, and indeed, *Piccadilly Jim* itself was printed by the *Post* a full year before its hardcover publication.

What a pair of gams!

CAB CALLOWAY'S HEPSTER'S DICTIONARY proved very popular, going through several reprints – the last of which was issued as a promotional item to accompany his appearance in the Hollywood film *Sensations of 1945* (1944), in which he sang 'We the Cats Shall Hep Ya', and also brandished an outsize book while singing 'Mr Hepster's Dictionary'. The latter tune explained that *jive talk* was now the language used by all the *jitterbugs* (jazz and swing fans), and clarified, for the benefit of cinema-going squares, the meaning of such terms as *hep cat*, *doghouse* (double bass) and *twister to the slammer* (key to the door).

Once again, this process showed that – just as 16th-century readers of Thomas Harman's *A Caveat or Warening for Common Cursetors Vulgarely Called Vagabones* could learn to talk the vagabond talk without ever having met one of the canting crew – you did not have to be rubbing shoulders with the hippest of the hep in some late-night Harlem swing joint in order to pick up the latest jive. Indeed, one classic term listed by Calloway (and much later associated with the Beats) was the word *dig*, meaning 'comprehend, understand', which had gone mainstream in the most public way when included in the Gary Cooper film *Ball of Fire* (1941). This is hardly surprising, given that the picture also included Gene Krupa and His Orchestra, and the fact that the entire story was built around a group of decidedly square lexicographers attempting to discover how the hep folk talked, noting down phrases like *killer diller* along the way. Cooper's co-star Barbara Stanwyck played a character named Sugarpuss O'Shea, much given to utterances such as 'What's buzzin', cousin?', while the trailer for the film screamed up-to-the-minute phrases like 'he's a solid sender', 'in the groove' and 'what a pair of gams!' Not to be outdone, *Life* magazine made it their 'Movie of the Week', and printed a slang glossary for the benefit of readers:

SHOVE IN YOUR CLUTCH – get moving
LOOSE TOOTH – incompetent person
SCREAMING MIMIS – jitters
CUT THE MEKENKES – stop talking nonsense
PATCH MY PANTYWAIST – term of amazement
BLITZ IT – hurry it up

Quite what the residents of London and many other British cities who were then being blitzed made of the latter expression is anyone's guess, but in among these entries *Life* also listed *dig me?*, meaning 'understand me?' This was relatively fresh-minted jazz slang, less than a decade old, but now comprehensible to anyone who could afford a cinema ticket or the price of a magazine. *Dig* has been co-opted by virtually every youth movement and music trend which has since followed, and continues to be used, whether seriously or ironically – a fate which unaccountably seems to have escaped *patch my pantywaist*.

Pimps, prostitutes and lonesome tramps

IN ADDITION TO THE AVALANCHE of hep-talk available in jazz records of the 1940s, the slang could also be learned from significant publications such as *Dan Burley's Original Handbook of Harlem Jive* (1944). Burley was a black journalist and magazine editor, who wrote a jive-heavy column called 'Back Door Stuff' in the *New York Amsterdam News*, and also a long-time jazz musician, working with some of the big names of the era. His 1962 obituary in *Jet* magazine, for which he had been associate editor, memorably described him as 'the poet laureate of straw-bosses and Southern sheriffs, of cornfield preachers and fifth floor walk-up flats, of barbecued pork and fried chicken, of pimps and prostitutes and lonesome tramps'. In the introduction to his most famous work, Burley himself cast an eye on the future, as follows:

> The proponents of Harlem jive talk do not entertain any grandiose illusions about the importance or durability of jive. They do not hope that courses in the lingo will ever be offered at Harvard or Columbia University. Neither do they expect to learn that Mrs. Faunteen-Chauncey of the Mayfair Set addresses her English butler as 'stud hoss,' and was called in reply, 'a sturdy old hen.'

Hoped for or not, the scenario in which jive language is studied on numerous university courses has most definitely arrived with a vengeance. Academics in recent decades have argued among themselves about the precise origins of certain words in the Harlem jive vocabulary, in particular suggested derivations from the Wolof language, brought over in earlier times by slaves. As Jesse Scheidlower of the *OED* commented in 2004, when dealing with the etymology of the word *hip* and its near-neighbour, *hep*:

The idea... that *hip* came from Wolof, a language widely spoken in Senegal and The Gambia, was first advanced, tentatively, in the late 1960s by David Dalby, a scholar of West African languages. The word *hipi*, meaning 'to open one's eyes,' was the putative source; Dalby also suggested West African sources for the American slang words *jive* and *dig*. Over time, Dalby's proposal was taken as fact by many people, particularly those who wanted to find African origins for English words. Even obvious problems with the etymology – such as the fact that Wolof does not generally use the letter 'h' – were ignored. (The word in question is actually spelled *xippi*.)

Indeed, anyone consulting the many thousands of entries in Pamela Munro and Dieynaba Gaye's *Ay Baati Wolof – A Wolof Dictionary* (1997) expecting to find the likes of *stud hoss*, or any word whatsoever beginning with 'st' or 'h', would retire disappointed. For what it is worth, if you once again refer to *A new dictionary of the terms ancient and modern of the canting crew* (1699), among the various slang terms beginning with 'h' you will find the following:

Hip, upon the Hip, at an Advantage in Wrestling or Business.

Nevertheless, although many of the origins of early hep slang remain obscure, the advent of recorded jazz, post-First World War, certain music-related feature films, and then the publication of the first collections of jive talk in the 1930s and 1940s, mean that a fair amount of that speech and its meanings have been preserved.

Jiving in a comin'-on fashion

THE EXTENSIVE GLOSSARY IN MEZZ MEZZROW'S *Really the Blues* (1946) hipped the squares to musicians' phrases like *cafe sunburn* (the habitual pallor acquired in such a nocturnal environment), *hipster* ('someone who's in the know, grasps everything, is alert'), *moo juice* (milk), *line your flue* (eat) and *groovy* ('really good, in the groove, enjoyable'). The last term word, frequently taken to be a classic 1960s coinage, was the hip jazz term of the early 1940s. As Bing Crosby so memorably asked the King Cole Trio during his regular Kraft Music Hall radio show in 1945: 'Say, is it a solid fact that you guys can beat your chops, lace the boots and knock the licks out groovy as a movie, whilst jiving in a comin'-on fashion?', to which Nat suavely replied, 'That is *precisely* the situation.' However, as evidence of how far into the mainstream such a term had already spread by then, a 1944 *Life* magazine article about white twenty-four-year-old fashion designer Betty Betz and her 'Teen Age Betty' range of clothing showed her sketching 'a slick mouse [girl] in a jive suit groovy as a movie', and commented of another garment, 'it's sheer murder, Jackson, and we ain't clickin' our teeth when we pass the word that the hems are wide enough to cut a rug'. Whether this met with the approval or comprehension of the magazine's oldest readers, some of whom would have been born not long after Lincoln's assassination, is an interesting question.

Bing Crosby and Nat Cole were broadcasting from Sunset and Vine, out in Hollywood, a long way from Harlem, but radio jive also spread down to the segregated South, where deejay Lavada Durst – known as Dr Hepcat – began *talkin' that talk* on station KVET out of Austin, Texas, from 1948 all the way through until 1963, with a show called *The Rosewood Ramble*. As a popular black jockey on a white station, he broke quite a few of the assumed ground rules, and in 1953 he also issued his own booklet of slang, *The Jives of Doctor Hepcat*, which, instead of just listing individual words, set out a wide selection of fine hepcat dialogues for use in a variety of situations. It helped that

Durst himself was a two-fisted, pounding boogie pianist who cut the excellent self-penned record 'Hattie Green' for local Austin label Uptown in 1949. In short, he knew the territory, and when it came to describing piano playing, this is what his booklet recommended:

> Here's a cat that lays a group of ivory talking trash and strictly putting down a gang of jive. The situation is much mellow, it's many fine and understand gates it will tighten your wig.

Although it was written in the early 1950s, the language in *The Jives of Doctor Hepcat* better reflected the jazz scene of the war years, of *jitterbugs*, *zoot suits* and the golden days of boogie woogie: 'Say, that's a real crazy combo blowing at the club, you can believe they can put the wheel on any deal, every sound is hip to the tip. When they put up some wild riffs it ain't no sin to take off your skin and dance around in your bones.' However, other sections of Dr Hepcat's jive foreshadow some of the language later employed by modern-day rappers, with his talk of musicians who *rock the house* and of *Jacks and Jills from flytime cribs*. Here is a prime example of his rhyming hep-speak:

> Aces to your places it takes bulling jive
> To keep the joints alive.
> Like cool, frantic, and dead in the know
> And some bronze kitty with a most able floorshow.
> Up in three places and let some pass
> And then pull in to port where the cats are breathing natural
> > gas.

Spoken by Cro-Magnon man

IN THE SAME YEAR THAT DR HEPCAT was cutting his debut record, and future Beat writer Jack Kerouac was continuing the jazz-themed road trips across the US in the company of Neil Cassady and Allen Ginsberg which he would later fictionalise as *On the Road* (1957), Capitol Records in Hollywood issued their own guide to *clue-in* the squares to *be-bop*, the new sound in music. Babs Gonzales and Paul Weston's *Boptionary – What Is Bop?* (1949) was a small booklet, the core of which was the two-page dictionary of slang words compiled by Gonzales, billed as 'Professor Bop, Himself'. Terms which would later see service among the beatniks, rockabillies and even hippies surfaced here, such as *daddy-o* ('buddy or friend'), *gone* ('great') and *crazy* ('out of this world'), alongside others of more venerable vintage, such as *scoff* ('to eat' – which is London slang that appeared in the *Swell's Night Guide* of 1846).

Not everyone was impressed. A 1948 *Daily Mirror* article by Robert Cannell had the following to say about the new trend:

> Bebop is the rage among the 'educated jazz fans' in the United States. There are, too, bebop hairdos for males (I'm chary of writing men), there are suits of gay checks and unusual cut. And one of the hallmarks of the true bebopcat is a pair of dark glasses, a beret... and a goatee beard. They also speak a weird kind of slang which changes so rapidly that not all 'bebopcats' can understand each other... Musicians playing bebop can 'float away' and express themselves in the way that they feel. My only complaint, however, is that they don't float far enough.

If this sounds like British provincialism in response to swinging new ideas from across the Atlantic, the American press was often saying much the same thing. Novelist and journalist Robert C. Ruark, writing in the *Schenectady Gazette* in 1949, commented:

> Bop, as I understand it, is a kind of musical outrage for which some people profess a fondness. It is played by people who

wear goatees and berets. Its language has been compared to that spoken by Cro-Magnon man, obviously the mental equal of the modern bopster. ... A musician is a 'wig,' and if he's cool, he's groovy, which means he's lop pow, or OK. If one is bugged, he is annoyed by a zoo, or sad-looking chick, or a turkey, or square, or a clown, or a non-hip bopper. Any of the above may be defined as a drag, or just plain awful.

Babs Gonzales himself, who had a band in 1946 called Babs' Three Bips & A Bop, waited another two decades – in between working briefly for Errol Flynn as a chauffeur – before self-publishing his own thoroughly distinctive autobiography, *I, Paid My Dues – Good Times… No Bread, A Story of Jazz* (1967). From the superfluous comma in the title, via its verso-page declaration, 'Babs Gonzales – Creator of the Be-Bop Language', down to the name of his book company, Expubidence (a word of his own invention), this was the fine sound of a man doing things defiantly his own way. Over the course of 160 pages of bop speak, he told the story of his days hanging out with Charlie Parker, who stole his clothes ('Babs, baby, I'm sorry I downed your threads'), trying to earn lots of money (*enough bread to burn a wet mule*), dress well (*so sharp he's bleeding*) and persuade crooked club promoters to pay him at the end of the evening (*give me my bread or I take your head*). In an interview for a newspaper called the *Baltimore Afro-American*, conducted just days before his death in January 1980, Babs had this to say about his use of language:

> My thing is that I was brought up in the streets as a rapper whose next meal depended upon a clever turn of the word and I figured I could rap as well as any of these cats could play their horns. So, I started running down my rap on stage and the people dug it.

To modern ears, the sound of a bebop musician and scat singer, born in 1919, using the word *rap*, around the same time that the earliest hip-hop music such as 'Rapper's Delight' by the Sugarhill Gang (1979) was gaining attention, might sound strange, but – leaving aside its appearance in Dr Johnson's *Dictionary* two centuries earlier – the word had been current in US black language since at least the early 1960s. In Clarence Major's *Black Slang – A Dictionary of Afro-American Talk* (1970), *rap* was defined as 'to hold conversation; a long impressive monologue'. Mind you, maybe Babs simply had a fondness for late 19th-century slang words from the North of England, as recorded in Richard Blakeborough's *Wit, Character, Folklore & Customs of the North Riding of Yorkshire* (1898), which contained the following:

> Rap, *n*. A friendly chat.
>> Ex. – *Cu' thi waays, an' lets 'ev a pipe an' a bit o' rap.*
> Rap-off, *v*. To speak on the spur of the moment.
> Raps, *n*. Gossip, news

You done got hip

Jazz music spread jazz slang across the world, which was then adopted by the Beats, co-opted and modified by 1950s rock'n'rollers and rockabillies, and finally enshrined and mummified in popular culture in the 1960s, as the *hippies* (itself originally another jazz word) sat around uttering words like *groovy* and *man*, and calling their female companions their *old lady* – all of which were in regular use among 1940s bop musicians.

The story of how that language permeated the popular consciousness can be illustrated simply in song titles. Here, for example, is a short year-by-year journey in jazz and blues recordings, from 1921 to 1945, reflecting some of the hip words of the day:

'I Want a Jazzy Kiss', Mamie Smith, 1921
'Hep', Mitchell's Jazz Kings, 1922
'Oh! Sister, Ain't That Hot!', Dolly Kay, 1923
'How You Gonna Keep Kool?', The Georgia Melodians, 1924
'Everything Is Hotsy Totsy Now', The California Ramblers,
    1925
'Rock, Jenny, Rock', The Georgia Strutters, 1926
'Ain't Love Grand (Don't Get Funky)', John Hyman's Bayou
    Stompers, 1927
'Don't Jive Me', Louis Armstrong's Hot Five, 1928
'I'm a Front Door Woman with a Back Door Man', Lillian
    Glinn, 1929
'Horse Feathers', Cliff Jackson & his Krazy Kats, 1930
'Kicking the Gong Around', Cab Calloway & His Orchestra,
    1931
'Reefer Man', Cab Calloway, 1932
'Swing, You Cats', Louis Armstrong & His Orchestra, 1933
'Rock and Roll', The Boswell Sisters, 1934
'Boogie Woogie', Cleo Brown, 1935
'That Cat Is High', Tommy Powell & His Hi-De-Ho Boys,
    1936
'Killer Diller', Benny Goodman & His Orchestra, 1937
'Stomp It Out, Gate', Rosetta Howard & The Harlem
    Hamfats, 1938
'Jake, What a Shake', Louis Jordan & The Tympany Five, 1939
'Jitterbugs Broke It Down', Ollie Shepard, 1940
'Are You All Reet?', Cab Calloway & His Orchestra, 1941
'You Done Got Hip', Roosevelt Sykes, 1942
'Riffette', Freddie Slack & His Orchestra, 1943
'Groovy Like A Movie – Let's Get Groovy', Bonnie Davis &
    the Piccadilly Pipers, 1944
'Bebop', Dizzy Gillespie, 1945

So, imagine that you were an English schoolboy jazz enthusiast during that era, such as Humphrey Lyttelton, George
Melly or Kingsley Amis. By buying these records, reading
about them in specialist UK jazz publications such as *Melody*

Maker (established 1926), hearing some of them on the radio or occasionally having the chance to see them in Hollywood films, a working knowledge of contemporary hep slang could be acquired without ever having come within three thousand miles of a Harlem after-hours joint. And today, well-heeled teenage UK hip-hop fans whose backgrounds are public school rather than Public Enemy – or perhaps *Straight Outta Compton*, but in this case the Berkshire village of that name – similarly learn from songs how to talk in contemporary *gangsta rap* slang.

Sometimes, of course, Harlem even came to London, as when Cab Calloway and His Orchestra played a residency at the London Palladium in 1934 – following in the wake of visits by Louis Armstrong in 1932 and Duke Ellington in 1933 – where the effect was considerably more awe-inspiring than that produced by a hand-cranked gramophone. Music journalists in the 1970s would speak in hushed tones of the bone-shaking capabilities of Black Sabbath's PA system, but I once met an elderly gentleman who had the good fortune to have seen one of those Calloway Palladium shows, who gleefully compared the combined power and volume of that orchestra's swinging massed brass section to that of an airliner taking off above the front stalls. As Cab himself later recalled, 'people climbed all over the stage and then tried to tear off our clothes as we left the theatre every night'.

That crowd of British jazz fans would have long been familiar with words like *reefer* and *jive*. Similarly, as can be seen from the above list, songs mentioning *rock* and even *rock and roll* were already an established thing in the inter-war years, so that it was not remotely unusual when the announcer on the 14 January 1939 broadcast of the NBC radio show *Camel Caravan* told listeners, 'Look out now, hang on tight, 'cause here comes Benny Goodman with a real rocker, "King Porter Stomp"'. The phrase *horse feathers* – an expression meaning rubbish or nonsense

– was used as a title by Cliff Jackson and His Krazy Kats for their 78 rpm recording of suitably unhinged ensemble playing and scat singing, two years before the Marx Brothers appeared in their 1932 film of the same name. By the start of the 1940s, *jitterbug* had become the accepted term both for a new, acrobatic style of jazz dancing, and for the dancers themselves.

The word has stayed rooted in its time, but another slang expression which surfaced around the same time, *hip*, has stayed the course ever since, across numerous different spheres far removed from music. Likewise, when the Dizzy Gillespie Quartet released a 78 rpm instrumental entitled 'Bebop' in 1945, they could not have imagined that not only would it lend its name to an entire style of music, but also, in its shorter form, *bop*, mutate and spread across successive music genres over successive decades, whether it was the magisterial Gene Vincent and His Blue Caps on their 1956 debut 45 singing the praises of 'Be-Bop-A-Lula', or New York's finest, The Ramones, on their own debut twenty years later, introducing the world to the 'Blitzkrieg Bop' (1976). Twelve-year-old glam rock fans saving pocket money to buy a copy of David Bowie's 'Starman' (1972) – which also spoke of *hazy cosmic jive* – or T Rex's 'Jeepster' (1971), were known to the press as *teenyboppers*, and Marc Bolan himself as The Bopping Elf.

The new idol of stamping youth

By the 1950s, jazz had essentially become respectable, now that rock'n'roll was the convenient new whipping boy for the press and moralists. In Britain, it was the same music paper, *Melody Maker*, which in pre-war times had defended jazz from similar complaints, that now led the charge decrying the supposed new aural menace. This was partly a question of social background; broadly speaking, middle- and upper-class youth often favoured jazz, whereas the rockers and Teddy boys were largely working class, and it wasn't them who wrote articles for the media. The Queen's own sister was a high-profile jazz enthusiast, prompting the *Melody Maker* to memorably observe, in an article deploring any link between that type of music and recreational drug use, 'Is the public to believe that because Princess Margaret likes jazz she smokes a hokum pipe? Or that Clarence House is an opium den?'

Despite this supposed divide, the language of early rock'n'roll utilised numerous slang words which had been current in popular music for decades. Indeed, as Louis Armstrong said in 1956, when asked by the *Daily Express* for his opinion of rock'n'roll, 'it reminds me of some lively old hymn music we used to sing back home when I was a boy... there's a little change here and there, but it's all about the same'. Despite the seismic shock waves caused by the man *Picture Post* called 'Elvis the Pelvis Presley, the New Idol of Stamping Youth, High Priest of the Rock'n'Rollers', half the bands jumping on the rock bandwagon in Britain were actually composed of former or current jazz musicians looking out for the main chance. Meanwhile skiffle, the home-grown proto-rockabilly music bashed out by teenagers on countless tea chests and washboards from Limehouse to Liverpool, was a direct offshoot of the jazz revival, and took its name from the New Orleans term dating back more than half a century. One of the most successful skiffle 45s, 'Don't You Rock Me, Daddy-O' – a top ten hit in 1957 for the Vipers Skiffle Group – is a textbook example of how jazz slang persisted into the new era. The band took their name from a 1930s term for marijuana smokers, while the title of the song name-checked two further jazz terms; *rock*, which dated back in this context to the 1920s, and *daddy-o*, a hip term of address since the 1940s.

Of the new breed, Gene Vincent and the Blue Caps, who, along with Jerry Lee Lewis, remained the favourite of the hard-core rockers for decades to come, not only walked the walk, they also very much talked the talk. When not serenading 'Be-Bop-A-Lula', Gene and the boys were hanging out on 'Bop Street' (1956), which opened with a brief interlude of spoken jive ('Tell me, cat, where's that *di*-rection?') and then launched into a blizzard of hep speak alongside Cliff Gallup's breathtaking guitar runs. A day earlier, they'd recorded a song called 'Bluejean Bop', which their record label promoted with an advert that read, 'ROCK with Capitol – Just "Dig" This Special Release!'

In the new rock'n'roll universe, men were still *cats* or *hep cats*, and women were *chicks*, *dolls* or *dames*, although they, too, could be like the boys, according to Eddie Arnold's 1954 hillbilly bopper 'Hep Cat Baby', about a woman much given to saying *real gone* and *dig this*. There were a couple of independent US record labels named Hep, and Carl Perkins sang about having a 'Jive After Five' (1958), while Little Richard explained in 'Slippin' & Slidin'' (1956) that he had *done got hip* to someone's *jive*, and furthermore, his gal was a *solid sender*. Meanwhile, out on the further shores of rockabilly, David Ray sang 'Jitterbugging Baby' (1959), while Larry Terry proclaimed magnificently, and at full volume, that he was undoubtedly a 'Hep Cat' (1961). Continuing the jazz language theme among the rockers, there was Boyd Bennett's 'The Groovy Age' (1956), and also Johnnie Shelton & His Rockabillies telling the world about a place called 'Groovy Joe's' (1958). In Memphis, pioneering female rocker, recording engineer and label owner Cordell Jackson wrote and sang about a 'Bebopper's Christmas' (1956), in which a 'real gone Santa' comes *boppin' in*, and the following year out of North Carolina came Don Hager & the Hot Tots with 'Bebop Boogie', whose lyrics also managed to include the words *jive* and *jitterbug*. Of course, not everyone in that particular music scene was drawing on jazz words to put their message across: over in Central City, Kentucky, the duo Tag & Effie ploughed their own singular linguistic furrow when they laid down that self-penned classic of hill-country love gone wrong, 'Baby You Done Flubbed Your Dub With Me' (1958). Trade paper *Billboard* gave the latter a favourable review, and, in the same issue, commented approvingly of another fine tune, 'Looking', by Texas rockabilly Royce Porter, that it 'builds and achieves a funky quality', which certainly suggests that the F word was current in music circles in a variety of contexts before its specific meaning narrowed in the late 1960s.

Hippy hippy shake

THE REVIEW PAGES OF *BILLBOARD* magazine are useful for charting the emergence of slang words into the US music world, and thus on into general public use, since they covered a wide variety of genres – from jazz, blues, doo-wop, gospel, R&B and swing to hillbilly, country, rock'n'roll, pop and show tunes. For example, in 1949 jazz saxophone player Cecil Payne released a booting rhythm & blues instrumental entitled 'Hippy Dippy', which the magazine was pleased to call 'one of those tenor-bary sax groan-and-moan deals with a big beat and some fresh themes'. The word *hippy* or *hippie*, which also surfaced, for instance, in Douglass Wallop's 1953 hepcat crime novel *Night Light*, originally just denoted someone who was hip. When Montana rockabilly Chan Romero wrote and sang his superior original version of the song 'Hippy Hippy Shake' in 1959, the word had no whiff of Merseybeat, let alone long hair or joss sticks, about it, and as late as 1964 it could be found being used in its original slang sense in a British tabloid newspaper toothpaste advert, to mean the coolest teenager at a party:

> Does Your Mouth Say Dreamboat? – You've got to be a sweetie with a mouth like this. Just watch yourself reflected in other people's eyes. The shyest boy will light up like a Roman Candle when you pass by, the toughest hippie of them all will find his cherished rudeness melt… So use Gordon Moore's Cosmetic toothpaste to tint your gums petal pink, polish your teeth to soft-shining brightness.

Within three years, the word appeared several times in its brand-new guise in a news report on the front page of the same paper, when ballet dancers Rudolf Nureyev and Dame Margot Fonteyn were arrested 'at a San Francisco "hippie" party' in the Haight-Ashbury district. 'There', the paper informed its readers, 'the hippies live in squalid communal flats. Many take drugs and believe in free love.'

So, if distinguished dancers from the Royal Ballet – Fonteyn was approaching fifty at the time – could find themselves roped by the press into the hippie phenomenon, the general public might be forgiven a certain amount of confusion regarding the music-derived language spoken by this apparently new and *switched-on* generation. Luckily, a blizzard of articles in that self-same press was there to offer friendly assistance to the terminally square. 'Are you confused when you hear statements like "He's in that Warhol bag?" or "[dance craze] The Jerk is fab" or "The royal family's gone kinky at last?"', wrote Gloria Steinem in a 1965 issue of *Life* magazine. Her inclusion of words like *fab* and *kinky* clearly showed the influence of the so-called British Invasion of bands which had followed in the wake of the initial American success of the Beatles since the beginning of the previous year. 'If a visiting Englishman referred to your wife as "a gear bird"', she continued, 'would you hit him?' By way of further clarification,

Steinem advised that 'it is essential to avoid such Old Hat terms as Hip, Bop, Cool, Beat, Beatnik, Cat, Crazy, Fink and Old Hat'. So, apparently, *hip* was no longer hip, *cool* had become uncool, and *beat* and *beatnik* had taken a beating.

The sordid hipsters of America

OR PERHAPS NOT. Indeed, it seemed that no one had informed *Life* magazine's own editors, who two weeks previously had run an article about trendy young matador El Cordobés, accompanied by the headline 'The Beatnik of the Bull Ring ("He wears his hair long, appears in jeans, speaks in slang…")'. The word *beatnik* itself is a rare example of a slang term whose origin can be precisely dated and explained. The Beat Generation – deriving from the jazz musician's slang word *beat*, meaning tired or exhausted – themselves had been floating around in various forms since the late 1940s; their name came to wider public attention with the publication of Jack Kerouac's novel *On the Road* in 1957. Reviewing the book in the *New York Times*, Gilbert Millstein called it 'the most important utterance yet made by the generation Kerouac himself named years ago as "beat"', and indeed, the novel itself contained a passage which spoke of 'the sordid hipsters of America, a new beat generation that I was slowly joining'. The following year, however, the spectre of the *beatnik* reared its much-publicised head, courtesy of a writer at the *San Francisco Chronicle*, Herb Caen, who, on 2 April 1958, sent the term out into the world via his column, deriving the latter part of his made-up word from the recently launched Russian space satellite, Sputnik. As he later told *Chronicle* journalist Jesse Hamlin, 'To my amazement, it caught on immediately. The *Examiner* had a headline the following day about a beatnik murder. I ran into

Kerouac that night at El Matador. He was mad. He said, "You're putting us down and making us sound like jerks. I hate it. Stop using it.'"

Perhaps Kerouac had a premonition of the way the next couple of years were to be played out in the media. In music, films, on television, in books and magazines, a veritable avalanche of bongo-tormenting, guitar-strumming, poetry-reciting beatniks invaded the popular consciousness. As far as the general public was concerned, this sudden outbreak of *beardy-weirdies* was mostly a subject for ridicule, tinged with a certain amount of jealousy on account of the numerous stories of jazz-themed orgies supposedly taking place in dark beatnik cellars. Jack Kerouac put out an LP himself in 1959, *Poetry for the Beat Generation*, reciting his words over a jazz piano backing, but it was a crowded market, and he found himself competing against up-tempo swingers like 'Bongo Beating Beatnik' by Joe Hall & the Corvettes (1959), 'Beatnik Girl' by the Bi-Tones (1960) or the hit instrumental 'Beatnik Fly' by Johnny & the Hurricanes (1960). Closest to home was the satirical song 'The Beat Generation' (1959), by Bob McFadden and Dor. The latter name concealed real-life folk singer and beat poet Rod McKuen, and both of them lived long enough to see punk pioneer Richard Hell use their song as the inspiration for his era-defining single 'Blank Generation' (1975).

Tomorrow Is Dragsville, Cats

WITH A PREDICTABLE EYE for a sales opportunity, in 1959 Hollywood released a film brilliantly entitled *The Beatniks*, and another called, yes, you've guessed it, *The Beat Generation*. Reinforcing the jazz connection, publicity material for the latter included photos of 'beatnik favourite Louis "Satchmo" Armstrong playing his famed trumpet in a "beatnik" hangout', singing the title song of the film. Cream of the celluloid crop, however, was a 1958 film aimed squarely at the rocking fraternity, *High School Confidential*, whose opening title sequence featured none other than Jerry Lee Lewis belting out the song of the same name to an audience of real gone teens from the back of a flat-bed truck. Large sections of the film are conducted in hep slang, as the music-crazy school students fall prey to an ambitious teenage drug dealer, and are much given to sayings like 'in the bread department I am nowhere' (I'm broke) or 'I'm looking to graze on some grass' (I want to buy some marijuana). One of many highlights is a beatnik club scene in which Phillipa Fallon as a beat poetess recites a veritable dictionary's-worth of hep phrases over a jazz backing ('Tomorrow is dragsville, cats, tomorrow is a kingsize drag'). This fine performance, with lyrics written by Mel Welles, was released as a 45 rpm single by MGM records that year, backed by another excerpt from the film, in which John Drew Barrymore explains the story of Christopher Columbus entirely in hep-speak to a classroom of *studs* and *gassers* (boys and girls). Meanwhile, West Coast jazz fans could slip into a comfortable toga and relax to the righteous sounds of an LP entitled *Romesville* (1959), featuring Rafael 'Googie' René and a starry cast of players such as Earl Palmer and Plas Johnson laying down the beat on tunes such as 'Caesar's Pad' and 'Cool It At The Coliseum' (sic). What further worlds could the jazz-crazy beatnik vibe now conquer?

The answer, perhaps not surprisingly, was revealed to primary-school-age readers of a 1960 edition of the *Popeye* comic called 'Poopdeck Goes Beatnik', in which the spinach-hungry sailor's ninety-nine-year-old father, Poopdeck Pappy, opens a nightclub for the beards-and-beret set in the cellar of Popeye's house, with signs in the garden reading 'Pappy-O's Pad Party' and 'Welcome All Kool Cats'. For a time, Pappy drives the hepcats wild in the basement by reciting nursery rhymes, which the assembled throng of *blown minds* take to be beat poetry ('Li'l Bo Peep lorst her crazy sheep...'), but when his son evicts him, marches down the street brandishing placards which read 'Me Son Is A Square', 'Popeye Don't Dig It' and 'He's Like Wasted'. It had taken just two short years from the invention of the name and Kerouac's complaint that 'you're putting us down and making us sound like jerks' to the whole scene being held up for ridicule to an audience of eight-year-olds – who were presumed to know already what a beatnik might be, or else the joke would have had no meaning.

By this stage, a vast array of hip terms beloved of the jazz community had found their way, via popular music and then through many other forms of media, into all parts of the mainstream. As the sixties hove into view, a startling number of the words with which the supposed counterculture would identify itself were already so familiar to the unhip world that it is only a surprise that music's avant-garde clung to them for as long as they did. Some of those words, old as they were, have nevertheless come to define the era, so that, for instance, the sound of the Mindbenders singing 'A Groovy Kind Of Love' (1966) seems like a quintessentially 1960s experience. Few of those hearing it on their radios that year, or since, were aware, not just of the word's years of service as jazz terminology, but of its slang meaning in Victorian England, where it applied to someone stuck in a groove, or a rut – in short a square – defined thus in Farmer and Henley's *Slang and Its Analogues* (1890):

GROOVY, *Adj.* – Settled in habit; limited in mind.

NINE

It Takes a Record
Company with Millions
to Push Us Forward

Toppermost of the poppermost

LISTENING TO POPULAR MUSIC RADIO STATIONS at almost any time over the past five decades, you could be forgiven for thinking that recording studios had only been invented circa 1960, because the music from any of the decades prior to that is so poorly represented. Anything earlier than the pop culture explosion which saw the emergence of Motown, Merseybeat, The Stones, Hendrix and James Brown has generally been presented in the media – and often regarded by the public – as ancient history, whereas the music of the 1960s era is still not sidelined in this way, despite now being half a century old. Hence a proportion of the slang which appears in those recordings also has a tendency to remain current, since each new generation is exposed to it. Many of those words were old even at the time, but what *was* new, however, was the sheer scale of the money to be made from riding the groovy bandwagon, to a place once sarcastically described by John Lennon as the *toppermost of the poppermost*.

The potential scale of the revenue from all things *fab* and *gear* was not immediately apparent to everyone. Beatles manager Brian Epstein clearly had no idea of how much money could be made for the band from the wave of pop hysteria surrounding them, famously signing a merchandising deal which gave away an astonishing 90 per cent of the profits deriving from the avalanche of plastic guitars, badges, Beatle wigs and other spin-offs that proceeded to sell in their millions. He, like most people in the music business, behaved as if none of this would last, but these days surviving members of certain 1960s bands are still touring stadiums, long accustomed to a country house and chauffeur-driven limousine lifestyle. They had the good fortune to arrive on the scene at precisely the moment when popular music and its language went thoroughly mainstream, and even the most staid parts of society began to pay lip-service to all things *trendy* and *switched-on*. The spread of the cult words of the new movement via radio, television, film and print media was fast and effective. To take just one example, when the Beach Boys sang about having *good vibrations* in 1966, it was simply a matter of time before a significant slice of the planet became aware of the phrase and its meaning.

In the 1960s, words like *groovy*, *mod*, *far out* and *swinging* poured out of transistor radios and invaded numerous areas of everyday life, from adverts for cleaning powder to children's shoes. There was serious money to be made – at least for some – and if you weren't *with it*, you were probably already dead, *man*.

Come rock and roll me over

ONCE THE FIRST WAVE OF ROCK'N'ROLL broke through onto hit parades and radios around the world in the mid-1950s, its largely teenage fan base was exposed to a considerable amount of music-related slang. Sometimes it was simply a case of the title, such as when Detroit pop crooner Guy Mitchell's single

'Rock-A-Billy' reached the No. 1 spot in Britain in May 1957, which would have been the first time that many UK music fans had encountered the word. Guy was essentially a middle-of-the-road entertainer, rather than a rocking wild-man, yet on this disc he used hip phrases like *blow my fuse* and *go man go* – the latter having gained international attention when Carl Perkins wrote and sang the original version of 'Blue Suede Shoes' (1956). By contrast, although Carl's 45 was a pure-bred slice of Memphis *rockabilly*, most people in England would have simply called it *rock'n'roll* at the time.

People had been singing about *rocking* and *rolling* in blues, jazz and then R&B records since the 1920s, generally as a slightly less X-rated way of referring to the time-honoured business of *horizontal athletics*. For several centuries prior to that, sailors had used the expression *rock and roll* to denote the action of a ship at sea – although it is also possible to read an earthier meaning into the words of the traditional shanty 'Johnny Boker', first quoted in the nautical memoir *On Board the 'Rocket'*, by Captain Robert C. Adams (1879):

> Oh, do, my Johnny Boker,
> Come rock and roll me over,
> Do, my Johnny Boker, *do*.

Back on dry land, in 1936 the *Yorkshire Post* gave notice of the following event, designed to raise money for Leeds Royal Infirmary:

> January 29 – 'Rock and Roll', a revue presented by British Legion Women's Section (Otley Branch), Mechanics' Hall, Otley, 7.30pm.

At first sight, this seems remarkably advanced, but it appeared just as American vocal harmony trio the Boswell

Sisters were enjoying a huge hit on both sides of the pond with a song called 'Rock and Roll' (recorded October 1934), which was mentioned in a 1935 *Daily Express* poll as one of the ten favourite popular songs among their readers, so the women of the Legion very likely named their revue after it. However, as the lyrics make clear, the rocking and rolling in question is once again the movement of a ship, and the Boswell Sisters promoted it with an appearance in the feature film *Transatlantic Merry-Go-Round* (1934), a gangster tale set on an ocean liner, seated in a model rowing boat, and dressed in sailor suits.

Dig that ocean motion

IN BRITAIN, THE PHRASE ROCK AND ROLL as a term for describing the motion of the sea continued to occur every so often in newspaper reports of the 1940s and early 1950s, and as late as 1953 could be found in a report of two men who had so refreshed themselves at the bar in Victoria Station that they missed their train to Carshalton and woke up on the boat train instead, when 'a steady rock and roll told [them] that *something* was wrong'. A year later, however, the phrase had a totally different meaning as far as the UK press and public were concerned, largely thanks to Bill Haley and His Comets. They first entered the UK charts in December 1954 with 'Shake, Rattle & Roll', which had first been cut a few months earlier by legendary Kansas City blues shouter Big Joe Turner. Turner's original was full of double-entendre slang, some of which was toned down in the Haley version, but the band still left in the part in which the singer's *one-eyed cat* (penis) was attracted by a nearby *seafood store* (vagina), which apparently escaped the attention of radio-station censors. Even so, it was clear from both recordings that this was a song about male–female relationships, whereas the subject of the first tune to use the title, Al Bernard's entirely different 'Shake Rattle & Roll', released back in 1919, was gambling, and the shaking, rattling and rolling of a pair of dice.

It was Bill Haley's 'Rock Around The Clock', following close behind 'Shake, Rattle & Roll' into the UK hit parade, which really put the slang word *rock* into worldwide parlance as a musical term. The song stayed only two weeks in the British charts, peaking at number seventeen, but then made a triumphant return ten months later after being used as the title music to the film *Blackboard Jungle* (1955), when it went all the way to number one. Fired with enthusiasm, the *Daily Mirror* immediately cast around for the next dance sensation, The Fish, which they judged 'zany enough to start a craze' in British dance halls – 'As one musician said in awe when he watched the rocking-and-rolling throng below him: "Brother, dig that ocean motion!"'

By July 1956, even the journalists at *The Times* deigned to notice the new phenomenon, and, with an air reminiscent of a BBC film crew making a documentary deep in the rainforest, informed their readers that Bill Haley's new film, *Rock Around the Clock*, 'extols the virtues of "rock an' roll"', and portrays 'American youth finding fulfilment in what seems to be a mingling of primitive dance and ritual'. By mid-September, the same paper was reporting that the film had been banned in 'Birmingham, Belfast, Bristol, Liverpool, Carlisle, Bradford, Blackburn, Preston, Blackpool, Bootle, Brighton, Gateshead and South Shields', suggesting that your chances of viewing it were severely diminished if you happened to live anywhere beginning with the letter B. They did have one enlightened message from the Oldham watch committee, who decided against a ban while nevertheless displaying the uncanny clairvoyance common to censors through the ages: 'There is nothing wrong with the film. Although we have not seen it, we know all about it.'

A different article in *The Times* that month put the blame for any problems associated with rock'n'roll mostly upon the new singing phenomenon, Elvis Presley, under the decidedly non-judgemental headline 'US Scenes Recall "Jungle Bird House At The Zoo"'. However, their unnamed correspondent reporting from America seemed keen to assure readers that it would all be over by Christmas:

> But mercifully it is generally felt to be a passing fad like all the others, though many young people would no doubt like to lay their hands on the commentator who wrote in the *Denver Post* that 'this hoody-doopy, oop-shoop, ootie-ootie, boom-boom-de-addy boom, scoobledy Goobley dump is trash'.

Clearly, it was not just the sound, but the actual *language* of rock'n'roll that was getting up certain people's noses.

Gigging at the nuthouse

IN 1957, ELVIS HAD A SMASH HIT with the single 'All Shook Up', one of twelve of his songs which reached the UK top thirty that year. The expression used in the title was hardly new – for instance, a character in Rudyard Kipling's novel *Captains Courageous* (1897) utters the phrase 'well, you was shook up and silly' (although whether he was also acting *wild as a bug* the author does not record). However, the Presley song made enough of an impact that distinguished *New York Times* reporter Harrison E. Salisbury chose to call his fine 1958 book-length study of American juvenile delinquency and gang culture *The Shook-Up Generation*. Based, as the publisher's blurb explained, 'on personal observation and talks with the youngsters in the candy stores, on the street corners, in the rock'n'roll hangouts where they spend a great part of their lives', it featured a glossary of current slang terms, including the following:

BOP	To fight
COOL IT!	Take it easy!
DIG IT!	Get this!
FISH	An erotic dance similar to the burlesque house grind
GIG	A party
PUNK OUT	Display cowardice

Jazz musicians had been calling their one-night engagements *gigs* for several decades by this stage. When Humphrey Lyttelton published his 1957 autobiography *I Play as I Please – The Memoirs of an Old Etonian Trumpeter*, he explained the term for the benefit of his less hep readers, while recalling his early live appearances at a club in Chelsea called The Nuthouse: 'The "g" is hard as in "gag"… this is the slang expression for a single, one-night engagement as a member of a scratch band'.

As slang, *gig* was old indeed. It appears in the *Canting Crew* dictionary of 1699, where it could be either a nose, or 'a woman's privities'. By the time of John Camden Hotten's *A Dictionary of Modern Slang, Cant & Vulgar Words* (1859), a *gig* was simply listed as 'fun, frolic, a spree', which could also conceivably be had at a musical gathering of some kind, and is not far away at all from Salisbury's New York street gang meaning of 1958. Where the juvenile delinquents and the jazz musicians of that decade would have parted company, of course, would be over the use of the word *bop*, and as for *punk out*, well, it was almost another two decades before punk would be *in*.

Some 1950s slang has lasted the course, whereas other phrases failed to stay current. For example, in December 1954 Elvis stood in Sun Studio in Memphis and introduced the song

'Milkcow Blues Boogie' with a few words to his fellow musicians, Scotty and Bill, suggesting they should all 'get real, real *gone* for a change'. At the time, in that place, this was ultra-hip language. Fast-forward to 1978, and disco act Boney M could be found in charts around the world singing about deceased Russian 'love machine' Grigori Rasputin, declaring him a *cat*, who, apparently, *really was gone*, by which time such slang was roughly twenty years behind the times. *Cool* was still cool (daddy), but *gone* had long since, well, gone.

All mod cons

THE DAWN OF THE SIXTIES seemingly rendered much that had come before unhip as far as the younger population were concerned, including some of the music slang of earlier generations.

Through it all, however, a certain amount of hip slang just refused to die, even as the music that accompanied it assumed newer forms. Hence one of the most exciting English bands to emerge in the 1960s, The Who, made their debut statement – under the name The High Numbers – with a 1964 single called 'I'm The Face / Zoot Suit', which employed up-to-date youth slang in one title, but wartime jazz-speak in the other. As the record company advertising copy put it at the time:

> on their first disc outing,
> four hip young men from london say:
> **i'm the face**
> and wear:
> **zoot suit**
> (the first authentic mod record)

Calling yourself a *face* was current *mod* slang for someone who was a key player on that scene, a trendsetter, one to admire.

Mention of *zoot suits*, however, brings us right back to the days of Cab Calloway, but to the band – and to the teenagers watching them at their regular slot at the ultra-hip Scene club in Soho's Ham Yard – what they would have called a *zoot suit* was something distinctly less extravagant than the 1940s model. As for the word *mod* itself, well, by that point it was fast taking on a life of its own. *Record Mirror*, carefully briefed by the band's *ace face* manager Peter Meaden, was hardly shy about aligning them with the youth movement which had originated in London just as the fifties turned into the sixties:

> How mod are this mod-mad mob? VERY mod. Their clothes are the hallmark of the much-criticised typical mod. Cycling jackets, tee-shirts, turned-up Levi jeans, long white jackets, boxing boots, black and white brogues and so on to the mod-est limits.

Mods were tabloid fodder by then, courtesy of the well-publicised seaside disturbances at resorts like Clacton and Margate in 1963 and 1964. When not enjoying bracing days out at the beach, they were also making news in London: 'Girls screamed and chairs flew as fights between the "mods" and the "rockers" led to several casualties at the Lyceum Ballroom in the Strand last night,' said a front-page report in the *Daily Express* in May 1963. However, despite frequent mentions of the m-word in the newspapers, readers might well have been confused as to what exactly a *mod* was supposed to be, since the meaning of this slang word had shifted comprehensively over the previous ten years.

Secondary modernists

A RELATIVE OF MINE RECALLS being at a school dance as a teenager in 1953, and a boy asking her the mysterious question,

'Are you *trad* or *mod*?' This was almost a decade before the chart success on both sides of the Atlantic of *trad* clarinettist Acker Bilk – although it is not clear how many record buyers in Idaho were aware that *acker* was Somerset slang for *friend*, while the word *trad* meant so little over there that Richard Lester's UK music film *It's Trad, Dad!* (1962) was renamed *Ring-a-Ding Rhythm* for the American market. The division in the fifties over *trad* and *mod* was between traditional and modern jazz – the former exemplified in the UK by bandleaders such as Humphrey Lyttelton and Ken Colyer, and the latter encompassing the various strands which had evolved following the late 1940s bebop trend, played by musicians such as Miles Davis or Gerry Mulligan. In the same week that a key modern jazz figure, Dave Brubeck, made his UK debut in 1958, Kingsley Amis, normally a trad man, complained in his weekly jazz column for the *Observer* about the tendency of trad bands to play endless versions of 'When the Saints Go Marching In', 'one more performance of which will either give me the screaming ab-dabs or send me over to the modernists, body and soul'.

The word *modernist* cropped up regularly in Amis's jazz column that year. However, the following March a new development in the meaning of the word was reported in the same paper, when the writer Clancy Sigal interviewed a North London street gang called The Punchers. Sigal was from America, and numbered among his friends the likes of Nelson Algren and Studs Terkel, and it was his then-fashionable Stateside appearance which helped him gain the trust of the gang:

> This 'manor' – a North London tenement neighbourhood – is theirs by right of birth and conquest. They sit in all-night cafes, 'tooled up' sometimes with knives and 'choppers' and crank handles, and wait for 'pullings' (challenges), or else go out to meet and, in the last resort, create them. … My character

reference for the night was Allan, who had grown up with them 'on the manor' and owed them his pledged loyalty, even though now he was planning to marry and move away. He said: 'The way you cut your hair makes it easier for them to accept you. You're what we call a modernist.' It's the new trend with them, cutting their hair short *à la* St Germaine [sic] de [sic] Pres and listening to the Modern Jazz Quartet and searching hard for 'intellectual' words.

These were some of the young *modernists* whose name was later shortened to *mods*, who would then go on to clash with bike-riding, leather-jacketed *rockers*, especially when there were press photographers and newsreel cameras in attendance. By then, however, many of the original late 1950s modernists had abandoned the scene. In 1963, the year of the first beachfront scuffles, there were plenty of references to mods in the press, but the waters were already becoming muddied. Shirley Lowe wrote an article entitled 'Mod Or Trad?' for the *Daily Mirror* in March, but she was speaking strictly about different types of jazz fan, not the scooter-riding youth cult. However, when the paper's veteran show business correspondent, Donald Zec, referred to new pop sensations The Beatles in September as 'four cheeky-looking kids with Stone-Age hairstyles', many youngsters wrote in to complain. Rose, from Chelmsford, argued that 'Zec made them out to be thick-headed Rockers, but all their fans know them to be Mods', while 'Two Very Angry Fans' from Aldershot called them 'handsome Mod boys who deserve every penny they get'. Few people these days, when asked to name a mod group, would mention The Beatles, but the band were indeed photographed at a British seaside resort that summer, as the *Mirror* reported in August, although their antique full-body swimwear was more 1924 than 1964:

The sun is shining. On the beach, four young men in striped

bathing suits and straw boaters go into a song and dance routine. ... the four young men larking about on the sands at Weston-super-Mare are (left to right) Paul McCartney, John Lennon, Ring Starr [sic] and George Harrison – the Beatles, appearing at the local Odeon.

A selection of genuine mods were interviewed in 1963 by *Woman's Own* journalist Jane Deverson, who eventually, together with the writer Charles Hamblett, combined the results into the very fine book-length youth study *Generation X* (1964). One told them, 'a mod will pay up to thirty guineas for a suit and up to £5 for a shirt. Most popular is John Michael, the Mod Shop in Carnaby Street, Soho. The Dunn's shops are fab for hats. We pay up to £5 for shoes and £2.10s. for a hat.'

Many of the interviewees were aged fifteen or sixteen, so the fact that they could pay roughly three times what high-street retailer John Collier was asking for a suit that year – while a good pair of men's Hush Puppy shoes could be had elsewhere for £3.50 – gives an idea of the spending power helping to fuel the new teenage fashions. Deverson and Hamblett's book directly inspired the name of the 1970s punk band fronted by Billy Idol, but the phrase *Generation X* now means something else entirely in many people's minds, thanks to the 1991 debut novel by Canadian writer Douglas Coupland. He seems to have been unaware that it was already the title of a well-respected book, although the band themselves had name-checked it in various late 1970s interviews with the music press. In a 1989 piece of the same name from *Vista* magazine, Coupland wrote, 'British punk rock star Billy Idol calls them Generation X. Specifically, they are college educated people born between 1958 and 1968 to middle and upper-middle class families.' Given the overwhelmingly working-class backgrounds of the people interviewed in the 1964 book, this represented a major distortion of the meaning of the phrase, quite apart from the fact that the generation under discussion was an entirely different one, and the London punk band themselves were hardly singing about the lives of 'upper-middle class families'.

This is the famous Ringo here, gear fab

IN 1963, THE YEAR OF THE BEATLES' huge breakthrough, a rock band formed in Stockholm who called themselves the Hep Stars – a name which belonged more to the days of Calloway than the Cavern. They achieved great success in Sweden, and a certain Benny Andersson joined their line-up the following year, a decade before he and ABBA won the Eurovision Song Contest with his catchy but historically flawed summary of Bonaparte's behaviour at the close of a long and bloody career.

Hep was unhip in England and the US by then, but language was moving fast in those days. Consider, for example, the slang-heavy cover of issue number six of an American comic called *Go-Go*, published in April 1967, under the slogan 'We're So In, We're Out!'. 'Like WOW!' it shrieked. 'We got a brand new contest! "Name The Mod Swinging Group!"' Elsewhere on the same page, they invited their readership of twelve-year-old girls to 'Join the IN Crowd' and also to 'Turn On with Petula Clark'. Just a year or two earlier, some of these words would have been adult slang, and ultra-hip, now they were fodder for schoolchildren and the mass market. The use of the word *mod* here was some distance removed from the youth cult which originated in London half a decade earlier. Similarly, while it was only the previous year that acid-culture guru Timothy Leary had urged people to *turn on, tune in, drop out*, already *Go-Go's* editors were using *turn on* in a watered-down, non-drug- or sex-related sense.

The word *mod* was already a lost cause, operating as a short-hand for anything up to date and modern, which – since old was bad and new was good in the brave new world of the sixties pop-culture consumer – might also have been indiscriminately labelled *groovy* or *far out*. Then, in 1968, US television audiences were treated to a new crime show about a group of undercover American police named *The Mod Squad*, brought to the screen by producer Aaron Spelling (later responsible for *Charlie's Angels* and *The Love Boat*). Unsurprisingly, bouts of fisticuffs between cast members and assorted rockers on Clacton seafront were few and far between.

America may have taken the word *mod* to its heart, but how different things might have been if they had seized instead upon the linguistic possibilities presented by Lonnie Donegan's State-side successes. He blazed a trail from the UK into the US charts eight years before The Beatles, and then in 1960 Atlantic Records – impressed with how Lonnie's new music-hall-flavoured single 'My Old Man's A Dustman' had come from nowhere to the top of the British charts in just one week – took out a full-page advert in *Billboard* magazine, complete with a photo of the man himself peeking over the top of a cartoon dustbin. Virtually no one in America had a clue what a dustman was supposed to be, so the song was subtitled 'Ballad Of A Refuse Disposal Officer'. Since the lyrics themselves were shot through with cockney slang, the advert came weighed down with handy linguistic advice for the US consumer, thoughtfully provided to Atlantic by Donegan's manager, Cyril Berlin:

ENGLISH–AMERICAN GLOSSARY OF TERMS

Flippin' Skint –	'mighty broke'
Gorblimey Trousers –	'workman's trousers'
Council Flat –	'local government apartment'
Daisy Roots –	'cockney rhyming slang for boots'

Sadly, this expensive campaign failed to have the youth of America strolling down the road in a pair of *gorblimey trousers*, looking a *proper nana*, and muttering wistfully about the Old Kent Road, despite the fact that numerous folk singers in pubs the length of Britain were even then dressing up in their finest imitation Woody Guthrie attire and singing about dustbowls, shotgun shacks and a Mississippi river most of them had never seen. However, three years later, the worldwide success of The Beatles made the port city of Liverpool an object of transatlantic longing for some, and certainly helped popularise those slang words of approval *gear* and *fab*.

By the time of their second feature film, *Help!* (1965), such language was commonplace enough that a scene was included in which a Scotland Yard superintendent, played by Patrick Cargill, attempts to prove his mimicry skills to George Harrison by picking up the phone and saying, 'Hello there, this is the famous Ringo here, gear fab. What is it that I can do for you, as it were, gear fab.' *Fab* meaning *fabricated* was well established after the war, because of the name given to the temporary ready-made housing built at that time, *pre-fab*. There was also a detergent powder in the late 1950s called Fab. However, *fab*, as a shortening of *fabulous*, was certainly in use at the start of the sixties, before The Beatles had released a record or come to public prominence. The *Observer* columnist Pendennis, writing on the first day of 1961, pegged *fab* as playground slang:

> Our research unit which has been looking into children's vogue-words reports that, after several years' service, 'super' is right out of fashion – about as dated as 'top-hole' and 'ripping,' in fact. 'Super-sonic' is the modish superlative and, among the kindergarten set, plain 'sonic' is preferred. 'Fab' or 'fabulous' may still be used, however, without risk of being thought *passé*.

Yet *fab* had staying power, and millions of children would have then heard the word used frequently in the dialogue of the new TV series *Thunderbirds* (1964–6), in which glamorous Lady Penelope was chauffeured around in a pink Rolls with the number plate FAB 1. By this stage, the media had already begun referring to The Beatles as the *fab four*, encouraged by the band's press agent, Tony Barrow, who coined the phrase.

Nun of the above

THE SAYING THAT'S THE GEAR! as a term of approval appeared in a 1925 book entitled *Soldier and Sailor Words and Phrases* by Edward Fraser and John Gibbons, and had been shortened to *gear* by the 1950s. With the arrival of the music style known as *Merseybeat* or the *Liverpool Sound*, the public became accustomed to hearing the word used in interviews with groups from that port city. In 1964, when Gerry Marsden of Gerry and the Pacemakers was asked by the *Daily Mirror* to comment on the news that his group was to star in a feature film, he was reported as saying, 'It's fab, gear and lovely!', although Cilla Black, talking to the *Daily Express* a couple of months later, employed the term *fab gear* simply to mean *trendy clothes*. The word had come a long way since Jonathan Swift's day, when it functioned instead as a venerable term for what the *OED* properly refers to as the *organs of generation*, as used here in *A Tale of a Tub* (1704):

> And whenever Curiosity attracted Strangers to Laugh, or to Listen; he would of a sudden, with one Hand out with his Gear, and piss full in their Eyes, and with the other, all to bespatter them with Mud.

Oddly enough, the publication of Mark Lewisohn's epic work of Beatles scholarship *All These Years, Volume One, Tune*

In (2013) finally seems to have debunked the much-related story of John Lennon in the band's Hamburg days whipping out his own *fab gear* and urinating on a group of passing nuns.

They don't run trains there

AS THE HIPPIE ERA ROLLED into view, a good example of a slang phrase which was worked into the ground by everyone from *freaks* to old fogey broadsheet journalists was *far out*. Indeed, if a television comedy series today wanted to depict a typical acid casualty of the Summer of Love, then outfitting someone in a reeking Afghan coat, tangled fright wig and beads, and having them flash a peace sign while muttering, *far out, man*, would probably tick most of the boxes, so enthusiastically had some original hippies adopted the new counterculture code. As Anthony Haden-Guest remarked in a 1967 issue of *Oz* magazine, 'The British Empire spends 200 years unloading beads on the natives. In 9 months we get them all back again.' Elsewhere in the same issue, an equally deadpan attitude to prevailing trends was displayed by a firm selling newly fashionable light-show equipment for concerts, using the advertising slogan, 'TURN ON / TUNE IN / DROP US A FIVER FOR A HOT LINE TO INFINITY'.

As an expression, *far out* was well established before the sixties began, and is yet another example of a phrase which originated among jazz musicians before going mainstream some time later. Tracing the term through the pages of *Billboard* magazine, it surfaced, for instance, in a review of jazz saxophonist Earl Bostic's 'My Heart at Thy Sweet Voice' (1954), a modern jazz take on a French tune from the 1870s ('Bostic rides mighty far out on this classical melody from Saint-Saens' opera "Samson and Delilah".) Unsurprisingly, their reviewers also reached for those words again in 1959 when considering Jack Kerouac's jazz-backed spoken-word LP *Poetry for the Beat Generation* ('Most hearers will call the Kerouac manuscripts far out'). By 1962, *far out* had become an accepted category in the jazz world, as referenced in an article in *Billboard* which gave record-shop owners advice on how to arrange their stores:

> Gone are the days when a dealer could throw all his swinging merchandise in one browser box labelled 'jazz'... Leading lights in the avant garde or ultramodern category are Ornette Coleman and John Coltrane. These artists along with others in the far out groove seem to sell best to college clientele.

Coleman and Coltrane were serious artists, but *Billboard*'s reviewers also praised the 'far-out' dialogue and 'amusing jive talk' on veteran TV announcer Don Morrow's jazz-backed spoken-word LP *Grimm's Hip Fairy Tales* (1961), in which the likes of Hansel and Gretel received a beatnik makeover:

> These two little round cats with the square handles [straight names] shared a pad at the edge of Treesville with their Big Daddy, who was a flunky, and a Big Step-mama, who was slightly off-key. Man, she didn't dig the patter of little feet, no-wise...

In fact, by the latter half of the fifties, the term *far out* was so well grounded in jazz circles that it acquired its own ultra-hip slang variant, *they don't run trains there*. Its meaning at that time was more elastic, however. *Life* magazine, for instance, used it in a 1959 headline about the new US space exploration programme ('LIFE Is With It In A Far Out Era'), then in 1961 applied it to experimental theatre ('Samuel Beckett's far-out classic, *Waiting for Godot*, had a TV showing this year to a million viewers'), and cinema in 1963 (under the virtually unintelligible headline

'Foofs, Spoofs Are Far Out And Big'), before finally reporting on the making of the *Sergeant Pepper* album with a 1967 article entitled 'The New Far-Out Beatles'.

Once again, however, jazz and beatnik language was so successfully co-opted by the hippies of the sixties that to this day *far out* conjures up that decade. With the rise of the underground press in the second half of the 1960s, such words were then thrown around like confetti, in a setting far removed from the publications of the previous decade, so that by 1970 *Oz* magazine could be found running a cartoon showing a woman on the phone, entitled 'The Obscene Phone Caller And How To Handle Him', in which she is saying, 'Wow! FAR OUT!!! Really? Hold the line, I gotta go get my dildo! And some dope!' The times, as Bob so rightly observed, they were a-changin'.

Tolkien bit my generation

THE NEW COMMUNITY OF FREAKS, *potheads*, *groovers* and so-called *beautiful people* expressed themselves in the language found in songs of the era, a cross-section of which survives in the small ads they placed in publications such as the *International Times*, a London newspaper whose original run was from 1966 to 1973. Here was a place to find like-minded band members ('WANTED: Musically "turned on" Bass and Drummer'), genuine romance ('THREE RAVERS seek three dolly girls sexual days or nights. Photographs appreciated', and 'Due to temporary absence of wife, Kinky woman wanted') or simply experience the imminent arrival of the Messiah in Berkshire ('LOVE IN / LOVE OUT! GATHERING of the communes in wooded park. Free food. Light shows – films. 11 am. Big Red God descends from sky. Come in your thousands. Bring friends. Love. Peace').

These particular examples appeared between February and May 1968. Readers at that time could also find George Harrison being quoted in an Indica bookshop advert recommending *Autobiography of a Yogi* by Paramhansa Yogananda ('It's a far-out book, it's a gas'), while in the same issue, acid guru Timothy Leary was busy as usual spouting the new buzzwords of the doped-up generation in an article entitled 'You Are A God, Act Like One' (If you *'turn on'* without *'tuning in'* you will get psychotically *'hung up'*. Every *'bad trip'* is caused by the failure to *'tune in'*). His famous phrase, *turn on, tune in, drop out*, first surfaced in 1966, and then, in their 1967 song 'A Day In The Life', The Beatles expressed a serious wish to *turn you on*, earning a broadcasting ban from the BBC on account of the presumed drug connotations of the phrase. Leary himself had also dipped a toe in the LP market, once in 1966 with a purely spoken-word record titled after his famous slogan, then again in 1967, under the same title, but with a fashionably Eastern-influenced musical backing. There were tracks named 'Freak-Out', 'The Turn On' and also 'All Girls Are Yours' (which presumably came as reassuring news to the man in the *International Times* small ads experiencing 'temporary absence of wife').

Marc Bolan, who began as a mod *ace face*, then passed via garage rock and acoustic folk before emerging as a glam rock superstar, had a deep love of words and slang of all kinds, which he poured into his lyrics and his interviews of the time. As he explained to the underground publication *Gandalf's Garden* in 1968, promoting the debut LP by his duo Tyrannosaurus Rex:

> Names, strings of words, odd books gas me, names of herbs just break me up, freak me out completely, I can groove a whole story out of just the name of a herb. It represents so many images to me I have to write them down so other people can dig it.

As can be seen, there is a significant amount of jazz slang surviving in this typical example of 1968 London hippie language. In those days Bolan could title a song 'Frowning Atahuallpa (My Inca Love)', yet switch to 1950s slang when calling a track on the same record 'Hot Rod Mama'. His song titles over the next few years, not to mention his lyrics, provide a nice cross-section of slang from various decades. For example, the name of the B-side of 'Children Of The Revolution' (1972) reached back to the 1940s, 'Jitterbug Love', whereas other song titles employed contemporary US slang, such as 'Rip Off' (1971) or 'Main Man' (1972). One of his biggest hits was 'Get It On' (1971), a slang phrase that was defined as follows in Eugene E. Landy's *The Underground Dictionary* (also 1971, although oddly the expression was not included in Clarence Major's *Black Slang – A Dictionary of Afro-American Talk*, published twelve months earlier):

> GET IT ON v. 1. Have sexual intercourse. 2. Take drugs. 3. Go, leave.

For its American release, the T Rex single was retitled 'Bang A Gong (Get It On)', having appeared over there in a year when a band called Chase had a tune of the same name, and Edgar Winter's White Trash were also in the market with a different song entitled 'Let's Get It On'. The lyrics to Bolan's song used the phrase in the sexual sense, and this was also very much the case when Marvin Gaye entered the field with his classic 1973 LP *Let's Get It On*, as Marvin's own sleeve notes made clear for anyone foolish enough to think that the title might perhaps mean *let's go, leave*: 'I can't see anything wrong with sex between consenting anybodies. I think we make far too much of it. After all, one's genitals are just one important part of the magnificent human body'. Just in case anyone had still missed the point, one track included the sound of two people supposedly utilising their magnificent human bodies for just such a purpose, earning a credit on the sleeve from Marvin: 'P.S. Those sex noises on intro of "YOU SURE LOVE TO BALL" are Madeline and Fred Ross'. This, of course, was using the word *ball* as slang for sex – a common enough American expression by that stage, although it could also mean just having a good time. Back in 1958, the title character in 'Good Golly Miss Molly' by Little Richard *sure likes to ball*, and radio censors probably assumed that this was a relatively harmless phrase for partying or dancing, but the specifically sexual meaning already existed by that stage, and the phrase had appeared in William Gaddis's 1955 postmodern novel *The Recognitions*.

Crummy bleeding-heart punk with a big mouth

NOT EVERYONE MAKING A RECORD in the late 1960s was following the Maharishi, dressing up as a medieval bard, *getting it together in the country* or communing with their inner hobbit. Following on from the earlier primal garage band sounds of The Sonics, Them, The Downliners Sect or The Standells, the hugely influential example of The Velvet Underground, The Stooges and then The Modern Lovers and the New York Dolls eventually paved the way for the initial outbreak in 1976 of what came to be known as *punk rock*.

The word *punk* was an insult worn as a badge of honour. Punk had meant *whore* since the year 1575, and through its years as criminal slang it had been a term of abuse to throw at both men and women for nearly all of the time in between then and now. Clint Eastwood's gun-toting title character in *Dirty Harry* (1971) was hardly looking to flatter his opponent in the final showdown when taunting him with the often-misquoted words,

'You've got to ask yourself one question. "Do I feel lucky?" Well do ya, punk?' Similarly, in Donald Hamilton's 1966 crime novel *The Betrayers*, the word was used in exactly the same way:

> 'I'll just have to kill you, punk.'
> He licked his lips. 'Don't call me punk!'
> 'Why the hell not? You are a punk, just a crummy bleeding-heart punk with a big mouth.'

When New York punk rock emerged kicking and screaming from a small Bowery club named CBGB, equipped with Richard Hell's spiked haircut and ripped T-shirt and The Ramones' buzzsaw guitar sound and leather jackets, it also brought with it a language that suited stripped-down two-minute songs as opposed to some of the meandering, free-form *progressive* music which had held sway for some years. These were people whose notion of what constituted a decent song title was 'Now I Wanna Sniff Some Glue' (Ramones, recorded February 1976), as opposed to, say, 'Fanny (Be Tender With My Love)', a mainstream pop single by the Bee Gees released the previous month, which reached number twelve in the US charts. Back in August 1974, The Ramones were filmed at CBGB playing several songs, including a fine example called, significantly, 'Judy Is A Punk', and in the same year the original line-up of the band Television, with Richard Hell on bass, regularly performed his then-unrecorded song which provided the alternative name for the new movement, 'Blank Generation'.

When The Ramones played two hugely influential shows at the Roundhouse in Camden Town in July 1976, they brought their songs about *punks*, *runts* and *geeks* to the London outsiders who were forming bands such as The Clash and The Damned, and were also seen by the Sex Pistols, who had been gigging under that name since the previous autumn, but had not yet released a record. This was a month when primitive things were stirring in the musical undergrowth of the UK, but the overall musical climate was also such that *prog rock* mainstay Jon Anderson from the band Yes could release his debut solo LP three weeks after those Ramones shows – a concept album about a race of aliens and their journey through space, with the Tolkienesque title *Olias of Sunhillow*.

It's the buzz, cock

THE SEX PISTOLS WAGED VERBAL WAR on all manner of hippie language, deliberately employing the once-fashionable words of the previous generation – for instance, when filmed by Thames TV's *Today* show, on 1 December 1976. When the interviewer, Bill Grundy, sarcastically drew a comparison with the band's songs and classical music, saying, 'Beethoven, Mozart, Bach and Brahms have all died,' Johnny Rotten claimed that these were the band's heroes. 'Are they?' asked Grundy. 'Oh yes,' replied Rotten, dripping with fake sincerity, 'they really *turn us on*.' In the single 'God Save The Queen' (1977), his cry of *we mean it, maaan* parodied the hippie habit of ending most sentences with the word *man* – a usage derived from 1940s jazz musicians – and so the lengthened pronunciation, *maaan*, became a newly minted ironic slice of British punk slang. The first punk band I saw live was X-Ray Spex, promoting their debut single 'Oh Bondage, Up Yours!', in October 1977, playing to around fifty people in a half-empty hall in Portsmouth. The tiny advert in the local paper which had alerted me to the show also mockingly co-opted 1960s language, billing them as 'EXCITING LONDON BEAT COMBO X-RAY SPEX'.

One of the greatest punk bands of them all took their name from an instance in which outdated groovy language met a vintage cockneyism. In February 1976, a new musical TV series opened on ITV called *Rock Follies*, written by American dramatist Howard Schuman, who had moved to London in the late 1960s to avoid being sent to fight in Vietnam. *Time Out* previewed the series in an article headlined 'It's The Buzz, Cock!', which derived from the following dialogue spoken by Julie Covington's character, Dee:

> It's the buzz, cock. When you sing the rock music you get this buzz... I mean it ripples only not gently, in great waves, arms, fingers, groin, knees, toes, throat, mouth, head, loud, terrifically loud head buzz...

Calling people *cock* had been a familiar part of English speech dating back to the 17th century – 'Well done old Cocke,' says a character in Philip Massinger's play *The Unnaturall Combat* (1639) – but was already anachronistic by the mid-1970s, when it was more likely to be sniggered at because of the sexual double meaning, while the rest of the dialogue had more in common with scenes in the 1960s 'American tribal love rock musical' *Hair* by Jerome Ragni and James Rado. Nevertheless, something about the incongruity of the phrase appealed to Howard Devoto and Pete Shelley, and so they duly named their new band Buzzcocks. The fictional all-female group in the series were called The Little Ladies, whereas in real life the pioneering female punk band who formed in London that year chose a defiantly less twee-sounding name, The Slits.

It was an era in which punk shows were banned from venues, and certain punk records from the radio on account of their lyrics, but it was the Sex Pistols who fought the great punk language battle in the British courts, over their use of the venerable English slang word *bollocks*, which as standard English dates back a thousand years. As a plain word for the testicles it can be found in everything from Caxton's *The Myrrour of the Worlde* (1481) – 'their own genytoirs or ballocks' – to the Restoration poems of John Wilmot, 2nd Earl of Rochester ('the Charmes our Ballocks have'). In the sense of it being a term for an idiot, it was used, for instance, in 1916 by James Joyce in *A Portrait of the Artist as a Young Man* ('I'm a ballocks – he said, shaking his head in despair – I am and I know I am'). Numerous British children studied William Golding's novel *Lord of the Flies* (1954) at school in the seventies – and seem to have survived the experience, despite it containing the phrase *bollocks to the rules* – but somehow none of this prevented a prosecution being launched in 1977 as a result of the Sex Pistols' LP title *Never Mind The Bollocks*. A Nottingham record-shop manager was charged under the 1889 Indecent Advertisements Act for displaying publicity material relating to the album in his window, which resulted in a court case with experts on both sides debating whether the word *bollocks* was obscene, including John Mortimer, QC, for the defence, who said:

> This is a word that has been used countless thousands of times in this country not just in factories but in the corridors of law courts. It is part of life in 1977. One must consider whether there is a man, woman or child who does not know this word. One wonders whether a word which anyone can find in the dictionary which has been used since Bible times should be singled out for prosecution just because it is attached to a highly popular group of musicians.

The presiding magistrate, Mr Douglas Betts, eventually conceded the point, seemingly through gritted teeth: 'Much as my colleagues and I wholeheartedly deplore the vulgar exploitation of the worst instincts of human nature by both you and your company we reluctantly find you not guilty.'

Or, as most punks had long since concluded, legally speaking, the whole case was bollocks from start to finish.

TEN

BURN, BABY, BURN

Crumpet by gaslight

ALTHOUGH SOME RECORDS HAD MANAGED to slip through a fair amount of double entendres in earlier decades, as the 1960s gave way to the 1970s, censorship gradually eased even more, to the extent that slang references to sex and drugs in the lyrics and titles of songs became more openly acceptable. Sometimes they were surprisingly overt. A prime example would be Max Romeo's classic Jamaican rock steady single 'Wet Dream' (1968), which – in addition to its shy, retiring title – also enthusiastically included slang words such as *crumpet* and *fanny*, with a chorus in which the singer repeatedly begged the object of his affection to assume a horizontal position so that he could *push it up*.

It might be assumed that such a record would have difficulty in gaining airplay and sell only moderately, and certainly the BBC responded to its lyrics, as they had so often in other cases dating back as far as the 1930s, by imposing a ban. However, despite this, 'Wet Dream' spent nearly three months in the UK Top Twenty. A glance at the *Melody Maker* listings for the second week of July 1969 shows the record sitting happily right above 'Get Back' by The Beatles, 'My Way' by Frank Sinatra and 'Give Peace A Chance' by the Plastic Ono Band. Further up was a new entry from some band called the Rolling Stones entitled 'Honky Tonk Women', and near the top was 'In The Ghetto' by Elvis Presley, so not much competition there, then. By August, it was still going strong – and also sharing the spotlight with that classic piece of heavy-breathing romance, 'Je T'Aime… Moi Non Plus', by Serge Gainsbourg and Jane Birkin – finally slipping down the Top Twenty at the end of September, just as a newcomer called David Bowie was on the way up with a song named 'Space Oddity'. Strange to say, however, when radio stations these days frequently replay the classic hits of the sixties, they generally forget to programme Max Romeo's biggest hit.

Near-the-knuckle songs from the Caribbean were hardly unusual at that time. Jamaican rock steady singer Lloyd Terrel (aka Lloyd Charmers) issued 'Bang Bang Lulu' (1968), with lyrics that dated back to the 19th century in British and American versions, generally under the title 'Bang Away Lulu'. Then there were calypso artists such as The Mighty Sparrow from Trinidad singing a pimp-flavoured song disguised as the tragic tale of someone forced to part with the family pet, 'Sell The Pussy' (1970), or The Merrymen in Barbados boasting about the dimensions of their 'Big Bamboo' (1969), in which a man's girlfriend rejects sugar cane on the grounds that 'she liked the flavour but not the size'.

If all this sounds as if popular music was becoming ever more suggestive as time went by, consider for a moment the songs of million-selling Lancashire ukulele singer George Formby, such as 'With My Little Stick of Blackpool Rock' (1937) – banned by BBC radio for its various penis-themed double entendres as our hero's rock becomes *sticky* or gets stuck in his pocket, or the winsome 'I Wonder Who's Under Her Balcony Now' (1938) with its cunnilingus subtext, in which he imagines his ex is being kissed beneath the *archway where the sweet william grows*.

Jamaican *ska* and *blue beat* music of the 1960s was a solid favourite with the early mods in the UK. The latter term was basically an alternative name for ska, inspired by the UK record label Blue Beat, which released much of this material at the time, and indeed the words *blue beat* featured prominently in the collage of phrases which made up the cover of the original 1964 edition of Deverson and Hamblett's *Generation X*. Millie Small enjoyed a huge hit on both sides of the Atlantic with her blue beat cover of a mid-1950s song, 'My Boy Lollipop'. (The original, a US recording from 1956 by a teenager from New York, Barbie Gaye, is a ska recording in all but name.) When Smash Records then released Millie's *My Boy Lollipop* LP in the US in 1964, they billed her on the cover as 'The Blue Beat Girl', alongside the following handy explanation for record buyers: 'Some call it blue beat – others call it the Jamaican ska, but whatever you call it, it's a great new dance step.'

Alton Ellis's 'Rock Steady' (1966) was the first song to name-check the new type of slower rhythm which came to be known as *rocksteady*, while another early release in that style, Dandy Livingstone's 'Rudy, A Message To You' (1967), helped popularise the Jamaican slang name for the tough *rude boys*, or *rudies*, found in the dance halls of Kingston and on the streets. A decade later, during the reggae/punk crossover era in which the deejay at Covent Garden punk club The Roxy was Rastafarian Don Letts, and even Bob Marley was moved to record a song entitled 'Punky Reggae Party', the phrase was used by David Mingay and Jack Hazan as the title to their documentary film about The Clash, *Rude Boy* (1980).

By this stage, certain Rasta words – such as *dreadlocks* for their distinctive hairstyle – had become internationally known owing to the popularity of reggae music. Indeed, one incidental pleasure of reading the *NME* in the late 1970s was observing the unconvincing spectacle of a portion of their mostly white British staff peppering their reviews in all musical genres with Rasta and rude boy slang from Jamaica's Trenchtown district, such as *irie* (good), *bloodclaat* (an insult, literally meaning sanitary towel) or *I and I* (me), and occasionally rounding off their pieces with the expression *seen?*, meaning 'have I made myself clear?'

The word *Babylon* in Rasta terms usually referred to the system, the government or the police, as opposed to what was seen as the higher authority of their religion, or more loosely it stood for Western society generally, hence the title of Bob Marley's 1978 live tour LP *Babylon By Bus*. Given the word's biblical origins, it is not a surprise to find it being used a decade earlier in a non-reggae context, in this exchange from Edward S. Hanlon's 1968 novel of New York flower-power dropout slum dwellers, *The Great God Now*:

> 'You know what the hippie is, Leo?'
> 'Tell me.'
> 'He's God's warning to Babylon.'

Similarly, Eldridge Cleaver used the word in his 1969 book *Soul on Ice*, when summing up the attitude of armed black militant resistance to the Vietnam war:

> Why not die right here in Babylon fighting for a better life, like the Viet Cong? If those little cats can do it, what's wrong with big studs like us?

As for the term *reggae* itself, this dates back to the appearance in 1968 – in a slight variant spelling – of the single 'Do The Reggay' by The Maytals, and then, in the same year, another Jamaican vocal group, The Tennors, released a song called 'Reggae Girl'.

Sound system deejays such as Count Machuki and King

Stitt began speaking and vocally improvising over records at live shows from the late 1950s onwards, inspired by jive-talking US jazz and R&B deejays. A decade later, such experiments were finding their way onto records, and the talkover style itself was named *toasting*, a direct forerunner of hip-hop *rapping*. Toasters such as U-Roy would vocalise over pre-existing tracks and rhythms which were often several years old, and producers such as Lee 'Scratch' Perry, Clancy Eccles or Duke Reid became pioneers in that field, often stripping the tracks down to the essential drum and bass rhythms. Years later, in 1984, television presenter Jools Holland visited Jamaica to film a special reggae report for the Channel Four music show *The Tube*. Standing with Lee 'Scratch' Perry outside the gates to the producer's house, Holland asked about the significance of a rusting item of kitchen hardware impaled on the spiked railings of the outside wall. With unerring logic, Lee replied, 'It say that I am a toaster, and I am not a boaster, but a positive toaster.'

To pitch a boogie

THE LANGUAGE OF JAZZ has repeatedly surfaced in the music business, sometimes in ever more disconnected ways. Indeed, when Clarence Pine Top Smith recorded his landmark driving barrelhouse piano composition 'Pine Top's Boogie Woogie' back in December 1928, he not only laid down one of the definitive building blocks which would lead to up-tempo rhythm and blues and then rock'n'roll, he also comprehensively launched the slang word *boogie*, which has since travelled on a very long, strange course as a general term for dance and dancing. When one of the giants of the field, boogie pianist Albert Ammons, was interviewed by Doyle K. Getter of the *Milwaukee Journal* in 1943, he said that before the term existed, this style was known among players by a different name, *heavy bass*. As the article explained, 'the phrase "to pitch a boogie" for years in Chicago's Negro belt had simply meant "to throw a party"'. (The piece also mentioned that other musicians would have a *jam* with pianist Pete Johnson and his band – another jazz term which has stayed the course, among other things providing the name for Paul Weller's group in Woking three decades later.)

Big band *boogie-woogie* was one of the dominant sounds of the Second World War era, and, in country music, a parallel style known as hillbilly boogie developed in the late 1940s, while with the release of 'Boogie Chillun' (1948), John Lee Hooker began a lifelong association with the word throughout his illustrious career. By the 1970s, it could mean many things. There were long-haired good ol' boys down in Georgia playing a style which became known as *southern boogie*, but disco and funk outfits also developed a lasting fondness for the word as the decade progressed: 'Get Up And Boogie' (Silver Convention, 1976), 'Boogie Nights' (Heatwave, 1977), 'Yes Sir, I Can Boogie' (Baccara, 1977), 'Boogie Oogie Oogie' (A Taste of Honey, 1978), 'Blame It On The Boogie' (The Jacksons, 1978) and 'Boogie Wonderland' (Earth, Wind & Fire, 1979), to name just some of the obvious examples.

Since hip-hop music began its ascent in the wake of key releases such as the Sugarhill Gang's 'Rapper's Delight' (1979) and Grandmaster Flash & the Furious Five's 'The Message' (1982) – both of them released and co-written by Sugarhill Records label owner Sylvia Robinson, who in the mid-1950s had been one half of the superb R&B vocal duo Mickey & Sylvia – rap musicians have also demonstrated an enduring allegiance to the word *boogie*. There was New York hip-hop outfit The Boogie Boys (who had a hit called 'A Fly Girl' in 1985), and the same year also saw the formation of influential South Bronx group Boogie

Down Productions, while contemporary hip-hop includes artists such as the succinctly named Boogie (with his song 'Bitter Raps', 2014) and also A Boogie Wit Da Hoodie, whose repertoire includes the song 'DTB' (a title explained in the lyric, *fuck bitches... I don't trust bitches*).

As mentioned in earlier chapters, the slang word *fly* was in use in London two hundred years ago, and is recorded in the third edition of Francis Grose's *Classical Dictionary of the Vulgar Tongue* (1811):

> FLY. Knowing. Acquainted with another's meaning or proceeding.

By the time of the fourth edition, revised by Pierce Egan in 1823, the definition had expanded to also include the following: 'vigilant, suspicious, cunning, not easily robbed or duped; a shop-keeper or person of this description is called a *fly cove*, or a *leary cove*'. Which, of course, would make them, as California punk band The Offspring might have said in 1998, 'Pretty Fly For A White Guy' (1998). As it happens, running parallel to the word's frequent use in black 20th-century popular music – such as Martha Copeland's 1928 blues recording 'I Ain't Your Hen, Mister Fly Rooster' – the word had never really gone out of fashion in England during that time. For instance, in Margery Allingham's 1948 detective novel *More Work for the Undertaker*, one character says of her regular aristocratic sleuth, 'He's very fly, is Mr Campion,' and then, a quarter of a century later, the word occurs in a conversation between two of the stalwarts of John Le Carré's largely public school espionage team in *Tinker Tailor Soldier Spy* (1974), when Connie says to Smiley, 'Not that Aleksey Aleksandrovitch would have fallen for *that*, mind. Aleks was *far* too fly.'

Another slang term much used in hip-hop circles, and

with a similarly venerable history, is the business of calling your apartment your *crib*. In medieval England, the word was applied to the wooden stalls in which farmyard animals slept, but by Shakespeare's time it could also mean a small rough dwelling for human habitation. Eventually, it was established English criminal slang for a home. Once again, Pierce Egan's 1823 version of the *Vulgar Tongue* gives the details of its use as burglar's terminology:

> CRIB. A house. To crack a crib: to break open a house.

The term's journey to America can be logged, for instance, by its appearance in the glossary of Josiah Flynt's 1901 study of criminal life, *The World of Graft*, where he defines a *crib* specifically as a *gambling dive*, and in which *fly-cop* is slang for a detective, and to *squeal* on a fellow crook is also to *rap*. By 1967, *crib* could be found in *Trick Baby*, where a character fresh out of prison asks an acquaintance for help finding a place to stay:

> I gotta find a crib. I went to Thirty-seventh Street to find my foster-folks, but they've moved. Johnny, I'm glad you've got a short [a car], maybe you can help me find a crib and a clean two-buck broad.

His rap is strong

THE WORD RAP ITSELF has been slang for centuries, denoting all manner of things. For example, in the time of Henry VIII, the *OED* informs us, it meant 'the act of breaking wind', whereas in the *Canting Crew* slang dictionary of 1699, a *rapper* was 'a swinging great Lie'.

The generally accepted first use of the word *rap* in the modern context in a song lyric occurs in the 1965 song 'Michael

('The Lover)', by Chicago soul vocal trio the C.O.D.s, a Motown-influenced romantic dance number all about a smooth-talking charmer – 'the girls think that his rap is strong' – written by band member Michael Brownlee. Here was a song about a lover, not a fighter, but this was also a time when the civil rights struggle in America was making headlines, and a new mood was apparent on the city streets. The 25 August 1965 issue of *Life* magazine featured fifteen pages of riot photographs from the Watts district of Los Angeles following a week of unrest that month in which thirty-four people died, using headlines that highlighted some of the new words and slogans that were emerging: 'In A Roaring Inferno "Burn, Baby, Burn"' and '"Get Whitey!" The War Cry That Terrorized Los Angeles'. Reporter Marc Crawford and his photographer, both of whom were black, encountered some people who were in the middle of setting fire to a supermarket:

> At last, 'Whitey' was reacting to them. Set a fire and Whitey has to take cognizance of you: Whitey's buildings were burning. 'I wouldn't give a goddam if they burned my house down as long as I could get his,' one Negro said. 'Mine ain't worth a damn nohow. He's the one with everything to lose.'

The word *whitey* was enjoying a revival around this time, but a century before this it had been in use both in America and also in the early days of colonial Australia and New Zealand. Edwin Hodder, in his 1862 book *Memories of New Zealand Life*, records it being used by the indigenous population a generation or so earlier, while discussing the unsuitability of some of the newly arrived settlers as a food resource: 'If a Maori is asked if he "would like a whitey-man for ki-ki (food)," he will always answer, "Whitey-man no good ki-ki – too much the salt," it being generally believed among them that the immense quantity of salt consumed by the Europeans permeates their whole system.'

A year after Watts, the *Guardian*'s reporter Clyde Sanger returned to see how the district was faring, and commented on two of the new phrases being used on the streets:

> The slogan 'Burn, baby, burn,' was coined in those flames to hold currency until superseded this summer [1966] by 'black power'.

A month earlier, the latter phrase had been the subject of an editorial in *The Crisis*, the official magazine of the NAACP (National Association for the Advancement of Colored People):

> 'black' and 'power,' perfectly good words alone or in certain combinations, but loaded with racial dynamite when joined together in the phrase 'black power.' Like 'white supremacy,' it is a polarizing concept not only setting black against white and vice versa, but also black against all nonblacks. This is a late day for the Negro to start emulating the most despicable characteristic of certain white people. In a pluralistic society, the slogan 'black power' is as unacceptable as 'white supremacy'.

Black Power's Gon' Get Your Mama!

OTHER PEOPLE AT THAT TIME had different ideas, and 1966 was also the year which saw the formation of the Black Panther Party, a movement which would later have a significant influence on hip-hop, not least in the language they employed, in particular on the band Public Enemy. While the phrase *burn, baby, burn* had appeared in a different context in songs such as 'Disco Inferno' (The Trammps, 1976), Chuck D and Public Enemy made an explicit connection with the black nationalism of the 1960s, and one member, Professor Griff, was designated as 'Minister of Information', the same title which Eldridge Cleaver had held in the Panthers in the late 1960s. For some months in 1967 and 1968, there had been attempts to align the Black Panthers with the SNCC (Student Non-Violent Co-ordinating Committee), led by Stokely Carmichael, who was a member of both organisations. He was succeeded in the latter organisation by the tellingly named H Rap Brown, who briefly served as Minister of Justice for the Panthers. Commenting on how Brown came by this name, a 1971 profile in the *Sarasota Herald Tribune* had this to say, by which time he was on the FBI's 10 Most Wanted list:

> Born Hubert Gerold Brown, he earned the name 'Rap' because his fiery, persuasive speeches caused audiences to shout, 'Rap it to 'em, baby.' The tall, gangling leader became known as a militant firebrand who referred to whites as 'honkies'.

Honky was another interesting word which floated up through the black subculture in the second half of the 1960s. Black writer, folk singer and SNCC photographer Julius Lester summarised the linguistic situation as follows in his 1968 book *Look Out Whitey! Black Power's Gon' Get Your Mama!*:

> As Malcolm X once said, everything south of the Canadian border was South. There was only up-South and down-South now, and the whites in both places were 'crackers.' No more did you hear black people talk about 'the white man' or 'Mr Charlie.' It went from 'white man' to 'whitey'; from 'Mr Charlie' to 'Chuck.' From there he was depersonalised and called 'the man,' until in 1967 he would be totally destroyed by the one violent word, 'honky'!

This 1960s world of black activism and revolutionary talk was a familiar part of the household in which the young Chuck D was growing up, a decade and a half before he co-founded his hip-hop group Public Enemy, and there are sections on the official Public Enemy website today giving biographies of people like Eldridge Cleaver. The word *honky* as a term for white people has largely fallen from use in the intervening years since the 1960s – although the Beastie Boys released a B-side called 'Honky Rink' in 1992 which included the phrase *white people only* – but Chuck D employed it repeatedly in a song from the recent Public Enemy LP, *Man Plans God Laughs* (2015), entitled 'Honky Talk Rules'.

Both Public Enemy and the Beastie Boys were stalwarts of the Def Jam record label in the 1980s, which was founded by Rick Rubin in his room, number 712 of the Weinstein Dorm, on the campus at NYU in 1984. The following year – having already entered into business partnership with hip-hop promoter Russell Simmons (brother of DJ Run of the group Run DMC) – Rubin struck a deal with CBS Records for what he described at the time as 'a whole lot of money'. The label name derives from black slang, *def* for great, superb, *jam* meaning record, and this choice of words – especially the initials – were crucial, as Rubin told *Rolling Stone* in 2014: 'The logo was a big "D" and a big "J", and it really was about the DJ's place in hip-hop, being, in a way, equal to that of the emcees.' Flushed with their early successes with acts such as LL Cool J, the label took out a full page in *Billboard* magazine in April 1985, which simply said:

DEF JAM RECORDINGS
Our Artists Speak For Themselves
('Cause They Can't Sing.)

Yet again, though, the slang word *def* was one of those which had been floating around in jazz circles for some decades. Consider the very fine nineteen-minute short film *Ovoutee Orooney* (1947), which preserves a performance of the Slim Gaillard Trio at Billy Berg's Club in Hollywood the previous year, in which Slim holds forth in the *vout* slang language of his own devising.

The rolling opening titles go into some detail about what it terms his *slanguage*, before concluding:

> IT'S
>   OUT
>   OF
>   THIS
>   WORLD... BUT DEF.

Here, though, the word *def* would seem to be an abbreviation of *definitely*, whereas the *OED* gives the derivation of the hip-hop word as probably being a variant of the word *death*, which was how the linguistic commentator of the *New York Times*, William Safire, explained it in 1982, an ironic reversal whereby death is seen favourably, in the same way that the slang term *bad* meant *good*.

Fur Q

WHILE THE LANGUAGE OF BLACK POWER informed some of the more political hip-hop of the 1980s, by the early 1990s some sections of the genre had also become associated with the language of almost cartoon violence and sexism. In a 1992 episode of the BBC2 satirical TV series *The Day Today*, Chris Morris appeared as a fictitious rapper named Fur Q, talking about his habit of shooting random audience members, and seen firing a machine gun while singing a song called 'Uzi Lover', with its heart-warming sample lyric, *cock, bitch, cock, bitch, motherfucker*. Outlining his philosophy, he explains, 'You gotta kill people, to have respect for people.' If this sounds like a caricature, well, obviously, it is, but at the time of writing there is a North Philadelphia rapper called Lil' Uzi Vert – often referred to simply as Uzi – with songs like 'Moist' (2015), which talks about counting large amounts of money, throws in the word *niggas*, and claims *bitches* would like to suck him, and his voice makes them *moist*.

As for the word *respect*, it has come a long way since Otis Redding and then Aretha Franklin were asking for it back in 1965 and 1967. That song was all about mutual fairness in a relationship, but in street slang in recent decades *respect* has broadened out into a general term of approval, while the demand for *respect* has often been used as a thinly veiled excuse for a fight, when a person thinks they have been *dissed* (disrespected) by someone. Not everyone was demanding respect at the time that Otis wrote that song. Here, for instance, is working-class cockney-geezer-about-town Alfie, whose exploits began as a 1963 play of the same name by Bill Naughton, which he adapted into a novel in 1966, the year it was filmed with Michael Caine in the title role. At one point in the book, after a girlfriend says of another of her boyfriends that she doesn't love him, 'but I do respect him', Alfie thinks this to himself:

> That's a word I'd never use, respect. I don't even know what that means. Well, I do – but I've never respected anybody or anything in all my born days. It's not something you do or feel in my walk of life. And I'll expect to go to the grave not having been respected in turn. You can live without it. It's dying out everywhere.

Fine sentiments, but as predictions go, unfortunately it fell at the first hurdle.

Speaking of respect, the word *bitch* has been slung around as an insult in the English-speaking world since before Shakespeare's time. In his 1969 book *Soul on Ice*, Black Panther Eldridge Cleaver reflected on his own habitual use of the word in a letter from prison to his girlfriend:

> I have a bad habit, when speaking of women while only men

are present, of referring to women as bitches. This bitch this and this bitch that, you know.

Cleaver's book had a political intent, whereas the following year a series of crime novels of a more light-hearted nature began appearing, featuring a black private eye named Superspade who exudes a natural scent that somehow makes him irresistible to women. The language which runs through each of the books is a hip mixture of mostly current black slang. In the first, *Death of a Blue-eyed Soul Brother* (1970), the ultra-groovy hero turns a woman down with the words, 'Later, baby. Put those fire buns on ice. One of these days it'll be party time like you won't believe.' She angrily responds by saying, 'It will be cold in the hell of your mama's grave when I ask you again!' to which Superspade says, 'Don't play the dozens with me, bitch.'

The *dozens*, sometimes known as the *dirty dozens*, was an escalating round of insults traded back and forth between people in an argument – a term which dated back decades. Jelly Roll Morton recorded an unexpurgated version of the song 'The Dirty Dozen' when being interviewed by Alan Lomax for the Library of Congress in 1938, preserving lines he had learned around thirty years earlier in the Storyville district of New Orleans. Anyone who has noted the fact that hip-hop music is occasionally prone to using swear words – or indeed Fur Q, if he was in search of further lyrical inspiration – might also like to investigate Morton's rendition, which begins, *you dirty motherfucker, you old cocksucker* and continues on from there.

The Superspade novels appeared under the name B. B. Johnson, and on the rear of the first in the series, there was a cool author photo of a man of about twenty-five with a neatly trimmed Afro, wraparound shades and the overall look of a studious member of the Panthers. The only information given alongside it said, '"B. B. Johnson" is the pseudonym for one of Hollywood's most talented and creative black personalities.' Indeed it was – but he was not the man in the photograph. The real author was in fact fifty-five-year-old jazz songwriter Joe Greene, whose illustrious career included writing slang-inflected material for bandleader Stan Kenton – such as the tragic tale of one woman's search for accommodation, 'I'm Going Mad For A Pad' (1944) – as well as hits for artists like the Mills Brothers, Louis Jordan and Ray Charles. No wonder he had a wide range of slang at his fingertips when writing his crime novels. *Death of a Blue-eyed Soul Brother* was published the same year that another black private dick, John Shaft, hit the bookstands as the titular star of the novel by Ernest Tidyman – one difference, of course, being that Shaft's story was filmed the following year, accompanied by a magnificent Isaac Hayes soundtrack. Another incidental difference was that the author of the latter book was white.

Indie band, indie dustbin

GROWING UP IN BRITAIN in the late 1960s and then the 1970s, if you wanted to hear the new music, Radio One was still the dominant force, and on television *Top of the Pops* provided the weekly fix of chart music, its name sounding like a relic of a bygone era, within just a few years of its 1964 debut. Music genres arrived and then fragmented or mutated, and terminology became a badge of inclusion by which various scenes defined themselves. Some people moved easily from one genre onto the next in a seemingly logical progression – there were *glam rock teenyboppers* in 1971 who would then have called themselves *punks* in 1977, and a proportion of those further realigned themselves by the start of the 1980s under the name *goth*. This last term was a response to both the subject matter of the songs and the black clothes worn on the scene, which on occasion drew inspiration from classic post-war Hammer films, and also the Gothic novels of the 18th and 19th centuries. As slang, however, *goth* already had a venerable history; consider the following, from Farmer & Henley's *Slang and Its Analogues* (1890), in which the association derives not from vampires and Gothic churchyards, but rather the Visigoth army who sacked Rome in the year 410:

> GOTH – A frumpish or uncultured person; one behind the times or ignorant of the ways of society.

Goth was, and remains, a distinct scene unto itself, but much of the guitar music of the last thirty-five years has been filed under the catch-all term *indie* music – a phrase which by the end of the 1990s had become so debased that a further category, *indie landfill*, was developed in order to cover a multitude of generic, often record-company-promoted faceless guitar bands who had clearly spent more time combing their hair for the obligatory promotional video than in writing any kind of memorable material. The word *indie* surfaced in the late 1970s UK punk explosion, initially denoting independent record labels such as Chiswick, Stiff and Rough Trade on modest budgets, as opposed to major labels such as CBS or EMI. Punk fanzines like *Ripped & Torn* published their own charts as a way of nailing their colours to the mast, giving space to singles and LPs which were sometimes selling in their hundreds rather than tens of thousands. Then the music industry caught on, and the first official indie chart was published in 1980. As that decade progressed, it became common to refer to the kind of bands signed to these labels as *indie* bands, but by the early 1990s it was becoming hard to define what the word even meant. For example, a new band called Oasis could be seen topping the indie charts with the song 'Cigarettes and Alcohol' in October 1993, despite having signed to the Creation label just after half of the company had been bought by that well-known struggling indie concern Sony Music, the second-largest music company in the world.

In 1997, Noel Gallagher of Oasis was famously pictured at Downing Street shaking hands with new prime minister Tony Blair, a man who had apparently once harboured rock ambitions back in the 1970s. This was just one example of the Blair government's various attempts to court the youth vote, and in 2003 another involved the issuing of a radio advert aimed at teenagers, which tried to speak to them in their own slang. For this, the government was roundly mocked, not only in the media, but also in Parliament, when Michael Howard put the following question to Tony Blair, as *Hansard* reports:

> I have the text [of the advert] here, and it says: 'You cough up zip 'til you're blingin'', which, as the Prime Minister will know, means, 'You pay nothing until you're in the money.' The advertisement is promoting the Government's policy on student funding, which has yet to pass the House of Commons. Does the Prime Minister approve of that?

To be fair, other politicians had been down this route before, such as David Steele, MP, who featured as vocalist on a 1982 proto-rap single, 'I Feel Liberal, Alright' (1982), and the compliment has now been returned, with the rise of a style known as *chap-hop*, in which people in tweeds such as Mr B the Gentleman Rhymer *freestyle* over a banjulele accompaniment barbed songs of political comment such as 'They Don't Allow Rappers in the Bullingdon' (2012).

Eighteen-year-olds today have the chance to be into *techno, post-rock, hardcore, acid house, happy house, ragamuffin, death metal, thrash metal, dancehall, go-go, straight-edge, punk-funk, dubstep, trance, jungle, emo, grime, psych-rock, drum & bass, grunge, prog, UK garage, Balearic beat, Krautrock* and many, many more genres and sub-genres. Some have their own phrases and slang, but others are more rhythm-based, with language playing a secondary role.

Whereas in the past a particular genre often had a very strong, tribal sense of identity, these days some bands manage to encompass five or six apparently conflicting genres in the course of one album, which of course makes the music journalist's job linguistically tricky, and also that of the fans, when trying to describe their taste in music. Here, to take a recent example, is a line from John Mulvey of *Uncut*'s review of the album *Total Freedom* by Spacin' (2016), which employs a variety of slang terms from various decades: 'A fetishistically scuzzy psych-boogie band, whose choogles often accumulate a near-mantric, motorik intensity'.

Boogie, of course, has a venerable history, and *psychedelia* has been around since the sixties. There is no entry in the *OED* for *choogle* (or *chooglin'*, as it was often written in the 1970s), but it was a mainstay of music reviews back in those days as a way of describing a kind of easy-rolling playing. The word was popularised by Credence Clearwater Revival with a track on their *Bayou Country* LP (1969), entitled 'Keep On Chooglin'' (although in their case *chooglin'* was a slang term for sex). What particularly helps identify the description of Spacin' as modern is the unexpected combination of the word *chooglin'* with that of *motorik* (literally *motor activity* in German, but coined in this sense by journalists attempting to describe the machine-like 4/4 beat used by bands such as Neu! and Kraftwerk). That all these words can now be combined to label just one band shows how fluid the situation has become, musically and linguistically.

Of course, everything is cyclical. The trend among hip-hop artists and fans for wearing baseball caps backwards on the head might look like a development of recent decades, but reversing flat caps was common in pre-First-World-War England among young motorists with an urge for speed, who were known as *scorchers*, the object being to look as if you had been travelling at great velocity. 'It is quite reasonable that an outcry should be made against the scorching motor fiend,' wrote Ferdinand Long in the *Daily Express* in 1903. 'It is the goggle-eyed scorcher who presents a real menace to the earth's population, lamp-posts, trees, houses, etc.' Whether it be reversed headgear as a way of winding up straight society or defining your style, not to mention newspapers decrying the excesses of youthful drivers, most things have been done before.

It used to be that music slang, like music styles, came into fashion and then eventually gave way to the new, so that *hip* supplanted *hep*, *fab* was suddenly no longer *gear*, and saying *groovy* eventually became seriously ungroovy. No longer. Everything is in fashion simultaneously, and what passes for good taste in music these days can either look like open-mindedness, or no taste at all.

As things stand, to paraphrase Sun Tzu, if you wait long enough by the river, the bodies of every supposedly outdated trendy word and musical movement will eventually come floating by.

ELEVEN

Uniform Patterns of Speech

The disappearin' view of a racehorse

In Britain, until the later 1980s, if a tabloid had run a headline saying 'PC GONE MAD', it would have meant that a police constable had lost the plot, embarked on a rampage or otherwise blown a fuse. No longer.

Of course, the term PC in its original context is not slang, but simply a proper name for the ordinary rank-and-file police constable in the UK. However, over the years, officers of all countries have been called many other names, not all of them complimentary. It comes with the job, as local Florida official Sheriff Haskins calmly explains to Simon Templar in the crime novel *The Saint in Miami* (1940):

> 'Son,' he said, 'I've been compared to everything from the disappearin' view of a racehorse at Tropical Park to havin' my maw never find out what my paw's last name was. It ain't never got a rise out of me.'

There have been slang names for the police in Britain since before there was even a properly constituted force, and it was not until 1829 that the Metropolitan Police was founded. People known as *constables* had existed in one form or another in England since the 14th century, whose duty was to help keep order in the parish, but they were not part of some larger, organised body. Over here, police forces in general were believed to be the kind of thing used by despotic foreign rulers to subjugate their peoples, and the idea of setting up anything of that kind was bitterly resisted until the early 19th century. Nevertheless, in Stuart and Georgian times, the criminal community were well aware that assorted watchmen and parish constables were sometimes patrolling the night. If apprehended in London, the culprit would likely be sent for a *course of study* in 'Whittinton's Colledge' – a stay in Newgate prison, so called because London mayor Richard Whittington (c. 1354–1423) not only endowed a college but also rebuilt Newgate – to then be 'strictly examin'd at the *Old-Baily*, before taking their highest Degrees near *Hyde-Park Corner*' (being hanged at Tyburn). These ironic descriptions are taken from a publication called *Memoirs of the Right Villainous John Hall, the Late Famous and Notorious ROBBER, Penn'd from his own MOUTH sometime before his DEATH* (1714), which also includes the line 'out jump Four Truncheon Officers', which in this case is a slang term for some of the guards at Newgate, but still suggestive of things to come. There were a few law-and-order words listed in the short cant dictionary which formed part of this book – *cuffin*, a justice, *harminbeck*, a constable, and *scout*, a watchman – but in essence this was still a pre-police world, in which many of the criminals who were caught seemed to be the ones who loitered afterwards at the scene of the crime, or remained in their usual neighbourhoods, when some discreet fleeing might have been the better option.

Nabbed by the grunters

CONSTABLE AND OFFICER HAVE LONG been respectable names for the police, but the other variants employed by the general public, and sometimes the officers themselves, have generally been slang nicknames, ranging from the cosily descriptive to outright abuse. As noted in an earlier chapter, the 1811 edition of Francis Grose's *Dictionary of the Vulgar Tongue* defined the slang word *pig* as *police officer* – a usage confirmed in an 1823 article in *The Times* about the proceedings at Bow Street Magistrates' Court, in the case of a man named Murphy, who had been arrested in the act of picking someone's pocket. The report itself was entitled 'Police', although this was six years before Sir Robert Peel founded the Metropolitan Police (his name of course giving rise to the slang terms *bobby* and *peeler*). Nicholls, the official who made the arrest, is described in official terms as a *conductor of patrol*, but in his evidence to the court, a much more direct name was given:

> Nicholls added, that he saw the prisoner in company with young thieves at some rowing matches last week, when he pointed witness out to his companions as a *pig*, (a slang phrase for a police officer) and set them to hoot at him.

Unsurprisingly, the year that this article appeared was also the one in which Pierce Egan's revised edition of Grose's *Vulgar Tongue* defined *officers of justice* as *grunters*.

Since the British police were thus being roundly abused in slang terms before they were even constituted as an official body, it probably would not have come as too much of a shock to any former or serving members of the constabulary who happened to be watching the popular television word-based quiz *Blankety Blank* one evening in May 1979, when the answer to the riddle was supposed to be the word *police*. Most of the regular team of celebrities on the panel had duly inscribed this on their boards, and held them aloft at the appropriate moment. However, when it was the turn of Lorraine Chase, the cockney model turned actress, she had opted for something decidedly more colloquial:

FILTH

Here was a classic example of criminal slang, which first appeared in the 1960s, generally spoken as *the filth*. It was used in this form in G. F. Newman's hard-boiled novel of Metropolitan Police corruption, *Sir, You Bastard* (1970), which also contained a useful glossary of the kind of slang in use by police and criminals at that time. When investigating a recent robbery, the novel's main character, Detective Inspector Terry Sneed, says to a man who is *on the file of local talent* (a habitual criminal known to the police): 'It's understandable, John, you need a little extra. A blag [raid] was done up the road... Comes to about a monkey's [£500] worth of tom [*tomfoolery*, jewellery].'

In general, criminals and police have a vested interest in understanding each other's motives and language, and after all, they spend a fair amount of time in each other's company, and their jobs are inextricably linked.

When Alan Hunter's fine series character, Inspector George Gently of the CID, investigates a case involving an East Anglian motorbike gang of jazz-loving *ton-pushers* (aiming at speeds of 100 mph), *reefer-smokers* and *beats* in the novel *Gently Go Man* (1961), this stolidly respectable, middle-aged, pipe-smoking member of the force has to engage with their particular slang in order to have any chance of understanding what has happened. Described on the back cover as a *big-shot screw* (important detective), the inspector is given a tip by a local officer called Setters that the gang are usually to be found at a particular roadside hangout, in a dialogue between the two policemen conducted sarcastically in the jive talk of their quarry:

> 'Try the First and Last café' [Setters] said. 'You'll find it just out of town on the Norwich Road.'
>
>> 'Is it cool, man?' Gently asked.
>>
>> 'Bloody arctic,' said Setters.
>>
>> 'Like I may make the scene after a meal,' Gently said.

In post-war black America, a common name for a police officer was simply *the Man*. For instance, in the Harlem depicted in the novels of Chester Himes, it was enough for his two detectives, Coffin Ed and Grave Digger Jones, to utter just three words by way of an introduction, as here in *The Big Gold Dream* (1960):

> 'We're the men,' Grave Digger said, flashing his shield.
>
> 'You don't have to tell me, boss,' the doorman said.

They were fictional, but plenty of serving and retired US police officers later spoke to Mark Baker for his superb oral history *Cops – Their Lives in Their Own Words* (1985), and again, this sense of having to speak the slang of the street is reinforced:

> These young kids [police recruits] want to be a bunch of PR people. I told them, 'If you're going in there and talk, you got to talk their language.' When I go into a bar in a black area where the fights are going on, I just climb up on the bar, walk down it and kick everybody's drink off the bar. Then I says, 'Okay, motherfuckers, the Man's here. Let's take care of business.'

This somewhat *hands-on* approach would also have been the inspiration behind a fine post-war Australian name for the police, the *wallopers*.

Here comes the b— coppers

PERHAPS THE MOST WIDESPREAD and venerable slang name for a police officer, originally English, but also in common use in Australia and America for the best part of two hundred years, is *copper*. It has sometimes been speculated that this word derives from the shiny buttons down the front of 19th-century Metropolitan Police uniforms, since London's initial complement of 895 constables, who first patrolled the capital on 30 September 1829, wore blue swallowtail coats with a line of eight buttons. However, when seeking out criminals, their job was obviously to apprehend them, which, fifty years earlier, would have had them labelled a *nabber*, or *nabbing-cull*, as in Ralph Tomlinson's satirical poem, 'A Slang Pastoral' (1780):

> Will no blood-hunting foot-pad, that hears me complain,
> Stop the wind of that nabbing-cull, constable Payne?
> If he does, he'll to Tyburn next sessions be dragg'd,
> And what kiddy's so rum as to get himself scragged.

Tomlinson, incidentally, was a member of the Anacreontic Society – named after the Greek poet Anacreon, who extolled the properties of alcohol in his work – which met in a pub on the Strand called the Crown and Anchor, and he wrote the words to their drinking anthem, the 'Anacreontic Song', first published in 1778. Fellow club member John Stafford Smith composed the tune, to which in the 19th century was added a different set of lyrics taken from Francis Scott Key's 1813 poem 'The Defence of Fort McHenry', and that combination became known as a song called 'The Star-Spangled Banner'. So, just as large amounts of 18th-century underworld slang recorded by Francis Grose in Covent Garden – such as *fly*, *pad* and *crib* – eventually made the journey across the Atlantic and are still in use there today, a melody from that same London neighbourhood designed to spur on a convivial group of gentlemen imbibers, such as Dr Johnson and Sir Joshua Reynolds, has lived on to be regularly sung each year to the crowd at the Super Bowl in America by the likes of Janet Jackson, although whether the original members of the Anacreontic Society ever indulged in supposedly accidental *flashing* during their own performances is sadly not recorded.

From *nabbers*, it is a short step to *coppers*, whose most accepted derivation, including that of the *OED*, is from the verb *cop*, meaning 'to capture, catch, lay hold of'; thus, a *copper* is someone who *cops* you for a crime. By the 1840s, this word was certainly current in London, and was recorded in witness testimony during a trial at the Old Bailey on 11 May 1846, when Police Sergeant G9 (Edmund White) was giving evidence about having been assaulted when attempting to arrest a counterfeiting gang:

> When I first entered... a woman screamed very loud,'*Jim, Jim,* here comes the b— *coppers,*' and at that moment the money was thrown out – I have heard the police called *coppers* before.

Although already a slang word, eventually *copper* was itself adapted further into cockney rhyming slang, giving rise in the 1890s to *grasshopper*, copper (which led in turn to a police informer being known as a *grass*, by association), and also further rhyming names such as *bottle & stopper*, and *clodhopper*.

A cockney burglar character, in Dorothy L. Sayers's *The Nine Tailors* (1934), when describing another criminal literally lying low in the countryside, opts not for rhyming slang but for a different term, which dates to the end of the 1890s:

> He said the stupidity of the police was almost incredible. Walked right over him twice, he said. One time they trod on him. Said he'd never realised so vividly before why a policeman was called a *flattie*. Nearly broke his fingers standing on them.

Flattie, or *flat-foot*, conjures up images of the constable walking his beat for mile after mile, while another cockney character in a 1934 crime novel, *Murder Underground* by Mavis Doriel Hay, opts for an equally widespread slang name, saying, 'I don't want those busies around my place.' This word is suggestive of the term *busybody* – which dates back to the reign of Henry VIII – with the implication that the police are prying into someone's affairs. Just a few of the many other variants through the years have included *truncheonist* (1854), *rozzer* (1888), *bull* (1893, largely US), *bogy* (1924), *fuzz* (1929) and *PC Plod* (1971). One of the most famous UK slang names owes a great deal of its popularity to a TV series, *The Sweeney* (1975–8), in which much criminal argot is bandied about by police and criminals alike, and whose title derives from rhyming slang: *Sweeney Todd*, Flying Squad. In its debut episode, Detective Inspector Jack Regan introduces himself and his no-nonsense law enforcement methods to a young thief as follows:

> We're the Sweeney, son, and we haven't had any dinner. You've kept us waiting, so unless you want a kicking, you tell us where those photographs are.

As might be expected, the spin-off novels produced in the wake of the series also played their part in spreading criminal slang across the nation, such as book number six, Joe Balham's *The Snout Who Cried Wolf* (1977), which focused on a police informer. Edgar Wallace had written a crime novel about the same organisation in 1928, simply entitled *The Flying Squad*, in which their rhyming slang nickname did not feature (although it did make its first recorded appearance ten years later in another fine London novel, *The Gilt Kid* by James Curtis). However, the Wallace book contained some interesting contemporary slang, such as when a character named Ann, describing another woman's hair, comments, 'You may have seen her – she is a suicide blonde.' On being asked what this means, she then replies, 'She dyes by her own hand.' This phrase and its punning meaning duly survived the years and made the journey to Australia, prompting INXS to write the song 'Suicide Blonde' (1990), apparently inspired by singer Michael Hutchence's girlfriend Kylie Minogue using the same expression about her choice of hair colour.

There's an Old Bill by the stream

AT THE CLOSE OF THE FIRST WORLD WAR, many young British soldiers who had somehow managed to avoid being slaughtered in the trenches opted to join the police – a steady job, with a chain of command, a uniform and discipline, much as they were used to, but hopefully not quite as dangerous. A popular slang name for any ex-serviceman from the army at that time was an *Old Bill*, inspired by the character in the weekly magazine *The Bystander*, 'Old Bill' Busby. He was created in 1915 by the very popular trench artist Bruce Bairnsfather – a machine-gun captain with the Royal First Warwickshires, who began drawing and publishing ironic scenes of front-line life near Armentières at the start of that year, under the title *Fragments from France*, before being sent home injured after the second battle of Ypres. Old Bill had a pipe, a walrus moustache, balaclava helmet and a laconic attitude to the scenes of chaos around him.

After the war, the name adhered generally to ex-army personnel, and proved a lasting one, perpetuated by the formation of veterans' associations which used the name, as, for instance, in this item about the Prince of Wales from the *Manchester Guardian* in 1933:

During a visit to the exhibition of work by disabled ex-service-men held at the Imperial Institute, South Kensington, he was impressed by the idea under which members of the Old Bill Fraternity promised to purchase not less than five shillings' worth of goods made by war-blinded men. He immediately asked for an enrolment form and there and then paid his sixpence as the initial membership fee and responded to the invitation on the form of the cheerful figure of Old Bill, drawn by Bruce Bairnsfather, to 'put it there, mate', by placing his sig-nature 'along the dotted line.'

Similarly, in 1951, the *Daily Express* was happy to describe the 11th Earl of Egmont as 'the stocky little man with the "Old Bill" moustache', safe in the knowledge that their readers would understand the reference. It is hard to say exactly how the Old Bill moustache and attributes of the former soldiers were then somehow transferred in the public mind to the figure of the ordinary policeman on the beat. As for when exactly this transi-tion took place, the earliest citation found in the *OED* is from the great Frank Norman's 1958 prison memoir *Bang to Rights* – a book rich in working-class London slang of the time, using the author's own distinctive spelling and punctuation:

> Anyway I was out haveing a booz up one night when two old Bill's came up to me and told me they had a warrent for my arrest. Naturally I went potty and asked them what it was all about. One of the coszers [policeman, usually spelt *cozzer*, a blend of *copper* and *rozzer*] told me I was nicked for conning the old bag out of fifteen hundred quide...

This was something of an isolated instance, and the word then only really became widespread during the 1970s, although train robber Ronnie Biggs used the term in a 1979 tabloid inter-view from Rio, and he hadn't been in circulation in the UK since escaping from prison in 1965. Yet when a nineteen-year-old

Teddy boy involved in skirmishes with punk rockers down the King's Road in 1977 used the word as he was talking to reporter Andrew Stephen from the *Observer*, the paper still felt the need to include a translation in brackets for the benefit of their readers: 'If you have a bottle the Old Bill [police] can nick you for having an offensive weapon, see.'

That it was still a relatively novel expression is also suggested by Robert Barltrop and Jim Wolveridge's study of London vernacular, *The Muvver Tongue* (1980), in which the two East End authors asserted that 'no Cockney would use the cuddly-sounding "bobby" or even "bluebottle" for a policeman. "Copper" remains the universal word, and sometimes "flat" (short for flat-foot). "Rozzer" is mostly said by children, and the American "fuzz" has never got going among Cockneys. Recently "old Bill" has come into use, and seems to be growing in popularity.'

Pig's ear and a coffin nail

BACK IN THE MUD OF FLANDERS during the First World War, the original Old Bills devised a very rich selection of slang to help them cope with a world that had fast descended into a nightmare. This was a way of describing things, making fun of them, and mostly disguising the horror with a deadpan irony, because the reality was all too stark. The attitude itself was far from new – for instance, an 1873 edition of *The Standard* newspaper informed its readers that any regiment known for being in the forefront of any action was said, in army speech, to have the largest *butcher's bill*.

This slang came from the ordinary foot soldiers thrown into the middle of the chaos, rather than the self-important statesmen on all sides who had decided that a five-year bloodbath killing nineteen million people and maiming countless more was a sensible idea, and probably good for business.

Eric Partridge, the giant figure of 20th-century English slang scholarship, knew the argot of the First World War soldier at first hand, because he had been one himself. He was born in New Zealand in 1894, but his family had relocated to Australia by the time of the conflict, so he enlisted in the Australian army, and first saw service in Egypt, then Gallipoli and lastly on the Western Front, where he was wounded. He was on observation duty in the infantry at Sailly-le-Sec, near Amiens, on 21 April 1918, and saw the 'Red Baron', Manfred von Richthofen, shot down and killed just over half a mile away.

Having then moved to England after the war, initially to study at Oxford University, Partridge eventually founded a publishing company in 1927, which issued *Songs and Slang of the British Soldier* (1930), written by himself and fellow trench-warfare veteran John Brophy. The basic attitude of the enlisted man – very different from the sort of thing that MPs back home were making patriotic speeches about – is summed up pretty well in a song they sang, which appeared in the book in the following mildly bowdlerised form:

> I don't want to be a soldier,
> I don't want to go to war,
> I'd rather stay at home,
> Around the streets to roam,
> And live on the earnings of a well-paid whore.
> I don't want a bayonet up my arse-hole,
> I don't want my ballocks shot away.
> I'd rather stay in England,
> In merry, merry England,
> And — my bloody life away.

The world described in Partridge and Brophy's book is one

of sudden death, vermin and disease, in which soldiers might be struck down by *silent susan* ('a German high-velocity shell'), a *five nine* (ditto), *asiatic annie* ('a Turkish big gun at Gallipoli') or a *butt notcher* ('sniper', who kept score by notches on the butt of his rifle). They might well be feeling *crummy* ('itchy because of louse bites'), and thinking about the desirability – or the annoying absence of – *coffin nails* (cigarettes), *scran* (food), *pig's ear* (beer), a *bird* ('a young woman, especially in an amorous context') or a *piece* (ditto), which might well prompt them to *go on the razzle* ('make an expedition in search of entertainment') and maybe find a *kip-shop* (brothel) behind the lines. If they succeed, they will probably be called *jammy* ('Lucky; e.g. "he's a jammy bugger!"'), but on many occasions they would generally wind up with *nix* ('nothing. From the German *nichts*') – a situation which could also be summed up in one of the most ubiquitous slang words of those times, *napoo* ('finished; empty; gone; non-existent. Corrupted from the French *Il n'y en a plus* = there is no more').

A wound that didn't wind up killing you could be your ticket to *Blighty*, which the authors defined as 'England, in the sense of home'. This might be something very visible, such as the loss of a limb, but it could also be what the authorities came to call *shell shock*. The latter term was not, apparently, one much favoured by the troops themselves, as the longest-living British survivor of those days, Harry Patch, told the writer Max Arthur in the oral history *The Last Post* (2005):

> 'A bit rocky' was an expression you heard, but nobody ever used the phrase 'shell shock'. Somebody was wounded – but never 'shell shocked'.

Tom Thumb in yer i-diddle-dee

A GENERATION LATER, soldiers were once again coining slang on battlefields across several continents during the 1939–45 war. Anthony Burgess, who commented so astutely on language throughout his literary career, served in the British Army in the Second World War, and later, in a tribute volume to Eric Partridge, had this to say about military life in relation to speech:

> It was in the army that I learned to appreciate the great humorous stoicism of ordinary men and the way in which they expressed it in language. He [Eric Partridge], like myself, was fascinated by the slow folk development from trope to trope in the direction of greater sardonic truth. In 1939 soldiers were saying: 'The army can do anything to you but fuck you.' This, in 1941, had become 'The army can fuck you but it can't make you have a kid.' At the end of the war the army could give you a kid but it couldn't make you love it. I don't know what the latest embellishment is.

This sense of slang being passed on from one unit to another – and from one war to another – is very strong. Troops from New Zealand and Australia fought alongside British regiments in the First and Second World Wars, and each country's soldiers picked up expressions from the others, and indeed, all of them also inherited other slang terms which the 19th-century British Army had employed in its various overseas campaigns. Once American troops first arrived on European battlefields in November 1917, that cross-pollination of language spread further, and a similar pattern followed after their November 1942 debut appearance on European territory in the Second World War. Just to enrich the mix, words in use by one branch of the services would sometimes be adopted by another, so that, for instance, in the 1914–18 war, the Royal Flying Corps' habit of referring to aircraft as *crates* also passed into use among the *Tommies* in the trenches. British Army foot soldiers had been known as *lobsters* in the 18th and early 19th centuries, on account of their red coats, but from around the 1850s, the name *Tommy Atkins* supplanted it, eventually shortened to just *Tommy*. In the 1890s, the fictionalised adventures of Trooper Tommy Atkins were serialised in the *Penny Illustrated Paper and Illustrated Times*, which also helped spread military argot among the general public. In an 1895 episode entitled 'Trooper Tommy's "First War"' he adopts a stray dog that is fond of eating stray scraps of loaf, and Tommy explains that 'as all my room chums noticed his partiality for the bread, they named him "Rooty," that being the Army slang word for it'.

As with most other types of slang – except for the defiantly X-rated – newspapers and magazines have long enjoyed printing choice selections of military speech. In 1921, *The Times* encouraged its readers to contribute British Army words and phrases from the recent war, which were then published. One entrant, from November that year, came up with a fair list of 'typical expressions of general Army slang as he heard it', including *buckshee* (surplus, free), *lash-up* (fiasco), *wangle* (later defined by Partridge and Brophy as 'to procure goods or an advantage of some kind illicitly but without punishment'), *talking wet* (stupid utterances), *cushy* (comfortable, safe, easy) and *muck in* (to share items with your immediate comrades).

Once war had broken out again across Europe, civilians sitting in their Anderson shelters in October 1940 and awaiting the all-clear signal, as German bombing raids on London intensified, could have passed the time by catching up on current army slang and its origins in an edition of the *Manchester Guardian*:

> Although the Army in the first German War made some use

of rhyming slang, it was not allowed to displace many of the old soldiers' words derived from service in India. Some of them, it is true, are still current: in the battalion in which I am now serving (writes 'B') porridge is always 'burgoo' and jam is 'pozzie,' but instead of 'rooty and muckin' for bread and butter we hear of 'Uncle Ned' or 'strike me dead,' and 'roll-in-the-gutter.' The rot had begun twenty-five years ago. Tea was then almost always known as 'char,' but even so I can well remember a sergeant's saying he had got some 'Tom Thumb in his i-diddle-dee,' when he had scrounged some rum and put it in his tea.

Sometimes, of course, despite all the cockneyisms, tea in the British Army was simply tea, as in *Private's Progress*, Alan Hackney's 1954 novel of wartime conscript Stanley Windrush, where the soldiers head for the canteen for *tea and a wad* (cake or a bun). However, knowing the influence of London jargon, Stanley's father, a keen student of old popular songs, asks him in a letter to look out for anyone singing a tune entitled 'Gorblimey innit all right, eh?', whose lyrics he is eager to learn.

Everything's FUBAR in Skunk Hollow

IN AMERICA, EVEN IN PEACETIME, *Life* magazine was always keen to keep its readership aware of military slang trends. '"Shut-eye" is army slang for sleep,' they declared in 1937, employing a phrase which had been British forces' slang since at least the 1890s. Three years later, a corporal in the medical department at Fort McIntosh, in Laredo, Texas, wrote a letter to *Life* claiming that 'we have just about the best slang there is... When I say we, I mean about 17 boys here at the hospital.' The examples he provided included *lapping it up* (drinking beer), *pocket lettuce* (paper money), *chili bowl* (a haircut), *slum* (the main dish at any meal) and *Butch* (the commanding officer). Then in February 1941 – still ten months ahead of the Japanese attack on Pearl Harbor which brought America into the war – the *Manchester Guardian* wrote an article giving numerous examples of US military speech, claiming that 'even an expert of contemporary slang would be lost in the Army camps without a special dictionary':

> 'Blame Hitler' is the answer to all complaints of every variety. 'The old man in the poodle palace' is the commanding general in his headquarters. 'Mit-flapping' (from the slang 'mit' for hand) describes a soldier who tries to win the favour of a superior officer... Regular enlisted men are called 'goons,' while the new recruits are 'jeeps' and 'yard birds,' whose barracks are 'Jeepville' or 'Skunk Hollow.' ... A soldier with long experience is 'dog face,' and the man who shines the officer's boots is 'the captain's dog robber.'

The word *goon* had been an insult for two decades by then – meaning a stupid or oafish person – and would come to be the preferred term Allied servicemen in POW camps used for their German guards – so it is interesting to see it being applied here by ordinary soldiers to their own selves. This was all good clean fun among troops who were on home bases, in a country not yet at war, but in May 1945 information about this kind of slang could perhaps be classed as a military secret, as an article in a New Zealand paper, the *Auckland Star* – based on a report from the British United Press correspondent in London – made clear:

> When the Germans began the Ardennes offensive last December, Lieutenant-Colonel Skorzeny, Nazi master spy, dispatched 150 spies, with American accents, behind Allied lines in the war's most ambitious sabotage operation... They were put into American prisoner of war cages to pick up an accent and slang. They were instructed in American customs, even down to the method of opening a packet of cigarettes. The spies were then issued with American uniforms, weapons and jeeps, but the

Germans made two errors. They did not issue identification discs and they gave the men poor forgeries of American identity cards.

All but ten of the men were either shot while escaping or executed, making the botched operation in US Army slang at the time either a *SNAFU* (situation normal – all fucked up), or probably its more serious variant, *FUBAR* (fucked up beyond all recognition). The former phrase was widespread enough that a disaster-prone cartoon character was created by the US Armed Forces Motion Picture Unit in 1943 under Frank Capra named Private Snafu, who was used in a series of training cartoons shown to soldiers, which were directed by leading figures in the field such as Chuck Jones and Fritz Freleng. Knowing their audience, they spelled out the meaning of the word letter by letter at the beginning, pausing a little before *F* and then saying *fouled up*, aware that army viewers would be familiar with the real version. Indeed, in October 1944, when a Broadway play by Louis Solomon and Harold Buckman entitled *SNAFU* opened at the Hudson Theatre, *Billboard*'s reviewer Bob Francis commented:

> According to [producer] George Abbott's press department, *Snafu* in army slang, means 'situation normal, all fouled up.' G.I. Joe may tell you different, but that at least is a fair approximation.

By the time of the Vietnam war – a conflict of murky origins even for the better informed of those who were drafted, in which young men were taken from a land in which *turning on, digging thy self* or simply *letting it all hang out* were touted in some circles as valid career choices and were then flown direct to a war-torn jungle – the language of US combat troops had become even more stark. New recruits were no longer a *jeep*, they were an *FNG* (fucking new guy), food was not called *slum* but usually *beans and motherfuckers* (a C-ration staple of lima beans and ham), *FUBAR* had mostly given way to *fugazi* (fucked up), *pogue* was an insulting term for non-front-line military personnel (as opposed to the London Irish band The Pogues, who shortened their name from Pogue Mahone, which is Gaelic for *kiss my arse*), and, as ex-combat soldiers explained to the writer Mark Baker for his oral history *Nam* (1981), the slang phrase *double veteran* meant 'having sex with a woman and then killing her'.

Absorbing the milder parts of this slang during your first few weeks in Vietnam was part of the induction course, as Tim O'Brien wrote in his memoir, *If I Die in a Combat Zone, Box Me Up and Ship Me Home* (1973):

> I learned that REMF means 'rear echelon motherfucker'; that a man is getting 'short' after his fourth or fifth month; that a hand grenade is really a 'frag' [fragmentation grenade]; that one bullet is all it takes and that 'you never hear the one that gets you'; that no-one in Alpha Company knows or cares about the cause or purpose of their war; it is about 'dinks and slopes', and the idea is simply to kill them or avoid them. Except that in Alpha you don't kill a man, you 'waste' him.

As a rule, it was the enlisted men at the lower end of the military hierarchy who came up with the slang, but in this particular war one of the commanders at the top coined a phrase which has since passed into the language, usually rendered as *bomb them back into the Stone Age*. This came from the 1965 autobiography of United States Air Force General Curtis E. LeMay (*Mission With LeMay: My Story* – co-written with MacKinlay Kantor), and although he later apparently sought to qualify the statement, the original seems relatively unambiguous:

> My solution to the problem would be to tell [the North Vietnamese communists] frankly that they've got to draw in their horns and stop their aggression or we're going to bomb them

into the Stone Age. And we would shove them back into the Stone Age with Air power or Naval power – not with ground forces.

Scab lifters and gronk boards

FOR AN ISLAND NATION, sea terms have always been a significant part of everyday speech, and over centuries the Royal Navy has built up a large body of slang. When my grandfather joined the navy in 1942, at the start of four years of wartime service, he was given the current edition of the *Manual of Seamanship*, issued by the Admiralty, which contained much useful information concerning navigation, signalling, naval routine, hammock-slinging, life-saving and suchlike. The final chapter dealt with 'Sea Terms and the Boatswain's Call'. Here, alongside more specific expressions such as *athwartships* ('at right angles to the fore and aft line'), lay some words and phrases which have since passed into more general use. *Cracking on* is defined as 'to set more sail', which has now become a way of saying to *hurry up*. A *granny's knot* was defined as 'a term of contempt applied when a reef knot is crossed the wrong way', and a *trick* was a 'spell a man has at the wheel, look-out, chains, etc.' – all words that dated back a long way into the age of sail, and which could also be found in Admiral W. H. Smyth's exhaustive 19th-century reference work *The Sailor's Word-Book: An Alphabetical Digest of Nautical Terms* (1867). The latter contained many technical expressions, of course, but also some fine examples of what the author defined as *galley-slang* – 'the neological barbarisms foisted into sea-language' – and with a due sense of civic pride, I note that my home city made an appearance in the phrase *point-beacher* – 'a low woman of Portsmouth'.

Of course, one thing that the *Manual of Seamanship* and the

Sailor's Word-Book omitted in their lists of nautical terms was the vast profusion of downright smutty slang words to be found on board ship in every generation – a state of affairs acknowledged by the book reviewer of the *Glasgow Herald* in 1886, when praising a new seagoing tale for children entitled *Spunyarn and Spindrift* by Robert Brown:

> We have seldom read better nautical slang. It is not a faithful reproduction, of course, for the habitual language of the forecastle is simply foul, but it is a refined preparation of the real thing, and quite refreshing in its vigorous suggestiveness.

Forty years after my grandfather joined the navy, my cousin David Yates served on board HMS *Antrim* through some of the most intensive air–sea fighting of the Falklands war. When he wrote his book describing those times, *Bomb Alley – Falkland Islands, 1982* (2006), he included a glossary of below-decks navy terms which also displayed a vigorous suggestiveness, such as *pig* ('an officer'), *scab lifter* ('any sickbay staff'), *pongoes* ('any member of the army') and *gronk board* ('noticeboard for displaying pictures and other lewd female memorabilia'). In addition to this, having responsibilities in the ship's catering section, he provided a further Naval Cook's Glossary, decoding the meaning of such gastronomic highlights as *colon collapser* (vindaloo), *leper's hankies* (pizza), *germolene sandwiches* (deep-fried spam fritters in a bread roll), *mermaid's piss* (vinegar), *frog in a bog* (toad in the hole) and, for the discerning palate, *excreta à la Kontiki* (French garlic kidneys on toast).

Whether such delicacies were also available to the sailors in the Royal New Zealand Navy in 1944 is hard to say, but a report in the *Evening Post*, from Wellington, noted that examples of current Navy slang are:– Up Spooks (tot of rum), Gate (idle chatter), Ash-cans (depth charges), "Get a bottle" (reprimand), Plew (tea), Gish (anything extra, like leave)'.

The US Navy was also calling depth charges *ash cans* at that time, as an article in a 1940 issue of *Life* magazine by Oliver Jensen about their nautical slang records, which, given that both navies were active in the Pacific, is hardly surprising. Jensen recorded a fair few current American expressions, such as calling the women they met on shore leave *sea gulls* ('because they follow the fleet'), but, as is usual with occupational slang, many of them had a more venerable history. He writes that they refer to 'the chaplain as *padre* (whatever his denomination) and the chaplain's assistant as *Holy Joe*', the latter expression having appeared three-quarters of a century earlier in John Camden Hotten's 1874 edition of his *Slang Dictionary* as 'a sea-term for a parson'. Similarly, using the word *chow* as a term for 'food in general' would not have surprised the 19th-century British Army in India, as recorded in Yule and Burnell's classic work on the language of those days, *Hobson-Jobson: A Glossary of Colloquial Anglo-Indian Words and Phrases* (1886): 'Chow is "pigeon" [pidgin English] applied to food of all kinds'. Looking back a little further, W. H. Smyth's *The Sailor's Word-Book* (1867) contains the entry *chow-chow*, defined as 'eatables; a word borrowed from the Chinese'.

Finally, Jensen rightly remarked that 'many a common slang expression like "down the hatch" and "tell it to the Marines!" has come from the sea'. At the time he was writing, in 1940, the former was relatively new as a drinking salutation. The first listing in the *OED* dates from a 1931 article in H. L. Menken's magazine the *American Mercury*. A search through British newspapers of the early 20th century for this phrase only reveals stories about people or objects falling down the hatch of a ship. However, in July 1936, the *Daily Express* published a report on the return to Southampton of two members of the crew of a 'runaway Grimsby trawler' which had made a journey all the way across the ocean to the colony of British Guiana in South America. One of them raised his pint to their reporter and said, 'Here's down the hatch. Here's to England again.' However, *tell it to the marines* – an expression of disbelief or scorn at an unlikely story – is of far older vintage, being first recorded in John Davis's 1806 novel of the Royal Navy at the time of Lord Nelson, *The Post-Captain – Or, the Wooden Walls Well Manned; Comprehending a View of Naval Society and Manners*, in which it appears as something of a recurring mantra, such as: '"Belay there!" cried the captain; "you may tell that to the marines, but I'll be d— if the sailors will believe it."' The original meaning, therefore, casts the marines in the role of gullible dupes as compared to ordinary seamen, but over the years, once the expression became popular in America, the sense has been altered. The new implication is that you might tell such a stupid story to other people and they would accept it, but if you told it to the US Marines – who have supposedly been everywhere and seen everything – then they will recognise it for the nonsense that it is. This variant, unsurprisingly, seems to be the one favoured currently by the marines themselves.

In a flap with a corker

IF SALTY OLD SEA-DOGS COULD at one time be identified on the stage and in comic books by their fondness for expressions such as *belay there!*, so too might the slang of an RAF veteran in the years following the Second World War be easily distinguishable. For instance, the young legal clerk Mr Drudge in Margery Allingham's 1948 crime novel *More Work for the Undertaker* is an ex-fighter pilot, and certainly talks the language:

> Well, I've been chinning with the old Skip and he says Bang

on, jolly good show, first ray of light they've shown. Here's the essential gen.

It was not just crime-fiction readers who encountered such language at the time. Schoolchildren with a taste for the works of Captain W. E. Johns could find it liberally sprinkled through his work, as in *Biggles Takes the Case* (1952): '"Suppose you give me the gen," requested Ginger, slipping into R.A.F. jargon,' while Biggles himself in the same book is heard to exclaim, 'Suffering Icarus! That certainly is a bone-shaker.'

Some authentic wartime examples of such speech found their way into the newspapers even as the Battle of Britain raged overhead in the summer of 1940. A photo report in the *Daily Express* on 6 August that year showed various fighter pilots under the headline, 'They Have Just Been Destroying Messer-schmitts', with a caption saying:

> 'Plummers' (slang for armourers) feed belts of 'ammo' (ammu-nition) into the wing machine-guns. ... A sergeant-pilot has his mascot painted on his 'Mae West' (rhyming slang for vest).

Anyone searching for more examples of such speech might perhaps wish to consult a thirty-six-page pamphlet by one 'H. W.' (Ernest L. H. Williams), entitled *What's the Gen? – R.A.F. Slang, Illustrated*, published hot on the heels of the Battle of Britain in 1942, whose cover cartoon showed vividly how the term *Mae West* was not simply rhyming slang, but also a literal comment on the supposed resemblance between an inflated life-jacket and the chest of the Hollywood film star. As the author explained in his preface: 'Many of the expressions are new. Some are old. Others cannot be included for a variety of reasons.' To take just a few examples:

> *squirt, to give a*   to open fire

body snatcher, a	a stretcher bearer
gen, the	the low down; correct information
wind in your neck	shut up
Queen, a	a star performer of the fair sex
flap, in a	over active
mixed death	various types of ammunition
crack at, to have a	to try
six letter man, the	Hitler
humid	without personality, wet
cart, in the	in trouble
kite, a	an aircraft
good show, a	a meritorious performance
corker, a	a mine, or sometimes a young woman
bind, a	an irksome task, performed with difficulty; a bore

The word *bind* was immortalised for BBC radio listeners in the title of the comedy series *Much-Binding-in-the-Marsh*, set on a fictional RAF base, which began broadcasting in 1944 and ran in one form or another for a decade. A year after it started, Eric Partridge published *A Dictionary of RAF Slang*, in which he considered the origins of such language, as compared to that of the army and the navy:

> The Air Force had a small body of slang even when it was the Royal Flying Corps. The RAF has many more slang terms than were possessed by the RFC, although the total number of its terms is very much smaller than those of the two senior Services.

Although they existed, only a handful of Royal Flying Corps slang words made their way into British newspapers during the First World War, owing to the more formal nature of the aerial combat reports issued by the authorities. One such term – which appeared in a British pilot's first-person account of a dogfight with a German fighter, published in *The Times* in

February 1916 – happened to be the term *spit-fire*, meaning the sight of a gun muzzle-flash ('a series of "spit-fires" from his centre shows he has opened fire with his machine gun').

In his 1945 dictionary Partridge, who served in the RAF from 1942 to 1945, illuminated the origin of the word *gen*: 'Not, as many suppose, from "genuine"... No; *gen* is from "for the *gen*eral information of all ranks," common to the three services.' His other definitions explore various situations encountered by aircrew, such as becoming *tangled in the soup* ('to be lost, or go astray, in a fog') while flying over *the ditch* ('the sea; especially the English Channel'), and having to *footle around* ('to circle in search of a target') while keeping clear of *flaming onions* ('anti-aircraft tracer shells and/or bullets'), before letting loose their *sack of taters* ('a loadful of bombs, delivered grocery-wise') and hoping that they will arrive *bang on!* ('All right! Correct! In Bomber Command: from a bomb dropped bang on (exactly on) the target.') On returning safely to base, the logical course of action might well be to then get *supercharged* ('in a drunken state') as quickly as possible, also known as being completely *shot up* ('very drunk').

On the beam with that chicken

EMPLOYING AIR FORCE SLANG could sometimes cause unexpected problems. In 1943, an American newspaper called the *Lewiston Daily Sun*, from Maine, published a report under the headline 'NAZIS THREATEN TO TRY FLIERS AS "WAR CRIMINALS"... Nazi Propaganda Says it Has Proof "Gangsters" Control U S Air Force'. This state of affairs had arisen on account of the nose decorations and slang-derived slogans painted by American aircrew on the fuselages of their bombers, prompting the proposed trial of captured US airmen shot down near Bremen, said to have flown under the nickname *Murder Incorporated*:

> It was pointed out here that if the planes and crews actually did bear such names it would indicate nothing more than the flippancy of young soldiers who in the same vein have given their planes such names in American slang as 'Boomtown' and 'Susie Q'.

On a less serious note, a year later another newspaper, the *Pittsburgh Press*, traced the spread of US Air Force slang to other services, and then into general parlance, as a result of military collaborations with Hollywood during the making of films such as the Darryl F. Zanuck wartime propaganda vehicle *Winged Victory* (1944). Among their examples, they considered the new phrase – also popular with jazz musicians – *on the beam*:

> The latter means headed in the right direction, everything going right. It is applied to either thought or action. Thus, if a GI is pressing an ardent suit with the lady of his choice and says exultantly, 'I'm on the beam with that chicken', the layman can rest assured that everything is progressing favourably. Origin of 'on the beam' is easily traceable to flying by radio instrument – on a radio beam.

In the post-war era, some of those who had survived air combat drew on their experiences as the basis for novels. One of the finest examples was John Watson's story of a Bomber Command pilot and his crew, *Johnny Kinsman* (1955), a thinly disguised portrait of 158 Squadron, which flew Halifaxes out of RAF Lissett, just south of Bridlington.

Interestingly, the regular nickname in the book for the group captain – equivalent to the rank of colonel in the British Army – is *groupie*, a word which would have different connotations once the sixties hove into view (not that women who followed jazz musicians around were a novelty during the war years – they were simply known by a different slang name, *band rats*).

Watson had been a fighter pilot and then a bomber pilot, winning the DFC after having flown thirty-four operational tours. The death rate among aircrew in his book is steady and relentless, to the extent that almost everyone the reader meets eventually succumbs, but this is not handled in a sensationalist way, and all through it the slang used by these characters is realistically deadpan and offhand. 'Widdowson, sir, has pranged,' says an officer, reporting a crash. 'But he *can't* have,' replies the squadron leader. 'Not in that lovely new aircraft.' Then, later on in the book, after Kinsman's badly damaged plane has limped back to base:

> 'Aircraft bent?' the Wingco asked.
>> 'A little, sir.'

In the end, ex-Pilot Officer Tim Vigors of 222 Squadron got to the heart of an impulse which lay behind much of the outwardly callous or offhand-sounding wartime slang evolved by all three services when he wrote in his autobiography, *Life's Too Short to Cry* (2006, quoted in Max Arthur's oral history of the Battle of Britain, *The Last of the Few* (2010)):

> Death and wounds among our companions became commonplace and were taken with an exaggerated lightness which we found was the only possible way to bear the losses and remain sane.

TWELVE

The Last Word

Beware of geeks bearing gifts

Among the leading 'futurologists' and 'trend consultants' last year was New York outfit K-Hole, whose 2013 white paper on youth trends coined the term 'normcore' (denoting 'finding liberation in being nothing special', ie dressing in nondescript fashion as a sort of fashion statement). Now K-Hole has released its latest bullshit bible. Ostensibly all about 'doubt' as a cultural trend, it touches on 'chaos magic' and the concept of 'weaponising burnout' and ends with the authors claiming that they are 'swimming in a universe of squirrels.'

Private Eye, 18 September–1 October 2015

SLANG USED TO COME FROM THE STREET, from the *working stiffs*, the *grafters*, the *frails*, the *jack-rollers*, the *winchester geese*, the *hep-cats*, the *old lags*, the *mollies*, the *lobsters* and the *jug-bitten*. Much of the time, it still does, but it is fighting against a tidal wave of fake language deployed by committees of marketing executives or by focus groups in the pay of politicians, all desperately seeking to look cool. In today's online information blizzard, countless billions of words are sent out into the fray in the hope of causing a *Twitter storm*, perhaps *trending* on Facebook, or else gaining a ludicrous number of plays on YouTube, alongside the tap-dancing kittens and the latest celebrity *wardrobe malfunction*.

It is not uncommon to see people walking down the street wearing T-shirts or baseball caps proudly emblazoned with the single word *GEEK* or *NERD*. The latter term first appeared as the name of a creature in the 1950 book *If I Ran the Zoo* by Dr Seuss (Theodor S. Geisel), who, when asked by the computer publication *PC Magazine* in 1987 how he had come up with it, responded that 'he had never heard the word before he drew that character'. Many of those now adopting the former term are probably unaware that for much of the 20th century a *geek* was basically the lowest job in a travelling carnival freak show, the person in the tattered wild-man costume and fright wig who bit the heads off live chickens and snakes for the amusement of an audience of local *rubes*. *Billboard* magazine's side-show pages used to be full of fairground bosses advertising for geeks to work alongside other attractions, as in this typical line-up from an outfit touring Oklahoma in 1949, which included 'L Williams; May Williams, sword ladder and electric chair; Fay Dill, four-legged girl; [and] Jimmy McLeod, who joined recently with his pin cushion and fire act'. A few months later, the magazine ran a satirical report about a protest march of:

> 500 geeks [who] decided to hoof it from burg to burg in full regalia. When we say 'full regalia' we mean 500 stringy or matted long-hair wigs, 500 mother hubbards and leotards, 500 sets of wolf-like three-inch tusks, and each with his face smeared with brick color grease paint.

Clearly, anyone these days making do with just a GEEK baseball cap is missing out, and it is high time that wolf-like three-inch tusks came back into fashion.

Prior to its popularity in carnival circles, in 19th-century

Yorkshire a *geek* was simply a term for an idiot, a moron, a credulous simpleton, and was listed as such in the 1876 edition of Francis Kildale Robinson's *A Glossary of Words Used in the Neighbourhood of Whitby*. It is thought to be a variant of a much older slang word for a fool, *geck*, which derives from an identical German word of the same meaning. Dr Johnson defined *geck* in his *Dictionary of the English Language* (1755) as a term for someone 'easily impos'd on', and also quoted Shakespeare's use of the word. The similarity is further strengthened by the fact that in the *First Folio* of Shakespeare's works (1623), in *The Tragedy of Cymbeline*, the word was spelled *geeke*:

> Why did you fuffer *Iachimo*, flight thing of Italy,
> To taint his Nobler hart and braine, with needleffe ieloufy,
> And to become the geeke and fcorne o' th'others vilany?

Also to be found in Dr Johnson's 1755 dictionary was the following entry:

> COMPUTER. n. f. {from *compute*} Reckoner; accountant; calculator...
> I have known some such ill *computers*, as to imagine the many millions in stocks so much real wealth. *Swift*

Thus *geekes* were treading the boards in Jacobean England, and *computers* were alive and well in Georgian London, but it took until the last quarter of the 20th century for the two to join forces and bring about the *computer geek*.

As it happens, the October 1969 issue of the magazine *Computer World* announced, in suitably *geek*-friendly terms, the development of a new user language called *Slang*, 'oriented toward the solution of implicit nonlinear problems, such as simultaneous nonlinear algebraic equations, implicit ordinary differential equations, multipoint boundary value problems, maxima and minima, and calculus of variations'. Heady stuff.

In their song 'Suzy Is a Headbanger' (1977), The Ramones helpfully pointed out that the title character's mother was 'a geek', and these were still the days when the word conjured up images of people biting the heads off unsuspecting poultry. Similarly, a few years later, when an interviewer from the *NME* asked The Cramps to name their favourite film and they nominated Nick Zedd's *Geek Maggot Bingo* (1983, aka *The Freak from Suckweasel Mountain*), the subject matter under discussion was nothing to do with gadget-obsessed programmers in heavy-framed glasses. Times change, and the year 2011 saw the arrival of a Disney high-school film called *Geek Charming*. Suffice to say, one of these two celluloid contenders starred Richard Hell, and the other did not.

One year before *Geek Maggot Bingo* reared its bashful little head, an article about the supposed aphrodisiac effects of personal computer technology and language for the geek-about-town appeared in the magazine *Popular Mechanics* – appropriately enough, in a discussion of the term *RAM* (random-access memory) – which was surely a sign of things to come:

> There are now many computers that were bought with 4K of memory and are now fleshed out with 256K of bulging brainpower... Having a lot of RAM memory in the personal computing subculture is like walking into a bar with Miss Universe on your arm. People who would never once have considered inviting you to join them suddenly think you're a great guy.

Eventually, the newer meaning of *geek* prevailed, and in 2013 an article in the computer magazine *PC* made it clear to all interested parties that they had finally inherited the earth:

YOUTUBE'S GEEK WEEK KICKS OFF SUNDAY
Who run the world? Geeks. And YouTube is taking advantage

of our eminence by holding its first ever Geek Week from Aug. 4 to 10.

Fittingly, the whole thing was co-sponsored by an outfit called Nerdist.

In hock to your own image

THE RISE OF THE PERSONAL COMPUTER, followed by the sea of hand-held devices available today, has not only made *nerds* out of much of the population, the technology itself has enabled the instant dissemination of slang across the planet. In the past, the specialised argot of various groups might be in use for many decades among their core members before being gathered together in a newspaper article or book, but today anyone hearing an unfamiliar term can go online and track down a definition of sorts in seconds – although whether the information will be accurate is quite another matter. In addition, if you try searching the net for the meaning of some of the magnificent phrases recorded nearly two and a half centuries ago in Covent Garden by Captain Francis Grose – such as *Admiral of the Narrow Seas*, 'One who from drunkenness vomits into the lap of the person sitting opposite him', or *Riding St George*, 'The woman uppermost in the amorous congress, that is, the dragon upon St George' – it will be in the knowledge that someone, somewhere, from a government agency, is now monitoring your activity.

The crime writer John D. MacDonald saw it all coming as early as 1964, when his enduring individualist character Travis McGee considers the implications of credit cards and privacy, in the first novel of the series, *The Deep Blue Good-By*:

> They are the little fingers of reality, reaching for your throat. A man with a credit card is in hock to his own image of himself.

But these are the last remaining years of choice. In the stainless nurseries of the future, the feds will work their way through all the squalling pinkness tattooing a combination tax number and credit number on one wrist, followed closely by the L.T. and T. team putting a permanent phone number, visaphone doubtless, on the other wrist. Die and your number goes back in the bank. It will be the first provable immortality the world has ever known.

This lack of privacy is now in many ways self-inflicted. People have been telling slang-heavy stories to their friends in bars around the world for centuries, but now if they come home drunk and do it on Twitter or Facebook, using words that are judged to be 'inappropriate', they might find themselves hung out to dry by a modern-day lynch mob who can mobilise 200,000 signatures at the drop of a hat. Spend your teenage years plastering your social media accounts with all the latest slang and your own half-formed opinions, and in ten years or sooner they will come back to haunt you as prospective employers trawl old sites looking into your background. This is the point at which a self-posted photo of yourself collapsed on a party floor with a toilet seat around your neck and surrounded by zombie-eyed classmates – lovingly annotated with fifteen choice contemporary euphemisms for excessive chemical over-indulgence – starts to look like a potential barrier to a career as a future Archbishop of Canterbury. Or perhaps not.

Non-living person spinning in their grave

THROUGH IT ALL, THE AVALANCHE of slang across all forms of media continues. 'Scrabble Stays Dench With New Words', announced the *Aberdeen Evening Express* in May 2015, explaining that:

...a host of slang words used on social media, in texts and on the street are now available to fans of the traditional word game seeking to outplay their opponents. These include *obvs* (obviously), *ridic* (ridiculous), *lolz* (laughs), *shizzle* (form of US rap slang), *cakehole* (mouth), and *dench* (excellent).

The makers of Scrabble may have only just included it, but *cakehole* had been doing the rounds in British school playgrounds for over sixty years by this point, having begun as RAF slang during the Second World War. The other words are far more recent, but how long some of them will remain trendy now that the then Chancellor of the Exchequer George Osborne employed the first of these terms on a political talk show in April 2016 is an interesting question. As the *Daily Mirror* commented the following day:

> Pundits were baffled yesterday when [Osborne] unveiled the working behind his claim Brexit would cost £4,300 for every family in Britain. Mr Osborne smiled as he told ITV's *The Agenda*: 'That's a gravity model – a regression gravity model with a general equilibrium NiGEM model for the economy. Obvs!'

The Chancellor has form in this area, the paper explained, having recently outed himself as a fan of gangsta rap group NWA, enjoying tea at Downing Street with the band's Dr Dre a couple of years ago, and then in January 2016 being referred to by Ice Cube as *my homie*. Which, in certain circles, presumably qualifies as *dench*.

In 2014, footballer Rio Ferdinand ran into difficulties with the FA, having used the word *sket* in a Twitter message. This – as the print media were happy to inform the many millions of readers who had not encountered it before – is Jamaican-derived street-gang slang for a promiscuous woman. It is hard to believe that all the members of the FA Independent Regulatory

Commission were entirely familiar with the term before this matter arose, but in such ways these words become more widely known.

According to a March 2016 report in the *Daily Mail*, Facebook has now secured a patent in America to use artificial intelligence to 'trawl posts and messages for slang words before they get picked up by the rest of the crowd'. The object is apparently to 'better target its adverts to a wider range of social groups', and 'if the use is new, these neologisms will be added to a social glossary'. Unfortunately, their existing technology is apparently sometimes thrown by very old usages, as in the case of a venerable Welsh pub in the Brecon village of Llanfihangel Talyllyn, which has traded since 1840 as the Black Cock Inn. Sure enough, the landlord reported at the end of 2015 that the hostelry's profile had been suspended by Facebook for 'racist or offensive language' on account of their name.

Increasingly, language is being monitored – by private organisations, by governments, by student bodies and by sections of the general public. This has been a creeping process which has developed over the past three or four decades, now greatly enabled by internet technology. The critic Robert Hughes had this to say about the state of things in his 1993 book *Culture of Complaint – The Fraying of America*, published a few short years before the net would change everything:

> We want to create a sort of linguistic Lourdes, where evil and misfortune are dispelled by a dip in the waters of euphemism... Just as language grotesquely inflates in attack, so it timidly shrinks in approbation, seeking words that cannot possibly give any offence, however notional. We do not fail, we underachieve. We are not junkies, but substance abusers; not handicapped, but differently abled. And we are mealy-mouthed unto death: a corpse, the *New England Journal of*

Medicine urged in 1988, should be referred to as a 'non-living person.'

The fact is, the vast majority of the language and sayings documented in this book would now be unacceptable to someone somewhere, busily taking offence on behalf of everyone else.

Since the 1980s, a new wave of puritanism has emerged from US campuses under the cloak of *political correctness*, which increasingly seeks to ban anything it holds to be suspect. Witch-hunts are conducted against words, thoughts and modes of behaviour. Judgements are made, sentences passed, and appeals are futile. Ultimately, slang will have no place in this world, because the best of it is almost guaranteed to offend someone, somewhere.

Hold your vulgar tongue

TODAY, WE LIVE IN AN AGE in which pretty much every sexual activity known to the human race has been filmed and is available to view via the nearest computer or smartphone – which many people back in the 1960s would probably have considered a liberated and long-overdue state of affairs – yet numerous slang words for describing them would now be deemed unsayable. That same technological advance, however, has also made it possible to view real-life atrocity footage online, and brutality can be routinely filmed by the perpetrators using a cheap device carried in almost everyone's pocket. You can watch all of this at the click of a button, but mind your language when you talk about it.

Were Francis Grose alive in today's world, would his voice be heard, or might he in fact revel in the possibilities offered by new technology for tracking down new slang words and meanings, and the opportunities for publishing them independently online? Who knows? Perhaps a clue lay hidden in the definition he gave to the following piece of Exmoor slang, listed in his 1787 work *A Provincial Glossary, with a Collection of Local Proverbs, and Popular Superstitions*:

Bloggy, to Bloggy. To sulk or be sullen.

In the London of the 1780s, where Grose walked the back-alleys of Covent Garden, casual violence, heroic alcohol consumption and a multiplicity of sexual encounters were an everyday fact of life. The slang he preserved in his *Classical Dictionary of the Vulgar Tongue* addresses those events with an amused eye and evokes the realities of that time far more honestly than the corporate-speak and PC euphemisms of today could ever reflect our own. As for any potential offence caused by such language, Grose issued a mock-solemn apology for the slang terms which he had gleefully listed:

To prevent any charge of immorality being brought against this work, the Editor begs leave to observe, that when an indelicate or immodest word has obtruded itself for explanation, he has endeavoured to get rid of it in the most decent manner possible; and none have been admitted but such as either could not be left out without rendering the work incomplete, or in some measure compensate by their wit for the trespass committed on decorum. Indeed, respecting this matter, he can with great truth make the same defence that Falstaff ludicrously urges in behalf of one engaged in rebellion, viz. that he did not seek them, but that, like rebellion in the case instanced, they lay in his way, and he found them.

The following century, John Camden Hotten, in the preface to his own *Dictionary of Modern Slang* (1859), remarked that 'it is quite impossible to write any account of vulgar or low language, and remain seated on damask in one's own drawing-room'.

Luckily, I never had a drawing-room in the first place.

BIBLIOGRAPHY

Books

Robert C Adams, *On Board the "Rocket"*, Boston: D Lothrop & Company, 1879

William Harrison Ainsworth, *Rookwood: A Romance*, Philadelphia: Carey, Lea & Blanchard, 1834

Nelson Algren, *The Man With the Golden Arm*, London: Neville Spearman, 1959 (first published 1949)

Richard Allen, *Knuckle Girls*, London: New English Library, 1977

Margery Allingham, *More Work For The Undertaker*, New York: Pocket Books, 1950 (first published 1948)

Anonymous, *A Glossary of Provincial Words Used in the County of Cumberland*, London: John Gray Bell, 1851

——*The Life and Character of Moll King, Late Mistress of King's Coffee-House in Covent-Garden*, London: W Price, 1747

——*The Scoundrel's Dictionary: or, An Explanation of the Cant-words used by Thieves, House-breakers, Street-robbers, and Pick-pockets about Town, To which is prefixed, Some curious Dissertations on the Art of Wheedling: And a Collection of their Flash Songs, with a proper Glossary.* London: J Brownell, 1754

——*The Gentleman's Bottle-Companion, Containing a Collection of Curious, Uncommon and Humorous Songs; Most of Which Are Originals*, London, 1768

——*Harris's List of Covent Garden Ladies or Man of Pleasure's Kalender For the Year 1789 Containing the Histories and some curious Anecdotes of the most celebrated Ladies now on the Town, or in keeping and also many of their Keepers*, London: H Ranger, 1789

——*Harris's List of Covent Garden Ladies or Man of Pleasure's Kalender For the Year 1793 Containing the Histories and some curious Anecdotes of the most celebrated Ladies now on the Town, or in keeping and also many of their Keepers*, London: H Ranger, 1793

——*Sinks of London Laid Open: A pocket companion for the uninitiated, to which is added a modern flash dictionary, containing all the cant words, slang terms, and flash phrases now in vogue, with a list of the sixty orders of prime coves*, London: J Duncombe, 1848

——*The Pearl – A Journal of Facetiæ and Voluptuous Reading*, Oxford: Printed at the University Press, No. 5, November 1879

——*The Rakish Rhymer – Or Fancy Man's Own Songster and Reciter*, Paris: Lutetia, 1917 (first published 1864)

——*Essential Japanese Phrase Book*, Basingstoke: AA Publications, 1998

Max Arthur, *The Last of the Few – The Battle of Britain in the Words of the Pilots Who Won It*, London: Virgin Books, 2011 (first published 2010)

——*The Last Post – The Final Word from Our First World War Soldiers*, London: Phoenix Books, 2006 (first published 2005)

Herbert Asbury, *The Gangs of New York – An Informal History of the Underworld*, London: Arrow Books, 2002 (first published 1928)

Russell Ash & Brian Lake, *Bizarre Books*, London: Sphere Books, 1987 (first published 1985)

Philip Atlee, *The Green Wound*, London: Gold Medal, 1964 (first published 1963)

Bob Aylwin, *A Load of Cockney Cobblers*, London: Johnston & Bacon, 1973

B. E., *A New Dictionary of the Terms Ancient and Modern of the Canting Crew, in its Several Tribes of Gypsies, Beggers, Thieves, Cheats &c.* London: W Hawes, 1699

Richard Meade Bache, *Vulgarisms and Other Errors of Speech*, Philadelphia: Claxton, Remsen, and Haffelfinger, 1869 (first published 1868)

Nathan Bailey, *An Universal Etymological English Dictionary, Volume II*, London: Thomas Cox, 1737 (first published 1727)

——*Dictionarium Britannicum: Or a more Compleat Universal Etymological English Dictionary Than any Extant*, London: Thomas Cox, 1736

Mark Baker, *Cops – Their Lives in Their Own Words*, London: Cardinal, 1991 (first published 1985)

——*Nam*, London: Abacus, 1987 (first published 1981)

Paul Baker, *Polari – The Lost Language of Gay Men*, London: Routledge, 2002

Ray Stannard Baker, *Following the Color Line – An Account of Negro Citizenship in the American Democracy*, New York: Doubleday, Page & Company, 1908

Joe Balham, *The Snout Who Cried Wolf (The Sweeney No. 6)*, London: Futura Publications, 1977

Ronnie Barker, *Fletcher's Book of Rhyming Slang*, London: Pan Books, 1979

Robert Barltrop & Jim Wolveridge, *The Muvver Tongue*, London: The Journeyman Press, 1980

John Russell Bartlett, *Dictionary of Americanisms – A Glossary of Words and Phrases Usually Regarded as Peculiar to the United States*, Boston: Little, Brown and Company, 1848

——*Dictionary of Americanisms – A Glossary of Words and Phrases Usually Regarded as Peculiar to the United States, Third Edition, Greatly Improved and Enlarged*, Boston: Little, Brown and Company, 1860

Jerome Beck & Marsha Rosenbaum, *Pursuit of Ecstasy: The MDMA Experience*, Albany, N.Y.: State University of New York Press, 1994

John Bee, *Slang. A Dictionary of the Turf, the Ring, the Chase, the Pit, of Bon-Ton, and the Varieties of Life, Forming the Completest and Most Authentic Lexicon Balatronicum Hitherto Offered to the Notice of the Sporting World, etc*, London: T Hughes, 1823

——*Sportsman's Slang; A New Dictionary of Terms Used in the Affairs of the Turf, the Ring, the Chase, and the Cock-Pit; With Those of Bon-Ton, and the Varieties of Life, etc*. London: Printed for the Author, 1825

Alfred Bester, *Rat Race* (originally entitled *Who He?*), New York: Berkley Books, 1956 (first published 1953)

Jack Black, *You Can't Win*, Port Townsend, Washington: Feral House, 2013 (first published 1926)

Richard Blakeborough, *Wit, Character, Folklore & Customs of the North Riding of Yorkshire With a Glossary of Over 4,000 Words and Idioms Now in Use*, London: Henry Frowde, 1898

John G Brandon, *Nighthawks*, London: Methuen & Co., 1931 (first published 1929)

Angela Brazil, *For the School Colours*, London: Blackie & Son, 1918

Carter Brown, *The Wayward Wahine*, New York: Signet Books, 1960

John Brown, *The Chancer*, London: Panther Books, 1974 (first published 1972)

John Buchan, *The Thirty-Nine Steps*, London: Pan Books, 1982 (first published 1915)

Anthony Buckeridge, *Jennings and Darbishire*, London: Armada, 1967 (first published 1952)

Anthony Burgess, *The Right To An Answer*, London: New English Library, 1968 (first published 1960)

——*A Clockwork Orange*, London: Pan Books, 1964 (first published 1962)

William Burroughs, *Dead Fingers Talk*, London: Tandem Books, 1970 (first published 1963)

Cab Calloway, *The Hepster's Dictionary*, New York: Cab Calloway, 1939 (first published 1938)

Bernard Capp, *England's Culture Wars – Puritan Reformation and its Enemies in the Interregnum, 1649–1660*, Oxford: Oxford University Press, 2012

Raymond Chandler, *The Lady in the Lake*, London: Penguin Books, 1955 (first published 1943)

Raymond Chandler (Dorothy Gardiner & Kathrine Sorley Walker, eds), *Raymond Chandler Speaking*, London: Allison & Busby, 1984 (first published 1962)

Leslie Charteris, *The Saint in Miami*, London: Hodder Paperbacks, 1969 (first published 1940)

Agatha Christie, *The Murder on the Links*, London: Pan Books, 1961 (first published 1923)

Eldridge Cleaver, *Soul On Ice*, London: Jonathan Cape, 1969

Robin Cook, *The Crust On Its Uppers*, London: Pan Books, 1964 (first published 1962)

Myles Coverdale, ed., *The Byble in Englyshe, that is to saye the content of all the holy scrypture, both of ye olde and newe testament etc*, London: Richard Grafton & Edward Whitchurch, 1539

James Curtis, *The Gilt Kid*, London: Penguin Books, 1947 (first published 1936)

John Davis, *The Post-Captain – Or, the Wooden Walls Well Manned; Comprehending a View of Naval Society and Manners*, London: Thomas Tegg, etc, 1813 (first published 1806)

Robert M W Dixon & John Godrich, *Blues & Gospel Records, 1902–1943, Third Edition – Fully Revised*, Chigwell, Essex: Storyville Publications, 1982

Arthur Conan Doyle, *The Sign of Four*, London: Spencer Blackett, 1890

Pierce Egan (Charles Hindley, ed.), *The True History of Tom and Jerry, or, The Day and Night Scenes, Of Life in London from the Start to the Finish! With a Key to the Persons and Places, Together with a Vocabulary and Glossary Of the Flash and Slang Terms, occurring in the course of the work*, London: Charles Hindley, 1858 (Egan's original first published 1821)

John S Farmer, *Musa Pedestris – Three Centuries of Canting Songs and Slang Rhymes, 1536 – 1896*, London: Privately Printed for Subscribers Only, 1896

John S Farmer and W E Henley, *Slang and its Analogues, Past and Present*, [London]: Printed for Subscribers Only, 1890, etc.

Philip Fenty, *Super Fly*, London: Sphere Books, 1973 (first published 1972)

Henry Fielding (R P C Mutter, ed.), *The History of Tom Jones, A Foundling*, London: Penguin Books, 1982 (first published 1749)

Ian Fleming, *Casino Royale*, London: Pan Books, 1963 (first published 1953)

——*Live and Let Die*, London: Pan Books, 1965 (first published 1954)

——*Goldfinger*, London: Pan Books, 1964 (first published 1959)

John Florio, *A Worlde of Wordes, or Most Copious and Exact Dictionarie In Italian and English*, London: A Hatfield for E Blount, 1598

Josiah Flynt, *The World of Graft*, New York: McClure, Phillips & Co., 1901

John Ford (S P Sherman, ed.), *Tis Pity She's a Whore and The Broken Heart*, Boston: D C Heath & Co., 1915

Kinky Friedman, *Greenwich Killing Time*, London: Faber and Faber, 1997 (first published 1986)

Peter Fryer, *Mrs Grundy – Studies in English Prudery*, London: Dennis Dobson, 1963

Fulchester Industries, *Roger's Profanisaurus Rex*, London: Dennis Publishing, 2005

Matt and Kathleen Galant, *The New Sexual Underground – The Real Book About Hippie Love-Ins, Group Sex Parties, Nude Happenings, Wife Swaps!*, New York: Bee-Line Books, 1967

Peter Gammond, *Scott Joplin and the Ragtime Era*, London: Abacus, 1975

John Garfield, *The Wandring Whore – A Dialogue Between Magdalena a Crafty Bawd, Julietta an Exquisite Whore, Francion a Lascivious Gallant, And Gusman a Pimping Hector. Discovering their diabolical Practises at the CHUCK OFFICE. With a LIST of all the Crafty Bawds, Common Whores, Decoys, Hectors, and Trappanners, and their usual Meetings*, London: John Garfield, 1660

Rodney Garland, *The Heart in Exile*, London: Four Square, 1961 (first published 1953)

John Gay, *The Beggar's Opera*, London: John Cumberland, n.d.

Bibliography

Robert S Gold, *A Jazz Lexicon*, New York: Alfred A Knopf, 1964

Babs Gonzales, *I, Paid My Dues – Good Times… No Bread, A Story of Jazz*, East Orange, New Jersey: Expubidence Publishing Corp., 1967

Babs Gonzales & Paul Weston, *Boptionary – What Is Bop?*, Hollywood, California: Capitol Records, 1949

William Green (Charles Hindley, ed.), *The Life and Adventures of a Cheap Jack, By One of the Fraternity*, London: Tinsley brothers, 1876

Robert Greene, *A Notable Discovery of Coosnage, Now daily practised by Sundry lewd persons, called Connie-catchers, and Crosse-biters*, London: John Wolfe, 1591

——*Greene's Groats-worth of Wit, bought with a million of Repentance, Describing the follie of youth, the falshoode of make-shift flatterers, the miserie of the negligent, and mischiefes of deceiving Courtezans*, London: William Wright, 1592

Ward Greene, *Death in the Deep South*, New York: Stacpoole Sons, 1936

——*Ride the Nightmare (Life & Loves of a Modern Mister Bluebeard)*, New York: Avon Publishing, 1948 (first published, 1930)

Judson Grey, *Twilight Girls*, Los Angeles, California: Epic Originals, 1962

Francis Grierson, *The Buddha of Fleet Street*, London: Hutchinson, 1950

Francis Grose, *A Classical Dictionary of the Vulgar Tongue*, London: S Hooper, 1785

——*A Classical Dictionary of the Vulgar Tongue, The Second Edition, Corrected and Enlarged*, London: S Hooper, 1788

——*A Classical Dictionary of the Vulgar Tongue, The Third Edition, Corrected and Enlarged*, London: Hooper & Wigstead, 1796

——*Lexicon Balatronicum – A Dictionary of Buckish Slang, University Wit, and Pickpocket Eloquence, Compiled Originally by Captain Grose, and now Considerably Altered and Enlarged, with the Modern Changes and Improvements, by a Member of the Whip Club, Assisted by Hell-Fire Dick, and James Gordon, Esqrs of Cambridge; and William Soames, Esq of the Hon Society of Newman's Hotel*, London: C Chappel, 1811

——*A Provincial Glossary, With a Collection of Local Proverbs, and Popular Superstitions*, London: S. Hooper, 1787

Francis Grose (Pierce Egan, ed.), *Grose's Classical Dictionary of the Vulgar Tongue, Revised and Corrected, With the Addition of numerous Slang Phrases, Collected from Tried Authorities*, London: Pierce Egan, 1823

Alan Hackney, *Private's Progress*, London: Panther Books, 1962 (first published 1954)

John Hall & others, *Memoirs of the Right Villainous John Hall, The Late Famous and Notorious ROBBER, Penn'd from his own MOUTH sometime before his DEATH*, London: F Baker, 1714

Donald Hamilton, *The Betrayers*, London: Coronet Books, 1971 (first published 1966)

——*The Interlopers*, London: Coronet Books, 1970 (first published 1969)

Dashiell Hammett, *The Maltese Falcon*, New York: Vintage Crime / Black Lizard, 1992 (first published 1930)

——*The Thin Man*, New York: Pocket Books, 1945 (first published, 1934)

Edward S Hanlon, *The Great God Now*, New York: Paperback Library, 1968

Daniel Hardie, *Exploring Early Jazz – The Origins and Evolution of the New Orleans Style*, San Jose: Writers Club Press, 2002

Thomas Harman, *A Caveat or Warening for Common Cursetors, Vulgarely Called Vagabones*, London: T Bensley, 1814 (first published 1567)

Mavis Doriel Hay, *Murder Underground*, London: The British Library, 2014 (first published 1934)

John Heidenry, *What Wild Ecstasy – The Rise and Fall of the Sexual Revolution*, New York: Simon & Schuster, 1997

John Hersey, *Too Far To Walk*, London: Corgi Books, 1968 (first published 1966)

Bevis Hillier, *John Betjeman – The Biography*, London: John Murray, 2007 (first published 2006)

Chester Himes, *The Big Gold Dream*, London: Panther Books, 1968 (first published 1960)

——*Blind Man With a Pistol*, London: Panther Books, 1971 (first published 1969)

Edwin Hodder, *Memories of New Zealand Life*, London: Longman, Green, Longman & Roberts, 1862

William Holloway, *A General Dictionary of Provincialisms, Written with a View to Rescue from Oblivion the Fast Fading Relics of By-Gone Days*, Lewes: Baxter & Son, 1839

John Clellon Holmes, *The Horn*, London: Penguin Books, 1990 (first published 1958)

Kin Hubbard (David S Hawes, ed.), *The Best Of Kin Hubbard: Abe Martin's Sayings & Wisecracks*, Bloomington, Indiana: Indiana University Press, 1984

Robert Hughes, *Culture of Complaint – The Fraying of America*, London: The Harvill Press, 1995 (first published 1993)

Alan Hunter, *Gently Go Man*, London: Pan Books, 1963 (first published 1961)

Christopher Isherwood, *Diaries, Volume One: 1939–1960*, London: Methuen, 1996

A S Jackson, *Gentleman Pimp*, Los Angeles: Holloway House, 1973

Louis E Jackson & C R Hellyer, *A Vocabulary of Criminal Slang, With Some Examples of Common Usages*, Portland, Oregon: Louis E Jackson, 1914

Stanley Jackson, *An Indiscreet Guide to Soho*, London: Muse Arts Limited, 1946

Giles Jacob, *A New Law Dictionary, Containing, The Interpretation and Definition of WORDS and TERMS used in the LAW; And also the WHOLE LAW, and the PRACTICE thereof, Under all the HEADS and TITLES of the same*, London: E and R Nutt, for D Midwinter etc, 1739 (first published 1729)

Hank Janson, *This Hood for Hire*, London: Roberts & Vinter Ltd, 1960

Mike Jay, *High Society – Mind-Altering Drugs in History and Culture*, London: Thames & Hudson, 2010

B B Johnson, *Death of a Blue-eyed Soul Brother*, New York: Paperback Library, 1970

Ben Johnson, *Volpone, or, The Foxe*, London: Thomas Thorppe, 1607

Captain W E Johns, *Biggles Takes the Case*, London: Hodder & Stoughton Ltd., 1952

Samuel Johnson, *A Dictionary of the English Language, Sixth Edition*, London: J F & C Rivington etc., 1785 (first published 1755)

Bibliography

Barry Johnston, *Round Mr Horne – The Life of Kenneth Horne*, London: Aurum Press Limited, 2007 (first published 2006)

James Joyce, *A Portrait of the Artist as a Young Man*, New York: B W Huebsch, 1916

George Kent, *Modern Flash Dictionary, Containing All the Cant Words, Slang Terms and Flash Phrases Now in Vogue, to Which is Added a List of the Sixty Orders of Prime Coves*, London: J Duncombe, 1835

Reg Kray with Patsy Manning, *Reg Kray's Book of Slang*, London: Sidgwick & Jackson, 1989 (first published 1984)

A J La Bern, *It Always Rains On Sunday*, London: Nicholson & Watson, 1945

Jack Lang (Gordon Williams), *The Hard Case*, London: Mayflower, 1967

Richard Layman, *Shadow Man – The Life of Dashiell Hammett*, London: Junction Books, 1981

Timothy Lea (Christopher Wood), *Confessions of a Private Dick*, London: Futura, 1975

John Le Carré, *A Small Town in Germany*, London: World Books, 1969 (first published 1968)

——*Tinker, Tailor, Soldier, Spy*, London: Book Club Associates, 1974

G Legman, ed, *The Limerick*, New York: Bell Publishing Company, 1979 (first published, 1953)

Michael Leigh, *The Velvet Underground*, New York: Macfadden Books, 1965 (first published 1963)

Curtis E LeMay & MacKinlay Kantor, *Mission With LeMay: My Story*, Garden City, NY: Doubleday, 1965

Julius Lester, *Look Out Whitey! Black Power's Gon' Get Your Mama!*, New York: Grove Press, 1969 (first published 1968)

Ted Lewis, *Carter*, London: Pan Books, 1971 (first published as *Jack's Return Home*, 1970)

The Lord Chief Baron (Renton Nicholson), *The swell's night guide, or, A peep through the great metropolis, under the dominion of nox: displaying the various attractive places of amusement by night. The saloons; the Paphian beauties; the chaffing cribs; the introducing houses; the singing and lushing cribs; the comical clubs; fancy ladies and the penchants, &c., &c.* London: H Smith, 1849

Humphrey Lyttelton, *I Play As I Please – The Memoirs of an Old Etonian Trumpeter*, London: The Jazz Book Club, 1957 (first published 1954)

Alexander McArthur & H Kingsley Long, *No Mean City*, London, Corgi Books, 1957 (first published 1935)

John D MacDonald, *Dead Low Tide*, Greenwich, Conn.: Fawcett Gold Medal, 1969 (first published 1953)

——*The Deep Blue Good-By*, Greenwich, Conn.: Fawcett Gold Medal, 1964

——*Soft Touch*, London: Coronet Books, 1967 (first published 1958)

——*The Neon Jungle*, Greenwich, Conn., Fawcett Gold Medal, 1960 (first published 1953)

Ross MacDonald, *The Doomsters*, New York: Bantam Books, 1959 (first published 1958)

Colin MacInnes, *City of Spades*, London: Four Square Books, 1962 (first published 1957)

Clarence Major, *Black Slang – A Dictionary of Afro-American Talk*, London: Routledge, Keegan & Paul, 1971 (first published 1970)

Bruce Manning, *Cafe Society Sinner*, New York: Beacon Books, 1960

Patrick Marnham, *The Private Eye Story*, London: Fontana / Collins, 1983 (first published 1982)

Richard Marsten (Evan Hunter), *The Spiked Heel*, London: Pan Books, 1958 (first published 1956)

Groucho Marx & others (Stefan Kanfer, ed.), *The Essential Groucho*, London: Penguin Books, 2000

George W Matsell, *Vocabulum; Or, The Rogue's Lexicon*, New York: George W Matsell & Co., 1859

David W Maurer, *The Big Con*, London: Arrow Books, 2000 (first published 1940)

Henry Mayhew, *London Labour and the London Poor; A Cyclopædia of the Condition and Earnings of Those That Will Work, Those That Cannot Work, and Those That Will Not Work, Volume III*, London: Griffin, Bohn, and Company, 1861 (first published 1851)

George Melly, *Rum, Bum and Concertina*, London: Futura, 1978 (first published 1977)

Mezz Mezzrow & Bernard Wolfe, *Really The Blues*, New York: Dell Publishing, 1952 (first published 1946)

Spike Milligan, *Adolf Hitler – My Part in His Downfall*, London: Penguin Books, 1974 (first published 1971)

——*Monty – His Part in My Victory*, London: Book Club Associates, 1976

George Moor, *The Pole and Whistle*, London: Four Square, 1966

Llyn E Morris, *The Country Garage*, Botley, Oxford: Shire Classics, 2012 (first published 1985)

Pamela Munro & Dieynaba Gaye, *Ay Baati Wolof – A Wolof Dictionary*, Los Angeles: UCLA Department of Linguistics, 1997

J J Murphy, *The Black Hole of the Camera – The Films of Andy Warhol*, Oakland: University of California Press, 2012

W.N., C.B, R.S. & J.G (J Woodfall Ebsworth, ed.), *Merry Drollery Compleat, Being Jovial Poems, Merry Songs &c.*, Boston, Lincolnshire: Robert Roberts, 1875 (first published 1661–1691)

Bill Naughton, *Alfie*, London: Panther Books, 1966

Samuel Naylor, *Reynard the Fox – A Renowned Apologue of the Middle Age, Reproduced in Rhyme*, London: Longmans, 1845

Peter Nichols, *Feeling You're Behind – An Autobiography*, London: Weidenfeld & Nicolson, 1984

David Nokes, *Samuel Johnson – A Life*, London: Faber & Faber, 2009

Frank Norman, *Bang to Rights*, London: Pan Books, 1961 (first published 1958)

——*Stand On Me*, London: Pan Books, 1962 (first published 1959)

Rictor Norton, *Homosexuality in Eighteenth Century England: A Sourcebook*, Updated 12 December 2014 <http://rictornorton.co.uk/eighteen/>

Bibliography

Tim O'Brien, *If I Die in a Combat Zone, Box Me Up and Ship Me Home*, London: Paladin Books, 1990 (first published 1973)

Cothburn O'Neal, *The Gods of Our Time*, London: Panther Books, 1964 (first published 1960)

George Orwell, *Nineteen Eighty-Four*, London: Penguin Books, 1954 (first published 1949)

George Orwell (Sonia Orwell & Ian Angus, eds.), *The Collected Essays, Journalism and Letters, Volume 3, As I Please, 1943–1945*, London: Penguin Books, 1978 (first published, 1968)

Eric Partridge, *A Dictionary of R.A.F. Slang*, London: Michael Joseph Ltd., 1945
——*Shakespeare's Bawdy*, London: Routledge & Keegan Paul, 1968 (first published 1947)

Eric Partridge (Abridged: Jacqueline Simpson), *A Dictionary of Historical Slang*, London: Penguin Books, 1972 (first published and revised 1937–61)

Eric Partridge (David Crystal, ed.), *Eric Partridge in His Own Words*, London: Andre Deutsch, 1980

Eric Partridge & John Brophy, *Songs and Slang of the British Soldier 1914–1918*, London: Frontline Books, revised edition 2008 (first published 1930)

Laurence Payne, *Birds in the Belfry*, London: Hodder & Stoughton, 1966

William Prynne, *The Soveraigne Power of Parliaments and Kingdomes: Divided into Foure Parts*, London: Michael Sparke, Senior, 1643

Madame Fuqueau de Pussy (Francis S Williams, ed.), *Le Grand-Pere et Ses Quatre Petits-Fils*, Boston: Hickling, Swan & Brown, 1854

Thomas De Quincey, *Confessions of an English Opium-Eater*, London: Taylor and Hessey, 1823 (first published 1822)

Lucian Randall & Chris Welch, *Ginger Geezer – The Life of Vivian Stanshall*, London: 4th Estate, 2002 (first published 2001)

Langford Reed, *The Complete Limerick Book – The Origin, History, and Achievements of the Limerick with over 3000 examples many of which are entirely new*, London: Jarrold's, 1932 (first published 1924)

Richard and Quétin, *English and French Dialogues, With Dialogues on Railway and Steamboat Travelling, and a Comparative Table of Monies and Measures*, London: Librairie Hachette & Cie, 1876

Brad Riley, *The Intruders – The Explosive Story of One Man's Journey into a Homosexual Jungle*, Hollywood, California: Private Edition Books, 1966

J Ewing Ritchie, *The Night Side of London*, London: William Tweedie, 1858 (first published 1857)

Jerry Rubin, *Do It! – Scenarios of the Revolution*, New York: Ballantine Books, 1970

J D Salinger, *The Catcher in the Rye*, London: Penguin Books, 1978 (first published 1951)

Harrison E Salisbury, *The Shook-Up Generation*, New York: Harper & Brothers, 1958

Dorothy L Sayers, *The Nine Tailors*, London: New English Library, 1984 (first published 1934)

Hubert Selby Jr., *Last Exit to Brooklyn*, London: Calder & Boyars, 1968 (first published 1964)

William Shakespeare, *Shakespeare As put forth in 1623 – A reprint of Mr William Shakespears Comedies, Histories, & Tragedies. Published according to the True Originall Copies*, London: Lionel Booth, 1864 (first published 1623)

Joseph T Shaw, ed., *The Hard-Boiled Omnibus*, New York: Pocket Books, 1952 (first published 1946)

Iceberg Slim (Robert Beck), *Trick Baby*, Edinburgh: Canongate Books, 1996 (first published 1967)

Captain Alexander Smith, *A Complete History of the Lives and Robberies of the Most Notorious Highwaymen, Foot-pads, Shop-Lifts, and Cheats of both Sexes in and about London*, London: 1719

William Henry Smyth (Sir Edward Belcher, ed.), *The Sailor's Word-Book: An Alphabetical Digest of Nautical Terms, Including Some More Especially Military and Scientific, but Useful to Seamen; as well as Archaisms of Early Voyages, etc.*, London: Blackie & Son, 1867

Jonathan Swift, *A Tale of a Tub: Written for the Universal Improvement of Mankind*, London: John Nutt, 1704

J Sullivan, *Cumberland and Westmorland, the People, the Dialect, Superstitions and Customs*, London: Whittaker & Co., 1857

Philip Thicknesse, *The Valetudinarians Bath Guide, or, The Means of Obtaining Long Life and Health*, London: Dodsley, 1780

Hurlo Thrumbo, ed., *The Merry Thought – Or, the Glass-Window and Bog-House Miscellany*, London: J Roberts, 1731

Ralph Tomlinson, *A Slang Pastoral: Being a Parody On a Celebrated Poem of Dr Byron's*, London: Printed for the Editor, 1780

Nick Tosches, *Dino – Living High in the Dirty Business of Dreams*, London: Secker and Warburg, 1992

Arthur Upfield, *The Mystery of Swordfish Reef*, London: Pan Books, 1970 (first published 1939)

Various authors, *Esquire's Handbook for Hosts*, London: Frederick Muller Ltd, 1957 (first published 1954)

——*Manual of Seamanship, 1937, Volume One*, London: His Majesty's Stationery Office, 1942 (first published 1938)

——*New Zealand at the Front*, London: Cassell and Company Limited, 1917

——*Oxford Dictionary of National Biography*, Oxford: Oxford University Press, 2004

——*Oxford English Dictionary*, Oxford: Oxford University Press, Online Edition, 2016

'Walter' (Gordon Grimley, ed.), *My Secret Life*, London: Granada Books, 1982 (first published 1882)

Ned Ward (Paul Hyland, ed.), *The London Spy*, East Lansing, Michigan: Colleagues Inc. Press, 1993 (first published 1709)

James Redding Ware, *Passing English of the Victorian Era – A Dictionary of Heterodox English, Slang and Phrase*, London: George Routledge & Sons, 1909

Alexander Warrack (Betty Kirkpatrick, foreword), *The Scots Dialect Dictionary*,
   Poole, Dorset: New Orchard Editions, 1988 (first published 1911)
John Waters, *Role Models*, London: Corsair Books, 2014 (first published 2010)
John Watson, *Johnny Kinsman*, London: Panther Books, 1957 (first published 1955)
Hillary Waugh, *Last Seen Wearing*, London: Pan Books, 1966 (first published 1952)
Noah Webster, *A Collection of Essays and Fugitiv Writings on Moral, Historical,
   Political and Literary Subjects*, Boston, Mass.: I Thomas & E T Andrews, 1790
——*An American Dictionary of the English Language*, New York: S Converse, 1828
Irvine Welsh, *Trainspotting*, London, Vintage, 1999 (first published 1993)
Attributed to Oscar Wilde and others, *Teleny, Or the Reverse of the Medal*. USA:
   St George Press, 2015
Charles Williams, *Aground*, London: Pan Books, 1969 (first published 1960)
Gordon Williams, *A Dictionary of Sexual Language and Imagery in Shakespearean
   and Stuart Literature* London: The Athlone Press, 1994
Kenneth Williams (Russell Davies, ed.), *The Kenneth Williams Diaries*, London:
   Harper Collins, 1994 (first published 1993)
Bill Williamson, *The Dee Jay Book*, London: Purnell Ltd, 1969
Clarence Winchester, *Let's Look at London*, London: Cassell & Co., 1935
P G Wodehouse, *Piccadilly Jim*, London: Herbert Jenkins Ltd., 1940 (first
   published 1917)
William Wycherley, *The Country-Wife, A Comedy Acted at the Theatre-Royal*,
   London: T Dring, 1688 (first performed 1675)
David Yates, *Bomb Alley – Falkland Islands, 1982, Aboard HMS Antrim at War*,
   Barnsley, South Yorkshire: Pen & Sword Maritime, 2006
Colonel Henry Yule & A C Burnell (William Crooke, ed.), *Hobson-Jobson – A
   Glossary of Colloquial Anglo-Indian Words and Phrases, and of Kindred Terms,
   Etymological, Historical, Geographical and Discursive*, London: John Murray, 1903
   (first published 1886)

Articles, pamphlets, etc.

Peter Ackroyd, 'Cardboard and Chains', *The Spectator*, November 17, 1979
Joseph Addison and Richard Steele, 'From My Own Apartment', *The Tatler*,
   October 4 – October 6, 1709
Advert for *Total Freedom* by Spacin', *Loud and Quiet*, Vol 3, Issue 75, 2016
'Advice To People Afflicted With the Gout', *The London Chronicle or Universal
   Evening Post*, December 30, 1773
Harriet Agnew and George Parker, 'Hedge Funds Boost Campaign to Keep Britain
   In the EU', *Financial Times*, November 12, 2015
Mike Ambrose, 'Democracy in Danger', *Morning Star*, February 4, 2002
Kingsley Amis, 'Dixieland Blues', *The Observer*, February 9, 1958
'Among The Leading "Futurologists"', *Private Eye*, September 18 – October 1, 2015
'An Enquiry Was Held At Kirkham', *Manchester Guardian*, June 25, 1904
Jack Anderson, 'Drug Catalog', *St Petersburg Times*, June 10, 1972
'Anecdote of George III', *The Times*, February 3, 1835

'Apothecaries Hall', *The Adelaide Independent and Cabinet of Amusements*, August 5, 1841

Christena Appleyard, 'Sell of the Century', *Daily Mirror*, September 8, 1980

'Army Slang – Novelties From The United States', *Manchester Guardian*, February 22, 1941

'At Mr Tho. Prichard's', *London Gazette*, August 24, 1682

'At the Bow Street Office…', *The Spectator*, March 9, 1839

Annie Aumonier, 'The Woman Tempted Me', *Daily Mirror*, January 2, 1906

'Ayr Results', *Daily Mirror*, September 18, 1937

'Backchat', *Daily Express*, October 22, 2003

Peter Bailey, 'You Can't Tell The Cops From The Robbers', *Ebony*, December 1974

Clive Barnes, 'Mods and Rockers', *The Spectator*, December 27, 1963

'Behind Lines Ardennes Offensive', *Auckland Star*, May 22, 1945

Starr de Belle, 'Ballyhoo Bros. Circulating Expo', *Billboard*, January 21, 1950

Beatrix L Bellingham, 'Egypt's War Against Traffic in Dangerous Drugs', *Illustrated London News*, February 1, 1930

Ross Benson, 'Granny Get Your Gun!', *Daily Express*, December 3, 1979

Jeffrey Bernard, 'Low Life', *The Spectator*, August 13, 1983

Jack Blanchard, 'End of the Peer', *Daily Mirror*, July 27, 2015

Dan Bloom, 'George Osborne Said "Obvs" And It Was A Bit Awks', *Daily Mirror*, April 19, 2016

'Bottoms Up', *World Weekly News*, January 21, 2003

H Addington Bruce, 'Slang's Dangers', *The Milwaukee Journal*, May 8, 1920

June Bundy & Leon Morse, 'CBS, NBC Share Laurels With Sock Pubserve Airers on Dope Menace', *Billboard*, July 28, 1951

Anthony Burgess, 'About the Bush', *The Observer*, August 14, 1983

Paul Byrne and Jane Kerr, 'Wills At 21: Happy Booze Day To You', *Daily Star*, June 20, 2003

Duncan Campbell, 'Gutted – Slang Book is Banned', *The Guardian*, June 24, 2006

Robert Cannell, 'Bebopcats Are Out On The Tiles!', *Daily Mirror*, November 16, 1948

Russell Gordon Carter, 'His Own Star', *Boy's Life*, March, 1931

'Casualties', *The Flying Post or The Post Master*, September 24, 1700

Ralph Champion, 'Monday in America', *Daily Mirror*, May 11, 1959

Rudolph Chelminski, 'Open Season On Drug Smugglers', *Life*, June 26, 1970

Ben Child, 'Dick Van Dyke: Brits Have Teased Me For 50 years About Mary Poppins Accent', *The Guardian*, October 10, 2014

'China and India', *The Economist*, December 30, 1843

'Chunder Report', *Woroni*, May 15, 1964

'Cocaine Habit in Italy', *The Observer*, July 3, 1921

Alistair Cooke, 'Increase in Drug-Taking By American Youth', *Manchester Guardian*, June 25, 1951

James Cooper, 'Probe Follows Rock-and-Roll Riot', *Daily Express*, April 1956

Douglas Coupland, 'Generation X – The Young and Restless Workforce Following the Baby Boom', *Vista* magazine, 1989

'Crack Pair Jailed', *Daily Record and Sunday Mail*, February 18, 2006

Marc Crawford, 'In a Roaring Inferno, "Burn, Baby, Burn"', *Life*, August 27, 1965

'Crescent Amusement Co.' advert, *Billboard*, June 25, 1949

The Critic, *The Truth*, December 22, 1912

'Dan Burley, 54, Dies of Heart Attack in Chicago', *Jet*, November 8, 1962

Ivor Davis, 'Margot Charges Dropped', *Daily Express*, July 12, 1967

——'This Is America', *Daily Express*, September 20, 1968

Victor Davis, 'You Will Never See Me Starkers', *Daily Express*, April 19, 1969

Dean Martin's Greatest Hits, Volume 2, LP sleeve notes, Reprise Records, 1968

Lizzie Dearden, 'Facebook Suspends The Blackcock Inn Pub's Profile over "Racist Or Offensive Language"', *The Independent*, December 23, 2015

Neela Debnath, 'Meghan Trainor Keeps Nicki Minaj Off The Top Spot In The Singles Chart With "All About That Bass"', *The Independent*, October 12, 2014

Robin Denselow, review of *Straight Outta Compton* by NWA, *The Guardian*, September 14, 1989

'"Dope"- Destruction in China', *Illustrated London News*, August 6, 1927

'Does Your Mouth Say Dreamboat?', *Daily Express*, November 10, 1964

Patrick Doncaster, 'It's Fab To Be In Films', *Daily Mirror*, February 4, 1964

Frederick I Douglass, 'Last Interview With Babs Gonzales', *Baltimore Afro-American*, January 26, 1980

'Dramatic Criticism', *Daily Express*, May 14, 1900

'Drugs By The L.', *The Prices of Merchandise in London*, March 25, 1674

'Drugs Won't Do', *Illustrated London News*, December 12, 1896

Dvorak, 'Origins of the Word "Nerd"', *PC Magazine*, May 26, 1987

Kenneth Eastaugh, 'The Queen of Satire Plays it Straight', *Daily Mirror*, December 6, 1966

'Eldridge Cleaver Announces Bid For U.S. Senate Seat', *Jet* magazine, February 26, 1986

'FA Explains Ferdinand Punishment', *Aberdeen Evening Express*, November 5, 2014

Martin Fagg, 'Black & White – review of *Soul On Ice*', *Church Times*, February 21, 1969

'Federal Men Hit Elks Club', *Pittsburgh Post-Gazette*, March 15, 1930

'Films Of The Week', *The Times*, July 16, 1923

'Finbarr Saunders & His Double Entendres', *Viz*, No 45, December 1990

Carmen Fishwick, 'London School Bans Pupils From Using "Innit", "Like" and "Bare"', *The Guardian*, October 15, 2013

Percy Flage, 'Chronicle & Comment', *Evening Post* (Wellington, NZ), October 19, 1944

'Foofs, Spoofs Are Far Out And Big', *Life*, December 20, 1963

'Ford Says He'll Quit Building Cars If Booze Ever Comes Back', *St Petersburg Evening Independent*, August 21, 1929

Frederick Forsyth, 'Who Dares Wins', *Daily Express*, November 30, 2007

'Forthcoming Marriages', *The Times*, May 31, 1962

Bob Francis, review of SNAFU, *Billboard*, November 4, 1944

Nicholas Garland, 'The Birth of Bazza', *The Spectator*, October 29, 1988

Marvin Gaye, Sleeve notes to the LP *Let's Get It On*, Tamla Records, 1973

'Gets 18 Years in First Reefer Murder Here', *The Afro-American*, May 27, 1933

'"Get Whitey!" The War Cry That Terrorized Los Angeles', *Life*, August 27, 1965

Doyle K Getter, 'What Is Boogie Woogie? Two Artists try To Tell', *Milwaukee Journal*, October 11, 1943

Nancy Gilbert, 'Drug Slang Becomes Part of Teen Vocabulary', *Spokane Daily Chronicle*, May 8, 1969

'Great Loves of Great Artists', *Life*, September 11, 1950

'Grovel', 'Talking About Uganda', *Private Eye*, March 9, 1973

'Guard Dies In Bungled Bank Raid', *Daily Mirror*, April 21, 1988

Anthony Haden-Guest & Keith Morris, 'Nothing But Flower Children', *OZ* no 7, October 1967

Jesse Hamlin, 'How Herb Caen Named a Generation', *San Francisco Chronicle*, November 26, 1995

Dashiell Hammett, 'The Golden Horseshoe', *Black Mask*, November, 1924

William Hickey, 'I Can't See Old Gladstone Getting "Hep"', *Daily Express*, November 14, 1955

Lorena Hickok, 'Slang Saves English from Dying, and Language Shark Proves It's True, and How!', *St Petersburg Times*, November 30, 1930

Peter Hitchens, 'Taking Risks On The Dark Side Of The Sunshine State', *Daily Express*, September 15, 1993

'Homosexuals in Revolt', *Life*, December 31, 1971

'House of Commons', *E Johnson's British Gazette and Sunday Monitor*, June 12, 1803

'How High Will These Numbers Go?', *Record Mirror*, July 11, 1964

Jane Howard, 'Telling Talk From a Negro Writer', *Life*, May 24, 1963

Ronald Howe, 'Fighting Crime, No. 4', *Daily Express*, March 24, 1950

Ruth Inglis, 'Happy Harry', *Daily Express*, February 17, 1979

'"It's The Buzz, Cock!"', *Time Out*, February 20 – 26, 1976

'I've Made a Real Pig's A*!@ of it!', *Daily Mirror*, June 21, 1993

Sammy Jay, 'The Original Slang Dictionary: Francis Grose's own Copy of his "Classical Dictionary of the Vulgar Tongue"', Peter Harrington, 2013

Oliver Jensen, 'The Navy's Slang And Humor', *Life*, October 28, 1940

James Johnson and Noreen Taylor, 'Rock Turns Back the Clock', *Daily Mirror*, March 17, 1981

J.S., 'The Snow Man', *Manchester Guardian*, March 23, 1926

'Kia Ora From NZ Airmen', *Auckland Star*, December 20, 1941

Herbert Kretzmer, 'So Comical – The Tale of Four Women', *Daily Express*, June 18, 1965

Susan Lamb, 'Jurors Get Lessons In Drug Jargon', *Gainesville Sun*, February 8, 1983

Mike Langley, 'Fans Ain't What They Used To Be', *Daily Mirror*, January 14, 1994

Leader column, *Nelson Examiner and New Zealand Chronicle*, November 23, 1844

Timothy Leary, 'You Are A God, Act Like One', *International Times*, Issue 25, February 2 – 15, 1968

'Let It Bleep', *Time Out*, February 20 – 26, 1976

Letter to *Life*, April 1, 1940

Bibliography

Letter to *International Times*, March 9, 1972

Letter to *The Spectator*, February 21, 1969

Letter to *The Teetotal Advocate*, April 3, 1843

'Letters From the Front', *The Times*, February 17, 1916

'LIFE Is With It In A Far Out Era', *Life*, September 14, 1959

Ferdinand Long, 'Don't Get Run Down: How to Protect Oneself Against the
    Motor Scorcher', *Daily Express*, May 8, 1903

'"Loneliest Peer" Finds Content', *Daily Express*, April 16, 1951

'Lord a Leaping', *The Sun*, July 27, 2015

'LORD COKE – Top Peer's Drug Binges With £200 Prostitutes', *The Sun On
    Sunday*, July 26, 2015

Shirley Lowe, 'Mod Or Trad?', *Daily Mirror*, March 2, 1963

Lucio, 'Army Slang', *Manchester Guardian*, October 3, 1940

Jack Maher, ' The Many Types Of Jazz', *Billboard*, April 28, 1962

'Maidstone Farmers Club', *South Eastern Gazette*, December 17, 1872

Sharon Marshall, 'Misery Is Not Up Our Street', *Daily Star*, March 6, 2005

Peter McKay, 'Boozing To A High Degree', *Daily Mirror*, March 9, 1981

'Medical Journals Are Discussing At Considerable Length', *South Eastern Gazette*,
    February 2, 1897

'Melody Men Roll Again', *Life*, August 25, 1961

Tony Miles, 'The Fish – It's The Latest Hug, Rock And Roll Dance', *Daily Mirror*,
    April 26, 1955

'Military Industrial Exhibition', *The Standard*, July 10, 1873

'Millions of Melons Rush East in Imperial Valley's Big Week', *Life*, July 15, 1940

Gilbert Millstein, review of *On The Road*, *New York Times*, September 5, 1957

Stephanie Mlot, 'YouTube's Geek Week Kicks Off Sunday', *PC*, August 2, 2013

'Mr Billing's Trial – Lord Alfred Douglas Cross-Examined', *The Times*, June 3, 1918

'Miscellany', *Manchester Guardian*, June 28, 1906

Hugh Moffett, 'U S of A, Where Are You?', *Life*, April 19, 1968

'More Questions About Those Four-Letter Words', *The Guardian*, October 29, 1960

'Movie Of The Week: Ball Of Fire", *Life*, December 15, 1941

Stephen Moyes and Graham Brough, 'He Mitre Had a Pew Too Many', *Daily
    Mirror*, December 9, 2006

'Mrs Cake the Baker's Wife Drives 'Em Bonkers', *Daily Mirror*, September 4, 1987

'Murders In New York', *Manchester Guardian*, May 8, 1913

'Music as Written', *Billboard*, June 6, 1960

Mike Nevard, 'Jazz in Danger', *Melody Maker*, June 30, 1956

'New Slang From America', *Daily Express*, September 23, 1926

'New York's Children Accuse…', *Life*, June 25, 1951

Andy Nickolds, 'Bazza Gets It On', *Time Out*, March 12 – 18, 1976

'Nightclubs, Vaudeville', *Billboard*, October 2, 1943

'Nixon Calls For a War On Drugs', *The Palm Beach Post*, March 21, 1972

'No Ban in Oldham', *The Times*, September 15, 1956

'No word has been received…' *Daily Mirror*, January 16, 1917

'Novel Archway For a "FANY" Bride', *Daily Mirror*, April 11, 1919

Ryan O'Hare, 'Keeping Up With The Cool Kids', *Daily Mail*, March 9, 2016

'On Saturday, An Old Woman', *Illustrated London News*, December 14, 1850

Paul O'Neil, 'The Only Rebellion Around', *Life*, November 30, 1959

—— 'The Wreck Of A Monstrous Family', *Life*, December 19, 1969

George Orwell, 'As I Please', *Tribune*, March 10, 1944

——'As I Please', *Tribune*, March 17, 1944

Our Own Correspondent, 'US Scenes Recall "Jungle Bird House At The Zoo"', *The Times*, September 15, 1956

Hannah Jane Parkinson, 'Lesbian app Dattch rebrands as HER after raising $1m', *The Guardian*, March 19, 2015

Tom Patch, 'Will the Talkies Change Our Language?', *Daily Mirror*, June 15, 1929

Pendennis, 'Uncle Mac's Prize Day', *The Observer*, January 1, 1961.

Gerard Piel, 'Narcotics', *Life*, July 19, 1943

Charlotte and Dennis Plimmer, 'The Princess is Very Likely Reading This At the Same Time As You Are', *Daily Express*, August 29, 1956

Pamela Vandyke Price, 'The Good Life', *The Spectator*, May 5, 1973

'Police', *The Times*, August 5, 1823

'Police', *The Times*, August 17, 1825

'Police Forces Unable To Handle Increasing Traffic in Cocaine', *Montreal Gazette*, April 29, 1983

'Postscript', *The Economist*, March 16, 1844

Angela Potter, 'Electric Chair Is Hot Item At Death Row Records Auction', *Orange County Register*, January 25, 2009

'Presley Fever Hits Britain', *Picture Post*, September 22, 1956

Tom Prideaux, 'They All Keep On Looking For Floogle Street', *Life*, July 28, 1961

Marjorie Proops, 'Sad Little Gay Girl', *Daily Mirror*, February 4, 1971

Ian Ramsay, 'The Too Blue Line', *Daily Mirror*, August 5, 1985

'Rap Brown In Carmichael Mold', *Sarasota Herald Tribune*, October 17, 1971

'Reefer Craze Seen Dying Out in Eastern Cities', *The Afro-American*, June 1, 1940

Review of *Baby You Done Flubbed Your Dub With Me*, *Billboard*, December 15, 1958

Review of *Grimm's Hip Fairy Tales*, *Billboard*, March 20, 1961

Review of *Hippy Dippy*, *Billboard*, September 24, 1949

Review of *Looking*, *Billboard*, December 15, 1958

Review of *My Heart At Thy Sweet Voice*, *Billboard*, March 6, 1954

Review of *Poetry For The Beat Generation*, *Billboard*, June 15, 1959

Review of *Rock Around the Clock*, *The Times*, July 23, 1956

Review of *Rookwood*, *The Spectator*, June 4, 1836

Review of *Spunyarn and Spindrift*, *Glasgow Herald*, February 24, 1886

Review of *The Gentleman Is A Dope*, *Billboard*, October 18, 1947

Review of *The Great Man*, *The New Yorker*, March 2, 1957

'Rhyming Slang', *Daily Express*, July 14, 1900

Edward Roberts, 'Ice Cube Calls George Osborne His "Homie" After Hearing He's A Long-Time NWA Fan', *Daily Mirror*, January 22, 2016

David Robson, 'There Really Are 50 Eskimo Words For "Snow"', *Washington Post*, January 14, 2013

Bibliography

'Rock and Roll', *Yorkshire Post*, January 25, 1936

'Rock – Scream', *Daily Express*, May 13, 1963

Robert C Ruark, 'A Great Cultural Contribution', *Schenectady Gazette*, May 21, 1949

Bill Sachs, 'With the Country Jockeys', *Billboard*, January 26, 1963

'Salford Hundred Quarter Sessions', *Manchester Guardian*, October 28, 1880

Clyde Sanger, 'Progress in Watts, but Tension Still', *The Guardian*, August 19, 1966

'Sayings and Doings', *The Satirist and Sporting Chronicle*, March 25, 1843

Jesse Scheidlower, 'Crying Wolof', *Slate*.com, December 8, 2004

Richard Schickel, 'Shock of Seeing a Hidden World', *Life*, November 1, 1968

Webster Schott, 'A New Guru For Stoneheads', *Life*, October 6, 1972

Kelly Scott, 'Suspected Leader And Members Of Major Drug Ring Arrested In
    Raid', *St Petersburg Times*, May 17, 1980

'Scrabble Stays Dench With New Words', *Aberdeen Evening Express*, May 21, 2015

Donald Seaman, 'They Went Thataway', *Daily Express*, October 24, 1953

'Selfie: Australian Slang Term Named International Word of the Year', *The
    Guardian*, November 19, 2013

'Sex, Religion, Drugs Verboten On Vanity Plates', *Eugene Register-Guard*, November
    17, 1980

'Shaping Up for a Laugh at Life', *Daily Mirror*, September 3, 1975

Neil Shapiro, 'Mighty Macho Memories', *Popular Mechanics*, October 1982

Wilfrid Sheed, 'Gay Life Gets a Sharp Going Over', *Life*, May 24, 1968

'Shop Man Cleared On Pistols LP Charge', *The Guardian*, November 25, 1977

'Sid the Sexist', *Viz*, Issue 56, October / November, 1992

John Simon, 'Ritual Murder', *New York*, February 10, 1969

Serena Sinclair & Beryl Hartland, 'Reach For Your Tweezers', *Daily Telegraph*,
    January 25, 1965

Clancy Sigal, 'The Punchers' Night Out', *The Observer*, March 1, 1959

'Sir Winston's Driver Told PC: I'm Sloshed', *Daily Mirror*, December 14, 1967

'Slang', *Daily Mirror*, December 16, 1925

'"Slang" Enters the Computer Industry To Eliminate Complex Math Solutions',
    Computer World, October 22, 1969

'Slang of the Criminal', *The Milwaukee Sentinel*, April 4, 1911

'Slanguage: American Slang As It Is Today', *The Manchester Guardian*, September
    19, 1929

Small Ads, *International Times*, Issue 24, January 19 – February 21, 1968

Joan Smith, 'The Blue Show in a Tory Phone Booth', *Daily Mirror*, July 29, 1972

Charles Smyth, Letter to the editor, *Church Times*, March 15, 1963

Jason Solomons, 'Who's Set To Be Big In 94?', *Daily Express*, December 31, 1993

'Squaresville U.S.A. vs Beatsville', *Life*, September 21, 1959

Cyril Stapleton, 'Rock-and-Rollers Shock Ted Heath', *Daily Express*, May 8, 1956

Andrew Stephen, 'We Just Love Your Punks v Teds', *The Observer*, July 24, 1977

Peter Stephens, 'Norma's Second Honeymoon', *Daily Mirror*, May 28, 1973

Michael Stone, 'What Really Happened in Central Park', *New York*, August 14, 1989

Gloria Steinem, 'The Ins and Outs of Pop Culture', *Life*, August 25, 1965

'Strange Slangs', *Daily Express*, January 25, 1932

Robert N Sturdevant, 'Nazis Threaten To Try Fliers As "War Criminals"', *The Lewiston Daily Sun*, December 23, 1943

'Suge Knight's Murder Trial Set For July', *The Guardian*, April 30, 2015

'Summary', *The Church Times*, September 19, 1863

'Take a Trip', *East Village Other*, March 3, 1970

'Teen-Age Betty', *Life*, August 14, 1944

'The Beatnik of the Bull Ring', *Life*, August 6, 1965

'The Dialect of 'Fast Young Men'', *The Watchman and Wesleyan Advertiser*, April 7, 1858

'The Following Pasquinade', *The Times*, September 16, 1786

The Harder They Come, LP sleeve notes, Island Records, 1972

'The New Opium Clipper "Wild Dayrell"', *Illustrated London News*, November 10, 1855

'The Nuisance of the Deadhead', *Daily Mirror*, October 5, 1910

'The Obscene Phone Caller And How To Handle Him', *OZ* no 31, November 1970

'The Opium Plague', *Illustrated London News*, April 8, 1843

'The Prince Joins "Old Bill Fraternity"', *Manchester Guardian*, November 18, 1933

'The Prospects of the Ministry', *The Watchman and Wesleyan Advertiser*, October 1, 1873

'The Theatres', *The Spectator*, November 12, 1836

'There will be exposed to sale', *London Gazette*, March 21, 1686

'They Have Just Been Destroying Messerschmitts', *Daily Express*, August 6, 1940

'Think of PUSSY', *Daily Mirror*, February 27, 1932

Thomas Thompson, 'The New Far-Out Beatles', *Life*, June 16, 1967

T.I.M, 'American Slang – "Wising the Booboisie"', *Sydney Morning Herald*, May 10, 1935

'Titles for Apothecaries and Druggists Shops', *London Gazette*, August 21, 1684

'Toby Tosspot', *The Morning Chronicle*, August 23, 1809

'Trooper Tommy's "First War"', *The Penny Illustrated Paper and Illustrated Times*, July 20, 1895

Tom Tullett and Howard Johnson, 'The "Squealer" Gives Yard 10 Names', *Daily Mirror*, August 14, 1963

'Turn On With Petula Clark', *Go-Go*, April 1967

'Two Girl Pat Men Come Home With "Sealed Lips"', *Daily Express*, July 14, 1936

W. H. R. of Folkestone, Letter to *Mayfair*, Volume 8, No. 12, December 1974

Bob Wade, 'North-south Divide? Just Move the Goalposts!', *The Journalist*, October-November, 2015

Loudon Wainwright, Jr., 'The View From Here', *Life*, March 31, 1967

David Walker, 'David Walker's Talking Shop!', *Daily Mirror*, November 9, 1937

Irving Wardle, Review of *Privates On Parade*, *The Times*, February 23, 1977

Keith Waterhouse, 'Picture of Innocence', *Daily Mirror*, May 28, 1973

Paul Welch, 'The "Gay" World Takes to the City Streets', *Life*, June 26, 1964

'Wets' Last Hopes', *The Times*, June 20, 1919

'Whore House Horror', *Daily Star*, August 15, 2001

Edward Wickham, 'Radio', *Church Times*, November 1, 2002

Bibliography

'Wills "Right To Swear"', *Daily Mirror*, June 21, 2003

'"Winged Victory" Cast Leaves Slang Legacy to Hollywood', *The Pittsburgh Press*, December 20, 1944

Graeme Wood, 'How Gangs Took Over Prisons', *The Atlantic*, October 2014

W.T.C 'The Slang Evil', *The Age*, April 21, 1923

'Yo Blair, How Are You Doing?', *The Guardian*, July 18, 2006

Matthew Young, 'Drugs Cops Raid at Lord Snorty Pad', *Daily Star*, July 28, 2015

'Your Astrological Week Ahead With Psychic Bob', *The Daily Mash*, July 29, 2015

INDEX

Index

Index

Index

Index

Index

Index

Index

Index

Index